CHANGE AND CONTINUITY

Influences on Self-Identity of Christian Dalits of Madiri Puram Village in South India (1915-2005)

CHANGE AND CONTINUITY

Influences on Self-Identity of Christian Dalits of
Madiri Puram Village in South India (1915-2005)

Etala David Solomon

2012

Change and Continuity: Influences on Self–Identity of Christian Dalits of Madiri Puram Village in South India (1915-2005) – Published by the Rev. Dr. Ashish Amos of Indian Society for Promoting Christian Knowledge (ISPCK), Post Box 1585, 1654 Madarsa Road, Kashmere Gate, Delhi-110006.

© Author, 2012

ISBN: 978-81-8465-248-2

Laser typeset by **ISPCK,** Post Box 1585,
1654 Madarsa Road, Kashmere Gate, Delhi-110006
Tel: 23866322, 23866323
e-mail–ashish@ispck.org.in   •   ella@ispck.org.in
website-www.ispck.org.

DEDICATED TO

Paul G. Hiebert

Elmer A. Martens

MBMSI

P. B. Arnold

And

E. Premaleela Solomon

For teaching me the meaning of Christian discipleship

Contents

ACKNOWLEDGMENTS

I praise God the almighty through Jesus Christ for carrying me through this challenging yet enjoyable pilgrimage of doctoral studies.

I am thankful to my mentor late Professor Paul G. Hiebert (1932-2007), who together with Professor Elmer A Martens invited me to make this journey in the United States of America. In unique ways, they helped me endure this post graduate studies' journey.

I am most grateful to my dissertation readers—Professors Robert J. Priest and Richard R. Cook at Trinity International University—for sharpening my thinking and writing. I am indebted to the Mennonite Brethren Board of Missions and Services International for their financial and moral support through mostof my programme. I am also grateful to Dr. Elmer A. Martens, Dr. Eloise Hiebert Meneses and Dr. Paul D. Wiebe for editing the first draft of this book and their encouragement toward publishing it.

I express heartfelt thanks to Rev. Dr. P. B. Arnold, President, of the Conference of the Mennonite Brethren Church of India, for granting and extending my study-leave. Also, I am grateful to Mennonite Brethren Board of Theological Education, India, for their recommendation under the Presidentship of Rev. Dr. R.S. Lemuel.

I thank the librarians of the following libraries for being a great help: The Rolfing Memorial Library, Trinity International University, Deerfield; Northwestern University, Evanston; Garret Evangelical Theological Seminary, Evanston; United Theological College, Bangalore; South Asia Institute for Advanced Christian Studies, Bangalore; Henry Martyn Institute, Hyderabad; Andhra Christian Theological College, Hyderabad; and Mennonite Brethren Centenary Bible College, Shamshabad.

Last but not least, I thank my dear wife Premaleela and our older daughter, Shiny, and her husband, M. M. Manavapal, our first grandchild, Melissa Pearl (Mini), and our younger daughter, Stuthi, for their patience and moral support during my study.

INTRODUCTION

The best way to impact India's Church is to understand the village church. According to the 2001 census, 70 per cent of Indian people live in villages. When the gospel enters a village culture, it offers remarkable changes in faith, community life, health and hygiene, social dynamics and education. Yet in definite ways, Christian Dalits of Madiri Puram village continue to live according to their traditional practices, social and economic statuses, rituals of passage and systems of governance.

No village people remain the same forever. Village India has been changing through pre- and post-Independence (1947). Some have conceptualised changes in reference to "Sanskritisation" (ritual mobility) and "Westernisation" (Srinivas 1967) among other dominant influences. For example, peasant family structures, their economies and their polity are in the process of change, despite continuity.

So, a rural church cannot do contextualisation in isolation. It grapples with the principles of the gospel and other "factors" in defining its "new-old" identity. Its native identity may be sometimes balanced, sometimes lopsided, yet it claims to be authentically indigenous. Village Christians exchange local faith symbols, adhere to caste categories and align with the dominant class for functional social stability. Peasant Christians in Madiri Puram village continue some Hindu ritual practices and observe *bhakti* (devotion). The local Christian community discerns what is biblical, what is cultural and what is negotiable. But biblical and cultural values intersect. In missiological terms, folk people in Madiri Puram village live a "split level" Christianity (Hiebert et al. 1999, 15-29). This research looks into their "split-level Christianity." It examines a Christianity that is "down to earth" and "existential" in focus. The Madiri Puram village church offers models of self-identity with regard to religion, culture, socio-economic status and politics. Geographically, Madiri Puram is a remote village in the state of Andhra Pradesh in South India. It is far removed from former white missionary supervision. In addition, till recent decades, it was not easily accessible by road to national ecclesial leadership.[1] Thus the church is run by the church *Panchayat* (council of five elders) since its inception (c.1915) and reorganisation (1973). Moreover, a pastor's influence is minimal in major decisions of the church. So the *Panchayat* of the church in consultation with the male heads of families governs the processes of contextualising, or accommodating the principles of the gospel, based on consensus–an agreement that is reached with the use of both Christian and other social values.

Research Problem

My research question is to discover "How do Christian Dalits of Madiri Puram village exhibit the influences of social change and continuity as their self-identity, in the areas of religion, culture, socio-economic status and politics?"

In the following section, I have subdivided the Research Problem into four questions.

Research Questions

- How is change and continuity exhibited in the religious symbols of Madiri Puram village and how does this define their Christian identity?
- How do Christians of Madiri Puram village resolve conflicts created by socio-economic status?
- In what ways do Christians of Madiri Puram village enact change and continuity in morality and life guidance?
- How do Christians of Madiri Puram village reach consensus in their church *Panchayat* (legal assembly)?

This leads me to consider the significance of this research.

Significance

My research will add to the missiological literature on the gospel in particular contexts. Specifically it will:

- Expand missiological thinking about "folk Christianity" (Hiebert and Meneses 1995, 215; cf. Hiebert et al. 1999, 90-91, 225, 369)
- Provide a better understanding of village Christian socio-economic identity struggles
- Provide a better view of church administration in the context of the local church *Panchayat*

- Supply stories about how village congregations handle morality and life guidance.

Scope and Limitations

My research offers a deeper insight into some of the aspects of village Christianity. I have tried to study peasant Christianity in its life setting. However, it has definite limits. This research will not talk about gospel and culture in urban areas like Mumbai, where migrant workers from rural India abound. It will not concern itself with Gypsies (*Lambadas*) within my research area but just village Christians in rural South India. In order to clarify my topic, I will do literature review.

However, since urbanisation is a major trend in postmodern India, I will briefly deal with some projections, reasons and challenges of migration to a city like Mumbai. Mumbai is one among the four mega cities in India, namely Delhi, Kolkata, Mumbai (Bombay) and Chennai (Madras). Moreover, people from my research area have migrated to Mumbai in good numbers compared to other mega cities just mentioned.

Rural Migrations to Urban Centres

Prem P. Talwar, an adjunct professor at the School of Public Health, University of North Carolina, notes the projection that 50 per cent of the population in less developed countries will reside in urban areas by 2015 *(http://www.auick.org/database/apc/apc02701.html)*. This projection is in contrast to his own estimation of 42 per cent of rural migrations to the mega cities of India like Delhi, Mumbai, Kolkata and Chennai (Madras) as on today.

Squatter Settlements

People migrate to cities for various reasons. They go in search of better employment or to escape under-employment in villages. Drought situations are another main reason for migration. Debenath Mookerji has rightly pointed out the difficulties in a slum thus, "A highly congested usually urban residential area characterized by deteriorated unsanitary buildings, poverty, and social disorganization" (Mookherji 1982, 476). A slum is also considered a place where there are decaying areas of crime, broken families and gross immorality. While a dark picture of slums may be true, for some theorists, slums have been providers of goods and services that are required by the non-slum population.

Vedulla K. Rufus has done a good historical survey on migrants to Mumbai. For instance, he quotes Pastor P. J. Prakasham's five reasons why poor people migrate from Maktal-Narayanpet, a neighbouring region to my research area. They are as follows:

- The Narayanpet-Makthal Taluka (county) is a dry area with little rain fall
- The area is prone to famine and drought
- There is no work year round for the people
- To support large families (six to seven children)
- People hope for a better life in Mumbai (Vedulla, 1992, 48-49)

Challenges in Mumbai

Once Telugus arrive in Mumbai, they face several challenges. Vedulla K Rufus (Ibid) observes the following problems:

- Marathi, the local language, is difficult to learn.
- No housing to live in or could not afford to rent, so settled in slums.
- Ill-treatment by local people and the government.
- No pastoral care (so if Christians, they were like sheep without shepherd).
- They had no mission schools or hostels to help educate their children.
- They had no health care facility like in mission-related areas.
- They had no burial grounds.

Urban Blessings

From a positive standpoint, there are certain blessings with exposure to the cities. Some of the youth who have gone to mission boarding schools or a college in a city like Hyderabad or Mumbai bring back singing or acting like "Cinema heroes." Some of these men and women become teachers in government schools. Owing to their better and stable economy, they build better houses; buy a motorcycle or a new plot of land over and above their limited ancestral land. They even hire tractors to level land. This replaces the labor-intensive social life by the use of machine. These are the markers I see with urbanisation.

However, my research village is unlikely to fall prey to large-scale urban migrations. As per 2001 Census, about ten male heads of the family migrated temporarily among a total of 1,104 Dalit population. So it is about 1 per cent of the population. As on today, they migrate not to the urban centres but to brook sides near a city suburb. They work as laborers in a sand transportation business. The sand is loaded by these workers on trucks. The business is owned by a city contractor.

My research progresses from a broad picture of social change and continuity in modern India and moves down to the specifics of a village-life setting.

Social Change and Continuity

Before proceeding further, it is necessary that I clarify what I mean by the terms social change and continuity. "Social change is a general term which refers to: change in the nature, the social institutions, the social behaviour or the social relations of a society, community of people, or other social structures..." *(en.wikipedia.org/wiki/ Social change)*. And continuity is an "uninterrupted connection or union" *(wordnet.princeton.edu/perl/webwn)*. In my research, "continuity" can also mean accommodation or modification.

A review of the precedent literature will impress on the importance of this book in the first chapter.

LIST OF ILLUSTRATIONS

LIST OF TABLES

Chapter 1

SOCIAL CHANGE AND CONTINUITY IN MODERN INDIA—PEASANT FAMILY, ECONOMY AND PANCHAYAT

My literature review will investigate how peasant families, their agrarian economy, and the forms of governance (Panchayat) have changed, specifically pointing to agents that cause such change and continuity. In my research, I will go intentionally to investigate and find influences other than those pointed out by renowned Hindu social anthropologists like M. N. Srinivas (Social Change in modern India, 1967). The late M. N. Srinivas has introduced seminal concepts like "Sanskritisation" and 'Westernisation" as agents of social change and continuity. Village Christian Dalits witness that the "gospel" has been the greatest factor in changing their worldviews over and above "Sanskritisation" and "Westernisation." For this reason, it is necessary to take a fresh look at change and continuity among Christians in Indian villages. Since "social change"[1] is a wide area, my focus will be on three aspects of social change among peasant communities, namely (1) family, (2) agrarian economy and (3) *Panchayat* (governance).[2] My dissertation interests lay in change and continuity among Christian and non-Christian Dalit people in Madiri Puram village with regard to culture, economics and polity, with religious change (conversion)

---

[1] Randy Schutt makes distinction between "social service" and "social change." He compares social service to one time help [e.g., reformation], while that of social change to an enduring solution to the existing problem: The difference between social service and social change is like the difference between giving a hungry man a fish so he won't be hungry and teaching him how to fish so that he will never again be hungry. Social service relieves the immediate situation, while social change alters the political, economic, social, or cultural institution or customs that created the problem. *(2007<http://www.vernalproject.org>)*

[2] "Panchayat" means village council consisting five elders elected for a year. The Council is headed by a "Sarpanch" (lead elder) chosen by rest of the four elders.

as the overarching subject. These people happen to be small-scale peasants, sharecroppers, tenant farmers and agriculture labourers. Change and continuity are the dynamics that I examine among my target population, beginning with family and social change.

Family and Social Change

Family is basic to meaningful existence. It is the foundational institution wherein learning or unlearning religious orientation, morality, manners, hopes and failures occur. It is within the home that we begin to draw lines between "ideal" and "real," "private" and "public." Family experiences become authentic measurements either for appropriation or negation of other experiences in our life journey.

In India, family "structure and practice" factor very much into one's honour or dishonour (Patel 2005). Joint and nuclear are the two major types of family in India. Within joint families there are (1) matrilineal and (2) patrilineal structures. The patrilineal joint family system is heavily influenced and affirmed by caste-based Hinduism, while the nuclear family is mostly associated with Dalit culture. Inheritance, economic viability, residence and shared work load are some reasons for the joint family system. Whether joint or nuclear, a family experiences, social change due to factors like "Sanskritisation" and "Westernisation" (Srinivas 1967). In the following pages, I have described two joint family systems, namely patriliny structures, to serve as a background to my subject, family and change.

Joint Family: Definitions

Tulsi Patel, a woman professor of sociology at the Delhi School of Economics brings together seminal articles on the Indian family. The essays were written over a period of fifty years (1952-2005). The articles in her volume *The Family in India: Structure and Practice* (2005) cover issues beyond the stereotypical categories of joint or nuclear. The volume discusses whether or not joint family in India is disintegrating and Indian families are emulating Western conjugal family. Patel's basic thesis is to project the tension between the changing, yet continuing structures of the family.

Matrilineal Influences

The Nayars of Travencore State in Kerala practice matrilineal joint families called *tarawad* (natal home). The Nambudiris (Brahmans) follow the patrilineal type. Both the structures have practices particular to them. Mother-focused families range from 20 to 30 members in a family. Patel's definition of matriliny is informative:

The relatively greater autonomy of women in the *tarawad* is a reflection of both the principle of matriliny and the consequent *tarawad* formation. Polyandrous unions, visiting husbands and ritually sanctioned Nambudiri husbands and children from these husbands were typical features of the *tarawad*. This family system was rather complex and posed a certain difficulty in fitting with the family in patrilineal society (Patel 2005, 25).

Over the years, matriliny weakened due to dominant patrilineal practices in the country. Patriliny is Hindu in origin, Brahman in focus and therefore, in general, has a higher prestige.

Patriliny Influences

Susan S. Wadley's definition of patriliny is worth noting. Wadley's ethnographic study among *Thakurs* (Brahmans) of Karimpur village near New Delhi made her to highlight the benefits of the patrilineal family. She likens the patrilineal joint family to a broom, in contrast to the nuclear family, which she compares to that of a single straw apart from the broom. A single straw cannot sweep. Thus she defines patriliny as "the ideal joint family . . . made up of a married couple, their married sons, their sons' wives and children (and possibly grandsons' wives and grandchildren), and unmarried daughters" (Wadley 2002, 11). Patriliny is honour-shame focused. It is based on property and economic stability. For Thakurs, a breakdown in family relationships results in more than just disharmony within the family. Wadley likens a break in the joint family to divorce in America. She wrote,

> For Karimpur's landowning families, which are more likely to be joint than are poor families, separating a joint family is traumatic, rupturing family ties, economic relationships, and workloads, as well as necessitating the division of all of the joint family's material goods (land, ploughs, cattle, cooking utensils, stocks of grain and seed, courtyards, verandahs, rooms, cooking areas, etc.). Separation (*nyare*) is, in fact, most comparable to American divorce. It also brings dishonor to one's family (Wadley 2002, 11).

For Wadley the joint family has multiple merits. The Hindu joint family ideal receives its inspiration from liturgical texts. The joint family is perceived to be equivalent to social and national unity. It is thought of in the sense of physical health of the male members of the family. This relates to the control of sexual behaviour by men. It improves the self-control of males, thus it indicates moral stamina or health. Joint family counts on production or work capital held in common. The patrilineal joint family treats its female members and children as subordinate to men or elders. Wadley describes the dangers of nuclear family:

> If society lives together (*samaj ikhatthe*), your self-control (*sanyam apka*) is maintained. If you live separately, you lose your self-control. You get a separate room. You get a separate cot. You have separate food. Everything becomes separate. This affects your health (*tandurusti*). But when you live together—you have your mother at one place, sister at another, *bhabhi* (older brother's wife) somewhere else, or a servant at some place—then self-control is not difficult. You don't have any place to indulge yourself [implied is food or sexual indulgence]. This is the greatest factor in good health. That is why it is essential for the family to live together. Now it is important to understand that all this is a gift of nature (*kudarat*). If it is not in men, then how can we blame others? This tendency to live separate is very dangerous.
>
> They say that if a young daughter is alone in a room, then even her father should not go into that room. She is the girl whom you have produced out of your own seed, out of your own body, and she is young. So you should not go into that room. So when our family lives together, then we get less time, and we get more opportunities to work. We would not even be able to think about it [sex]. That is why our health used to be good. (Wadley 2002, 13)

In addition, a joint family is also a sign of political strength in village affairs. Therefore a breakdown in joint family causes one to lose social power. My research will show that Christian Dalits in Madiri Puram village exercise social power not through patrilineal joint families but through caste courts or panchayat.

Traditionally, the joint family system is based on notions of caste endogamy and purity of blood. However, Indian sociology and social anthropology have identified the crises of the family that have resulted from inter-caste or inter-religious marriages (Patel 2005, 31).

What other factors force families to change?

Agents of Social Change: Sanskritisation and Westernisation

M. N. Srinivas, a renowned anthropologist, introduced two seminal concepts that affect social change in modern India: "Sanskritization" and "Westernization" (1967). For him, Sanskritisation is happening throughout Indian history, while Westernisation was introduced to India by the British (1750-1947). These two concepts have to do with different paths to social mobility.

What is Sanskritisation? Sanskritisation is a process by which a "low" Hindu caste or tribal clan changes its customs, ritual, ideology and way of life in the direction of a high, and frequently, "twice-born" caste (Srinivas 1967, 6). As such, positional changes may occur in individual caste over a period of time, but a structural change to the *varna* (colour) principle never occurs. Crucial to the immutable *varna* principle is ritual purity headed by Brahmans and supported by Kshatriyas and Vaishyas. The notion of varna dharma, or caste duty, was developed during the post Vedic period (600 B.C. to A.D. 300), and serves to enforce conformity to the "colour" principle. Ultimately, it simply means the supremacy of the Brahmans.

"Westernisation" is the second concept that the late Srinivas introduced. He prefers Westernisation to "modernity" or "urbanisation." For him modernity and urbanisation have limited spheres of reference, appropriate primarily to industrial and urban centres. But Westernisation is neutral (though not value free) and affects both urban and rural masses. Srinivas defines:

> 'Westernization' to characterize the changes brought about in Indian society and culture as a result of over 150 years of British rule, and the term subsumes changes occurring at different levels–technology, institutions, ideology, values (Srinivas 1967, 47).

For example, with regard to technology, Srinivas thinks of bulldozers doing the massive leveling of lands for agriculture. On the other hand, newspapers, road systems, postal services and others have created *Pax Britannica* (Srinivas 1967, 61), unparalleled to the ancient Indian petty kingdoms and their infightings. The resulting impact is on the whole culture, both urban and rural.

As to the institutions, Srinivas notes that education and law schools started by Westerners were "open" to all peoples, especially to Untouchables. The British judicial system raised a sense of equality and a consciousness of individual positive rights. Other traditional institutions, like the army and civil services, were also affected by Westernisation.

Effects of Westernisation

First, Westernisation birthed the "new elite" such as Raja Ram Mohan Roy, M. K. Gandhi, Tagores and Vivekanandas. These new elite were open to new political and cultural ideas and were influential in ushering in the new India.

On the political and cultural front, Westernisation has given birth not only to nationalism, but also to revivalism, communalism, "casteism," heightened linguistic consciousness and regionalism. To make matters more bewildering, revivalist movements have used Western-type schools and colleges, books, pamphlets and journals to propagate their ideas (Srinivas 1967, 55 -56; Bose 1994, 394).

Second, Westernisation paved the way for Dalit (Scheduled Caste) conversions to Christianity. Srinivas observes that converts to Christianity did not influence Indian society for the following three reasons:

- Converts generally hailed from lower castes
- Conversion alienated them from the majority of society
- Conversion did not change their customs but just their faith (Srinivas 1967, 60)

Thirdly, Westernisation helped abolish a few traditional evil practices, with the help of the "new elite" such as *suttee* (1829), "female infanticide, human sacrifice, and slavery (1833)" (Srinivas 1967, 47; Agnihotry 1987, 15; Srinivasan and Gary R. Lee 2004, 1115).

So far, we have considered how non-Christian sociologists view social change. In essence, Hindu sociologists refer to the influence of Hinduism for strong patrilineal joint family life. They do not take into consideration nuclear-structure families common among a majority of Dalits in India. Thus, it appears theirs is not a balanced view of reality. By way of contrast, the next section addresses how Christian social thinkers view social change in family life.

Changing Pattern of Family: Nuclear Influences

P. D. Devanandan and M. M. Thomas[3] have edited ten essays on *The Changing Pattern of Family in India* (1960). The authors bring to the fore the causes for, the consequences of and the remedies for the changing pattern of Indian family life. The main thesis of their book is "the traditional joint family system is giving way to nuclear family structures." The book makes three basic statements:

---

[3] The late Devanandan and Thomas were among the influential Christian social scientists in India. They have edited *Religion and Society*, an academic journal of fame for several consecutive years. M. M. Thomas was a self-made lay theologian-statesman. He had the honour of serving as Chairman, Central Committee of WCC (1975-1980). Thomas also had the distinction of being governor of the State of Nagaland, India (1990).

1. Traditionally, the three twice-born castes practiced the joint family system owing to *common ancestry and property.*

2. Low-caste people never lived in joint families. Three reasons are advanced for this difference from the high castes (see Devanandan and Thomas 1960, xiv, 27-29).

   a. Low Castes had no common property.

   b. They were not bound by the *jajmani* (patron-client) arrangements. The monetary economy and the payments in cash have ushered in a change. Hitherto, the low caste bond slaves were paid in kind. Therefore, poor people used to pool their resources together. Due to modernity, labour is hired on a contract basis rather than the traditional status basis.

   c. Unlike the first three castes, the low castes had not practiced rituals to honour their ancestors (*Shraddha*).

3. The Christian family in India is also changing and the authors offer New Testament remedies. The solution the authors offer is in the good news of the gospel of Jesus Christ. For example,

   d. Marriage and family life are distinct, but not a condition for fullness of Christian life (*ibid.,* 140)

   e. Sex, as we know it, belongs to fallen humanity (*ibid.,* 134).

   f. Marriage is of this world. As such, family is not a "bed of roses" but a community of grace and forgiveness (*ibid.,* 141-143).

What causes these changes?

Forces of Change in Family Pattern

The authors present three factors that affect changes in the family pattern:

1. New ideas - such as "rights of a human person"

2. New social sanctions-like the ban on "sati" (widow burning) or on "child marriage"

3. New social structures-such as "industrialisation" and "urbanisation." The traditional authoritarian models in the family needed modification.

What are the consequences?

The authors write that the above three factors have increased:

1. Respect for the human individual for maximum development.

2. Evaluation of human sexuality. For example, some aspects of traditional marriage are incompatible with modern values.

3. "Secularisation" in a "scientific," "democratic" and "socialist" age is real.

4. Increased belief in the value of "Western Civilization." For example, social institutions, such as "industrialisation" and "urbanisation", are judged on the basis of their contribution to human welfare. However, it is also agreed that Western civility requires "individualism."

Christian Gospel and Family Planning

One of the greatest challenges for India is population explosion. In relation to this issue, Devanandan and Thomas emphasise marriage as a divine institution that demonstrates the spiritual and moral unity of the couple. They write that coitus is not just for procreation but for the creation of "one flesh", in body, spirit and morality (Eph 5:31). This does mean that a Christian can practice family planning. But marriage is not essential for fullness of Christian life (Matt 19:11-12). Marriage is only for this world (Devanandan and Thomas 1960, 140).

Integrative Comment

The Indian joint family is influenced by Hindu liturgical morality and cultural values, such as "Sanskritization" (M. N. Srinivas 1967). Second, P. D. Devanandan and M. M. Thomas affirm that new ideas such as "human rights", new social sanctions like the "ban on child marriage" and new social structures such as "urbanisation" have ushered in the nuclear family. For these Christian writers, a family is also "a community of grace and forgiveness" (Devanandan and Thomas 1960, 143). It is changing in form, but unchanging in providing meaningful existence to human beings. For example, marriages in most cases are arranged by parents and elders.

From the discussion on the peasant family we move to view its economic life.

Agrarian Economy and Social Change

The Green Revolution is one of the greatest technological achievements of the 20th century. It ushered in a change of life for the better for millions of peasants. Awarded the Nobel Peace Prize in 1970, Norman Borlaug, the father of the Green Revolution, attests to its importance. This movement entered India in the mid-1960s.

I am indebted to Stanley A. Freed and Ruth S. Freed, *Green Revolution: Agriculture and Social Change in a North Indian Village* (2002), for my understanding of the impact of the Green Revolution (or agro-economics) in India. The Freeds, a couple from the USA, have associated with and written extensively about Indian culture and society for the last 45 years. Stanley Freed is now Curator Emeritus and Ruth Freed is Research Associate in the Division of Anthropology, American Museum of Natural History. They did extensive ethnographic study of the village of Shanti Nagar (pseudonym) in 1957-58 and 1977-78. These dates closely bracket the Green Revolution. Shanti Nagar is a village close to and within the Union Territory of New Delhi.

Green Revolution: Definition

Freed & Freed define Green Revolution from an historical and socio-technological perspective.

> In the mid-1960s, rural India passed through a period of rapid social and technological change. Because changes were especially evident in agriculture, the period is known as the Green Revolution. Although all of India was affected, the Green Revolution was particularly pronounced in the northwest: Punjab, Haryana, Delhi Union Territory, and western Uttar Pradesh. By the late 1970s, the Green Revolution had been adopted throughout its northwestern heartland, and this region had entered the post-Green Revolutionary period. (Freed and Freed 2002, 19).

Freed and Freed differentiate the changes in the 1960s from the 1970s. In the late 1950s, agriculture in Shanti Nagar was subsistence peasant farming at a low technological level, basically unchanged for decades. By the 1970s, agriculture had evolved into expensive commercial farming with modern technology.

The authors explain five major socio-technological innovations basic to the Green Revolution:

(1) The development of high-yielding varieties of food grains, especially wheat and rice

(2) Land consolidation

(3) Private tube well irrigation

(4) Mechanisation

(5) The use of factory fertilisers and pesticides

　　　　(Freed and Freed 2002, 20; Sabharwal 2001, 193).

New sources of energy, electricity and the internal combustion engine, which replaced bullock power and changed the financial infrastructure, enabling farmers to buy new equipment (tractors, tube wells and threshers), represented a fundamental change. The most visible results of the Green Revolution were substantial increase in the production of new high-yielding varieties of grain and increased prosperity for farmers, as well as for almost all villagers.

As agriculture was undergoing fundamental change, other important developments were also taking place. The educational level of villagers improved markedly. This opened the door to employment opportunities in modern occupations. Because of the Green Revolution and associated developments in education and employment, the economy of Shanti Nagar, whose principal component is still agriculture, was transformed. The villagers now lead a modern style of rural life supplemented by urban employment. These changes have also had the effect of enhancing social equality. The Freeds offer "four" helpful theories. I will consider just two of the four.

Two Theories: Modernisation and Standard

Two of the four theories that Freed and Freed delineate are relevant to my subject, namely modernisation and standard theory. The key to modernisation theory is the peasants' willingness to adapt and modify Western machinery. The peasants of North India modify their machinery;

> For example, in North India, tractors may be fitted out with a pulley and belt and be used to power tube wells, fodder cutters, gristmills and the threshing machines. Tractors often serve to haul produce to market in a cart in lieu of trucks and they are widely used for personal transportation. (Freed and Freed 2002, 24)

Adapting machinery for local need enhances effectiveness and is economical.

"Standard," the second theory, is about commercialisation and is rooted in the works of Marx and Lenin. Marx and Lenin foresaw riches "for the few" and poverty "for the many" from capitalism (Attwood quoted in Freed and Freed 2002, 24; Mazumdar 1993, 18). The Indian Government made a policy to promote the new technology of the Green Revolution. This decision was taken in response to chronic food shortages and dependence on foreign food aid. Proponents of standard theory expected that the Green

Revolution would enrich big farmers impoverish small farmers and create massive unrest among agricultural labourers. Thus, in their thinking, the Green Revolution would turn into a "red revolution." But the contrary happened. Some agricultural labourers began to participate and became agricultural entrepreneurs, taking land on contract.

It is noteworthy that the Green Revolution has a second phase.

Second Green Revolution in 1977-1978

The first Green Revolution during the 1960s centered on hybridisation, while the second Green Revolution was about genetically engineered seeds. Genetically engineered seeds enhance a farmer's economic predictability and social stability and provide incentive to invest in farming. Freed and Freed defined the second Green Revolution,

> The first Green Revolution was based on hybridisation. The second Green Revolution features modern genetic engineering, a technique for extracting a gene from a donor organism and inserting it into a recipient so that it becomes incorporated in the recipient's genome. If the source of the gene is a distant species that cannot be hybridised with the recipient, the new organisms that result from genetic transfer is said to be transgenic. (Lewontin quoted in Freed and Freed 2002, 251).

The authors also note that

> Plant breeders have successfully transferreda gene from the bacterium *Bacillus thuringiensis* into maize and cotton that causes them to produce an insecticidal compound, commonly called Bt toxin. When insects nibble plants protected by the powerful Bt toxin, they die. (Freed and Freed 2002, 251)

For example, the "Flvr Savr tomato" (Freed and Freed 2007, 253), patented by Calgene scientists, has a longer life than common tomatoes. So, the second Green Revolution is not so much about yield in the crop, but about making farming more efficient and conferring economic advantages.

What all this means is that Christian Dalits are subject to change because the farming world is changing. It means they can adapt cultural modes of expression for use in their missiology as my research will demonstrate.

So far we have viewed the farming economy from a male perspective, but Eloise Hiebert Meneses rightly draws our attention to the market economy as it is related to and operated by Dalit women who sell agro products.

Market Economy, Social Change and Continuity: Meneses

Eloise Hiebert Meneses is a fourth generation missionary child from South India. Her view of Dalit market women stems from a critical view of Hindu hierarchical society. The author's womanhood and her egalitarian [Western] background also contribute to how she looks at the status of market women in the Devaraj Market of Mysore city.

Meneses convincingly argues that to love the "poor, female, and Untouchable (*Dalit*) market women is to love the neighbor" (Meneses, *Love and Revolutions: Market women and social change in India*, 2007, 156). These women are categorised as social "other/s" by the Hindu caste system. For her, market exploitation is grounded in the religious texts of Hinduism. She writes that her target people experience "caste oppression in the rough tones, sharp words, and other remnants . . . daily from [their] suppliers and customers" (Meneses 2007, 180). *Rg Veda* 10.90 and *Manu Dharma Sastra* I.91 (Manu's Law Code) order the Sudra caste's subservience to the three upper castes forever (*ibid.*, 60, 91-92; Dumont 1970; Sen and Dreze 1999, preface). And they place the *panchama* or Dalit Castes below the Sudras.

Meneses regrets that, ironically, market women embrace "Sanskritisation" by painfully saving money to marry off their daughters (see Samuel 2002). Dowry is one expression of this adaptation. Dowry-giving was not the traditional practice among the Untouchables, but a later development. Dowry was and is the practice of high caste and wealthy people. Daughters of the wealthy were never allowed to work outside the home, so in order to compensate for her future indoor life in her husband's home, a dowry was given. Meneses, worries that "Sanskritisation" or "social mobility" has never meant "structural change," but only a limited "positional change" for Dalits (Meneses 2007, 88). Other modes of Sanskritisation adapted by these women include expensive rites of passage and an unhealthy hold on remarriage of their widowed daughters (*ibid.*, 180).

Besides religiously sanctioned poverty, Meneses explains the exploitation of market women by the global market economy. Dr. Manmohan Singh is the chief architect of the liberal economy policy introduced in 1991 (Meneses 2007, 164-165). As a result of this policy, the poor labourers suffer. Dev and Ranade note the grim situation:

> Currently (post 2004), the poverty rate is at its lowest since Independence. But there are still nearly 300,000,000 people living on less than $1 per day, and a bottom of 40 per cent of the population that are spending 78 per cent of their income on food alone. (Dev and Ranade quoted in Meneses 2007, 165).

Following Alexander and Alexander, Meneses writes that liberalisation produces two negative results: (1) An expanding middle class and (2) a drop in income for the poor. She cites Alexander and Alexander who point out that the market place is particularly welcoming arena for the latter because of its ability to "soak up" large numbers of uneducated and unskilled people and to keep them minimally alive (Alexander and Alexander quoted in Meneses 2007, 167; Bose 1994, 393). This, however, does not mean that government policies and higher classes value petty traders. In fact, the petty vendors are chased off by police and ruffians. Their presence is considered to be unruly because they are unlicensed sellers:

> The presence of these unruly traders selling on sidewalks and in storehouses, without paying licenses and taxes, evoke images of disorder of development gone awry, and of market failure. The sprawling urban barrios and sidewalks congested with women hawking wares, their children sitting beside them, bespeak the failure of development and government control. (Seligmnann quoted in Meneses 2007, 168).

Meneses' argument is that social change requires pro-poor economic policies. She suggests that true *national* well-being depends upon just distribution of wealth by the government (cf. S. S. Bhatti in Rajesh Gill. 2005, 81-83). For example, the Marxist government in Kerala has reduced poverty to 8 per cent while in [non-Marxist] Uttar Pradesh it is as high as 46 per cent. One of the reasons, states Meneses is the 86 per cent "adult female literacy" rate in Kerala as compared to Uttar Pradesh at just 26 per cent (Meneses 2007, 169).

Meneses reiterates that, as a result of adaptation to the majority culture poor market women are forced into economic stress and their widow daughters are withheld from remarriage. I fully agree with Meneses that we need to move beyond biological kinships to take a stand for the social "others," such as the Dalits of India, and specifically, the market women. However, one has a feeling that Meneses' thrust has positioned the "Hindu nationalists" as "social others." Perhaps this is due to her stand for the poor. I suggest that nationalists too should be embraced, of course on the grounds that they show "internal change" like others.

From economic concerns we turn to the Panchayat way of administration, which has been in operation in India's villages for ages. Panchayat governance runs on consensus and humane values.

Panchayati Raj in India

The concept of the village *Panchayat* is ancient.[4] Panchayat and democracy are two opposing models of governance. A Panchayat is a council of representative elders who make decisions for the group, while democracy is a tabulation of the undifferentiated votes of the whole population. The Panchayat symbolises a decentralised system of administration based on truth and justice governed by "consensus" (Hiebert 1974, 101-102).

For S. K. Dey, the Panchayat represents a code and a philosophy of life. The nation, according Dey, is an extension of family and must be governed by this code. Dey is concerned that democracy has no roots in India and at best is short-lived, if not totally illusory. He envisions the Panchayati Raj, as it exists in India, transcending the national boundary and becoming "World Panchayat" in the United Nations Organisation (Dey 1962, 121-122). This World Panchayat would assume the role of "mother" to the world family, dispensing the resources of the earth equally to every human being.

Panchayat and Ram Raj

Dey begins with Rama Raj (the rule of the mythical king Rama)[5] as the ideal of Panchayat. Rama was a "ruler–servant" of Ayodhya (Dey 1962, 4). He was the oldest son of the family. The Sarpanch, who is the leader of the Panchayat, is likened to Rama as the oldest brother, caring for the needs of everyone in a joint family. Traditionally, the Sarpanch (*Mukhiya* in Hindi) had four counselors

---

[4] The term Panchayat comes from "panch," meaning five. Thus, it is council of five elders in the village. In general, they were experienced, aged and headed by either by Brahmans [priest] or Kshatriyas (ruling caste) Their justice is mostly punitive. The greatest punishment would be social boycott. As such, Panchayat also means the court of justice.

[5] Sita, Rama's spouse, was abducted by Ravana, the king of Srilanka. Rama invades Srilanka as Ravana does not submit and rescues Sita. The story is that Rama built a bridge between the southern tip of India and Sri Lanka to wage war against Ravana. Today, there is an outcry by the Hindutva parties to resurrect the mythical story for political reasons. Karunanidhi, the Chief Minister of Tamil Nadu and an atheist by belief, has condemned the existence of such a passage to Sri Lanka and declares that whatever exists there is nature's gift. The rocky seabed there, which creates shallow water, is connected to the mythical story.

to advise him on village development and its administration. There were devilish minds (e.g., Ravana or Kaikeyi[6]) even in the ideal kingdom, the Ram Raj. The evil ones often the battle for a short period, but truth and justice prevailed in the end.

Dey, himself a son of a Sarpanch, eulogises Panchayati Raj as the best model for the governance of India even today. For him, the entire village functions on kinship. Each one addresses the other by *dada* (grandfather), or *chacha* (paternal uncle), or *mama* (maternal uncle); thus everyone, whether of a high caste or a low caste, is related to one another. Realistically though, the Panchayats have also undergone changes.

Democracy: Panchayat Raj and New Democracy

British rule, education, industrialisation, the press and finally Independence (1947) have thrust democracy upon India, creating, a people-focused rule. This is in contrast to Gandhi's vision for the ideal Rama *Rajya* to be in operation in the villages of India. Gandhi stressed (1) winning real freedom from the devil (lust and greed), who is inside the person (Dey 1962, 50) and (2) the merit of the Panchayat system of rule (since freedom from colonial rule was won), as uplifting the village as the hope for the nation. Bapu indicated,

> The Government of the village will be conducted by the Panchayat of five persons annually elected by the adult villagers, male and female, possessing minimum prescribed qualifications. These will have all the authority and jurisdiction required. Since there will be no system of punishments in the accepted sense, this Panchayat will be the legislature, judiciary and executive combined to operate for its year of office. ... Here there is perfect democracy based upon individual freedom. The individual is the architect of his own Government. The law of non-violence rules him and his Government. He and his village are able to defy might of a world. For the law governing every villager is that he will suffer death in the defence of his and his village's honour.

> This, however, does not exclude dependence on and willing help from neighbours or from the world. It will be free and voluntary play of mutual forces (Gandhi quoted in Dey 1962, 63).

Panchayati Raj and Synthesis

In the footsteps of Gandhi, S. K. Dey rightly points out that India

---

[6] Kikeyi, a wife of Dasaratha, the blind king (and father of Rama), had a son called Bharat. He was Rama's younger brother. Kikeyi played tricks to steal the throne for her son. By design, she sent Rama into wilderness to live for 14 years, while her son rules the nation. Finally, Rama returns and assumes the kingdom.

shall be regenerated based on the synthesis of three vital principles: cooperatives, Panchayats and village schools. (1) Cooperatives, or *sahakara* societies, cater to the needs of the village family and industry, such as cooperatives for brick-makers, masons, cattle-breeders, poultry and fishery men (Dey 1962, 98), that (2) Panchayats shall head both the planning and administration of village affairs. Further, (3) village schools are pivotal to developing any village, because education is necessary for building human character. Dey cites Swami Vivekananda, for whom education was not accumulation of abstract knowledge but "man making":

> The ideal of all education, all training, should be man-making. Education is not the amount of information that is put into your brain and runs riot there, undigested, all your life. We must have life-building, man making, character-making, assimilation of ideas. If you have assimilated five ideas and made them your life and character, you have more education than any man who has got by heart a whole library. If education is identical with information, the libraries are the greatest sages in the world, and encyclopedias are the *rishis*. (Vivekananda in Dey 1962, 105)

Dey is appreciated for his reference point that "Ram Rajya" is ideal governance for the village. Rama goes through trials but wins at the end. His kingship is god ordained. M. K. Gandhi, Tagore and S. K. Dey have illustrated that the strength of India lies in the welfare of the village. By contrast, in the new democracy, the author wishes that "liberty, equality and fraternity" (Dey 1962, 116) as envisioned by Jawaharlal Nehru, prevail.

It is my conviction that the welfare of the Church in India also lies in caring for the rural Church. Panchayat judgment is notably not perfect, but takes social life into consideration. It is based on consensus of male family heads rather than on the basis of judge of a court of justice. However, the Panchayat modeled after Rama Rajya prefers the hegemony of high castes, which seldom tolerates equality of life and justice to poor and marginalised groups (Dalits).

Unfinished Quest for Local Democracy and the Modern Village

The traditional Panchayat Raj as patterned after Rama Rajya, is an ideal "theocracy." This was the vision of M. K. Gandhi, Tagore and Dey. In contradistinction, Naya [modern] Panchayat has been in effect since 1978. Nehru's socialism is the root cause for this thinking. He wanted the entire nation to participate in nation building based on egalitarian principles. Local democracy is the method the secularist Nehru propounded (Girish Kumar 2006). Nehru and his grandson, Rajeev Gandhi (former prime minister), are the champions of turning Panchayats into local democracies. The 73rd amendment to the Constitution ushered this great change in 1992 (Kumar 2006, 23; contrast Ruud 2003, 200-202). To strengthen *gram sabhas* (village councils), "Block Development offices" or "Provincial development and district councils" or *Zilla Parishads* were introduced. Block development offices spearhead provincial development programmes. The key here is the close proximity of administrative networks coordinated by the District Council or Zilla Parishad.

Unfinished Quest for Local Democracy

In contrast to Panchayat rule, Girish Kumar presents seven benefits of local democracy (Kumar 2006, 297). I will summarise Kumar's ideas and then critique them. First, democracy expands the scope of social and political participation, especially for poor and the marginalised peoples (cf. Sudarshan 1997, 277-278). Second, it makes the system more accountable, responsive and transparent. Third, it ensures the efficient delivery of goods and services to the people, especially in the fields of primary education and health care thus helping with a judicious use of natural resources such as water and forest resources. Fourth, it enables people to articulate and voice their concerns. Fifth, it offers people a forum to exchange opinions (see also Ilaiah 2003, 149-169). Sixth, it provides a way for ordinary people to operate in the public domain and to practice the art of collective decision making without resorting to intimidation and violence. Finally, it functions as a nursery for upcoming leadership, nurturing and preparing leaders for higher-level institutions. In a nutshell, local democracy impacts the day-to-day life of common people by ensuring more democracy at the local level.

Laudable as the objective was, it is the marginalised people who are at the receiving end of disadvantage in the local democratic system. Of course, the democratisation of village politics has given room for common people to articulate their views. Their voice is heard in a limited way. But local democracies have embraced caste-based politics. For example, the Congress Party is said to be run by the Brahman or the Reddy elite. Caste politics does not let the poor win elections because the rich and well-to-do manipulate the votes of poor people. Since 1990, local democracies serve as basins for reserved seats for the Scheduled Castes, including women (see Prabhakar 2004, 263). But this has again allowed the rich and powerful to play games with the lives of the poor. Sometimes a village Panchayat reserved for a Dalit woman candidate is spoiled by low castes' themselves, prompted by high-caste political rivals the low castes field another woman candidate. Moreover at times, politics based on political parties enrage political hatred even division in the church.

Therefore, local democracies have helped common people; they have also opened the door to the rich to manipulate the polity of the village. All this points to the reality that village life is changed yet unchanged. The sin-sick world needs a change of heart at every juncture of life. My only hope is that the good news of the kingdom and the model life that the church offers become a solution for India.

Summary on Literature Review

Social change and continuity exist in tension in three areas of village life. First, joint or nuclear families are subject to social change due to influences like Sanskritisation (ritual mobility aspirations) and Westernisation (Srinivas 1967). Yet residue from traditional beliefs and practices remain. Second, the farming economy has increased productive yield due to two Green Revolutions in the 1960s and 1970s. The two Green Revolutions introduced high-yielding varieties of food grains, tube well irrigation, mechanisation, chemical fertilisers, and genetically engineered seeds that assured economic stability for farmers (Freed and Freed 2002). Scientific innovations led to the modifications of machinery, thrusting change and continuity (e.g. tractors modified for multi-purpose use). Yet the revolution in farming has not helped small farmers who are in the majority. Third, S. K. Dey's idea of *Rama Rajya* (Hindu theocracy) is the model for *Panchayats* in India (Dey 1962). In contrast, secular-minded Prime ministers Nehru and his grandson, Rajiv Gandhi, have further strengthened democratisation of the village government (Kumar 2006). So the traditional family, economy and governance live in creative tension.

The above survey of the literature brings me to clarify another term in my research, which is "self-identity." I will comment briefly on the self-image of the Madiri Puram village Christians prior to their conversion to Christianity. I say "briefly" for two reasons. First, the self-identity of the Dalits is a thesis by itself. Second, at this juncture, it is enough for me to introduce the subject so that we have a feel for the Dalit status in society.

Self-identity of Christian Dalits

Who are Christian Dalits? Traditionally, Christian Dalits were denied of "human dignity." They were treated as non-humans as a result of Hindu caste rigidities. Bishop M. Azariah defines the term "Dalit" succinctly:

> Interestingly, the Sanskrit word 'Dali' and the Hebrew term 'Dhalid' literally mean the same and refer to "the poor and the oppressed people." In India, the so-called 'Outcastes' or the 'untouchables' have recently taken the name Dalit as self-designation, thus rejecting and protesting against these and other demeaning labels given them by the dominant Hindu society during their long history. The list included 'A-varna' (casteless), 'Dasas' (Slaves), 'Chandalas' (cursed ones), 'Panchamas' (fifth people), 'Harijans' (people of a junior Hindu God), and 'Scheduled' Castes, etc. (Azariah 2000, xi; cf. Massey 1996, 3; Massey 1997, 1-3; Webster 1999,1)

Eloise Hiebert Meneses has compiled a description of the inhuman Untouchable social status in pre-British India:

1. The necessity of taking a bath if touched by an untouchable.

2. The requirement that untouchables ring bells as they walk to warn others of their approach

3. The requirement that untouchables wear spittoons to avoid polluting the ground.

4. The requirement that untouchables operate at night to avoid being seen.

5. The forbidding of untouchable men or women to wear shirts or shoes.

6. The forbidding of untouchable women to wear jewelry or face powder.

7. The segregation of untouchables into separate hamlets.

8. The forbidding of untouchables to walk through the caste village.

9. The forbidding of untouchables to use major roads or wells.

10. The refusal to seat or to serve untouchables in tea shops and restaurants.

11. The forbidding of untouchables to read the Vedas (to learn to read at all).

12. The refusal of priests and artisan castes to serve untouchables.

13. The forbidding of untouchables to enter Hindu temples.

14. The requirement that untouchables remove the village people's night soil.

15. The requirement that untouchables remove carcasses and corpses.

16. The forbidding of untouchables to own land.

17. The slavery of untouchables to land owners for agricultural labour.

Eloise then analyses these 17 requirements and puts them into four major categories. Numbers 1-6 symbolise "social stigmatisation," numbers 7-10 depict "social exclusion," numbers 11-13 describe "religious restriction," and numbers 14-17 subject the Dalits to "degraded economic status and tasks." In essence, the Dalits had minus self-identity (see Meneses 2007, 91-92). Upon conversion to Christianity, these Dalits, who were once "no people have become the people of God" (1 Pet 2:10).

However, the focus of my study is not on their status while being "without God" and "without hope" (Eph 2:12), but on how these converted Dalits indigenise their theology, culture, socio-economic status and polity as part of their identity. What reasons and what influences[7] cause them continue or discontinue their Christian tenets?

The next chapter will clarify my research design.

---

[7] An "influence" is understood as power to affect persons or events, especially power based on prestige etc; e.g., she "used her parents" influence to get the job. *(wordnet.princeton.edu/perl/webwn)*

Chapter 2

RESEARCH METHODOLOGY

My area of research will further expand our understanding of "folk Christianity" in village India. A number of noted scholars have already written a great deal on this subject (Hiebert and Meneses 1995, 215; cf. Hiebert et al. 1999, 90-91; 225, 369). However, I claim that my research will make (1) a significant contribution to missiological reflection on discipling indigenous churches. It aims at (2) a better understanding of village Christianity in its cultural setting. Apart from benefiting missiological thinking and cultural anthropologists, this study will also (3) inform social anthropologists in India and elsewhere. For example, in a situation where Christianity is blamed for being "foreign," harassed and persecuted, my research will celebrate the positive aspects of the national identity of the church despite its limitations as a minority religious group. Moreover, I plan to continue my research in the years to come to better serve the Lord, the Church and my nation.

Methodology: Qualitative Method

To gather the desired data for the above concern, I will employ the qualitative method. Data collection is in the shape of an ethnographic study done over a period of five months continuously, with a few breaks in between. My absences from the site have given me room for reflection and either modification in strategy or a chance to modify a particular questionnaire. My real data come from qualitative interviews, life stories and participant observations. Life stories are tested by interviewing others involved in the story so that truthfulness is confirmed.

This study is based on ethnographic descriptions, life stories, comparisons and analysis of data. By "ethnography" I use H. Russell Bernard's definition: "As a noun, it means a description of a culture, or a piece of a culture. As a verb (doing ethnography), it means the collection of data that describes a culture" (Bernard 1995, 16-17). Culture in this thesis relates to the Christian Dalits [Dalits] and non-Christian Dalits of Madiri Puram and its neighboring villages. These descriptions are based on people's responses to my questionnaire or on my observations and verification with several other people in the village.

"Case studies" are those stories that pertain to events in individual or community life stages, or to cultural experiences and expressions between 1915 and 2005. Stories include their success and failure. My key informants shared their stories either voluntarily or as part of their response to my questionnaire. Stories were shared because people trusted me. They wanted to communicate moral lessons to the family or church or to honour God (e.g., overcoming a temptation). Stories are people's own perspectives; my role is to learn and analyse them.

The ethnographic data on Christian Dalits will be compared with that of non- Christian Dalits in the village and region. For example, lists of deities and ritual practices of these two communities will match or mismatch.

I will then analyse the data based on themes and worldviews that arise.

Advantages in Choosing Madiri Puram Village

Madiri Puram was chosen among many possible villages in Gadwal, a geographic region. The general direction given to me by my former mentor, Paul G. Hiebert was to conduct research in a village different from my own region (c.250 kilometers distance away). How did I choose this particular village? I shared my research concern with one of my faculty colleagues. We were sharing the pulpit at the Uppala Camp MB Church Dedication and Gospel meetings (2003). Early that Sunday morning, this colleague of mine took me on a borrowed motorcycle to Madiri Puram village and introduced me to the church there—his mother church. Following our visit, I shared my first impressions with my mentor and he readily agreed that I proceed.

I have a passion for understanding the village church, partly because I come from a village and partly because most of the 850 Mennonite Brethren churches (as per estimates in 2008) are rural. In my chosen topic, change is mentioned first to indicate the influence of the gospel in transforming the lives of the village people. But the riddle is to understand the continuance of past traditional practices despite a century of Christian presence.

There are a number of advantages of choosing Madiri Puram village for field research. First, the village claims to be as ancient as the *Mahabharata War* (c. 3137 B.C., see Subhash Kak. www.ece.Isu.edu/kak/Mahabharatall.pdf-). The village considers *Shivalayamu* (Shiva temple), one of the two main temples in the village, to have been established by *Janame Jayudu*, the grandson of Arjuna (a major character in the epic *Mahabharata*). This traditional claim has lent stability to the village. Second, Madiri Puram is one of the twenty peasant villages in Waddepally Mandal (province) of the Mahabubnagar District. It satisfies my intention of studying a farming community. It is a remote village like many Mennonite Brethren villages in Andhra Pradesh. Third, it provides me with enough population to study. As per the 2001 census report, 4,535 people live in the village. That includes 3,421 high castes and 1,104 Schedule Castes (Scheduled Caste) and 10 Schedule Tribes (ST). Scheduled Castes and Scheduled Tribes together make about 24.35 per cent of the population. There is one migrant Mala family.

In addition, I have chosen four neighbouring villages in which to locate my non- Christian Dalit interviewees, namely Mundladinne, Julekal, Waddepally and Shantinagar.

Procedure

My instruments included living among the people, participant observations, using key informants and conducting interviews. I used qualitative questionnaires as a guide. I did not hand the questionnaire to respondents but kept a copy handy for my easy reference. Twenty-four key informants were chosen after careful thinking. Ten among them were women. The reason is very simple: women fill the church at every spiritual gathering. In line with this design, I stayed in Madiri Puram village for five months at a stretch (July-November 2005), and then for several shorter visits ranging from three days to a week during 2003 to 2005. My primary data come from comprehensive information, from field notes.

Thick descriptions include how Madiri Puram Christian Dalits (prior to conversion) used to worship Maremma, their clan goddess. Maremma was one of the spiritual powers that even resisted Jesus to begin with and won over forty of his disciples, but when Jesus threatened her with dire consequences, she backed off (see chapter 4 on Art and Architecture). The data will also highlight how the Reddy and Christian Dalits form the dominant Class in Madiri

Puram village (see chapter 7 on "Consensus in Christian Dalit Panchayats").

I have the "etic" (outsider) views (Hiebert and Meneses 1995, 14-16, 363- 364), which contribute objectivity and balance to the study. The focus though was to learn from "emic" (insider/people) perspectives. Like Malinowski, the goal of my ethnographic study is "to grasp the native's point of view, his relation to life, to realise his vision of his world" (quoted in James P. Spradley 1980, 3).

Participant observation was another effective method for gathering data. It helped me to grasp themes in people's stories and modify my follow-up questions. I agree with Bernard in that it is a way to "immerse" myself in the life of the people. It allowed me to take open-ended interviews, and many photographs, laughing in their joys and crying in their bereavement (Bernard 1995, 323-324). It is a non-intrusive method and helped me to mitigate people's doubts about my research intentions, life and work.

In field research, "key informants" play the major role in gathering data. Merriam-Webster's New Collegiate Dictionary defines a key informant as "a native speaker engaged to respect words, phrases, and sentences in his own language or dialect as a model for initiation and a source of information" (quoted in James P. Spradley, *The Ethnographic Interview* 1979, 25). Spradley goes on to say, "informants are a source of information; literally, they become teachers for the ethnographer" (*ibid.*, 25). On the other hand, key informants can pose us with some limitations. Carol A. Bailey replaces the term "key informant", and warns us of the dangers of using the term "key actor." A key actor has a personal perspective, can isolate ethnographer from some members and can dictate terms to a new field researcher (Bailey 1996, 55, 56). In the beginning, the villagers did not believe my good intentions. But gradually, I was able to learn the art of winning their good will and understand their frustrations. However, not all can be key informants. There is an element of discretion in choosing them.

Who Qualifies as a Key Informant?

Spradley correctly identifies "five qualifications" for attaining information from key informants (1979, 46), which are: enculturation, current involvement, an unfamiliar cultural scene, adequate time and that an informant should preferably be an analytic (see Spradley 1979, 46-54). Out of twenty-four of my key informants, ten of them were women. The simple reason is they make up half of humanity, and more so, the bulk of the worshippers in the church. Over a dozen non-key informants were interviewed — from former pastors in the village to high-caste opponents of the Reddy (village headman) and the Christian Dalits. The total number of people interviewed was 45, including the key informants. But only 24 key informants' views have been taken seriously.

Instruments of Research

For conducting interviews, using a "tape recorder" was quite handy, apart from occasional note taking. I did not use the tape recorder if people were sensitive about its use. For example, I did not use it as I interviewed the only Brahmin in the village. Sometimes I sought the permission of the interviewee to record our conversation. The interviews were in Telugu, our mother tongue. The data in the tapes were transcribed and analysed. By using audio tapes, I could return to hear the voices, accents and feelings of the subjects of my interviews, which helped me to analyse the information.

While formulating the questionnaire, I had a couple of sittings with Hiebert, my late mentor, who later gave his nod of approval for my questionnaire (see appendices I and II). Some questionnaires had to be modified for follow-up, to suit the interviewee's level of understanding, other times modifications were made while translating into Telugu. But I kept the key intent of the questions. So my primary data come from ethnographic descriptions.

Other Primary Data, Research Instruments and Procedure

We have already talked about using field notes as a major source for analysing the village Church in India. Themes or insights that come from field research materials were expanded into chapters. For example, studying political alliances between the Reddy and the Christian Dalits help us discover a new dominant class, perhaps unlike in other villages. In general, one would expect dominant castes to form a dominant class, which tries to retain the village culture. Such themes are from the perspective of the people.

The materials gathered also include some of the following. The first three sources are Church records. The church has maintained its (1) *Minutes* beginning from 1951 to 2005. As far as I know, no other village MB Church has taken such an interest in recording minutes of their annual general body meetings and important decisions. This dissertation has taken into account major themes, decisions, appointment of pastors and disputes and reconciliation (1982). I have also looked into (2) *Church Income and Expenditure Records*, which were mostly faithful with an occasional misuse of funds. I noticed that the resources of the church are seldom used to propagate the gospel. Another source is the membership list. The church goes by (3) *Festival Contribution Records* and not by individual baptism records. To support the pastor, each head of the household is supposed to pay a fixed contribution in cash or kind three times a year—Christmas, Good Friday and New Year.[1]

On a broad level, I had access to the (4) *personal files* of pastors. I have searched for relevant issues in their correspondence with government officials. The files include letters from government officials to pastors to vouch for the scheduled caste status of certain people from the Christian colony for economic benefits.

(5) *Photographs* were taken as part of the data. From a comparison of photography comes chapter 4 on "Change and Continuity in Art and Architecture." A photo comparison of the cowshed of the prominent Reddy with that of the photo of the church porches proved to be invaluable to missiological thinking. (6) Personal writings were gathered from people like R. Jakarayya, a social activist, who has written against caste discrimination in his script titled, *Harijanoddharana* (Upliftment of the Harijan). These resources have been helpful in evaluating the social status issues of the Dalit community.

The plan for analysis was as follows: Christian Dalit perspectives on change and continuity in religious, cultural, economic and political fields were compared with those of non-Christian Dalit views and behaviours. Research emphasised the gospel as the key influence on Christian Dalits. In this sense, the term "Christian" qualifies the Dalit and not vice versa. So, "non-Christian Dalit" indicates non-belief in Christ and a difference in worldviews. A case in point is that non-Christian Dalits have a scant sense of sin, heaven and hell.

---

[1] Each family needs to pay three fees per year:

(1) 32 sheirs of paddy (c. 40 kg) or Rs 150/-

(2) Good Friday contribution in cash Rs 20/-

(3) Christmas contribution in cash: Rs.30/-(4). Fee is paid by membership. There is no exemption in principle. Thus making the church self-supported and self-governing.

Professor Robert J. Priest, a renowned social anthropologist and missiologist helped me to view that, experience-near theologising is the best way to understand or respond to non-Christian Dalits' low view of sin. Following Clifford Geertz's (1977) lead, Priest contends that "Experience-Near Theologizing" is much more engaging cultures than "experience-distance" concepts like "missional theology", as proposed by Hiebert and Tite Tienou (R J. Priest in Ott and Netland eds 2006, 183).

Conclusion

Themes and *leads* from the data are taken into account in the developing of chapters. Difficult economic situations and official harassment of the Dalits make me identify with the struggles of the people. Dalits, in general, are harassed due to the caste prejudices of the bureaucrats. This also points to social justice meted out by Christian Dalits as a result of government policies. There is need to integrate theological education with that of its context, the village church.

Bonds with the non-Christian Reddy facilitate the church to resolve its major disputes under his leadership. However, the democratic voting system in India has made some Christian Dalits bypass the Reddy rulings for political reasons, though his word is final in ecclesial disputes. This may be unique to this village. On the other hand, Madiri Puram church is *Panchayat* (elders' council) run. The elders and the Reddy form the first and second hierarchy ladders (number one and two), putting the pastor into the third category, followed by the Word of God. But there are times when the church listens to the pastor's advice and repents of sin. So continuity and change are social dynamics that are open ended.

But all this means further research is needed. One suggestion is to integrate a seminary education with the church's specific context and then apply it to universal principles of mission. This research will enrich the study of folk Christianity.

Ethical Considerations

My informants were given an "Informed Consent Letter" both in Telugu and English; the letter was explained to them. The Telugu version was for their records and I received the English version with their signatures. I clearly explained to them that the data collected would only be used for research purposes and would not be made public. Their names and responses would be treated as strictly confidential, using pseudonyms. Except for the case of a couple of non-Christian Dalit informants, I see no human rights risks in my field research procedure. See Appendices I and II for "Questionnaire" and "Consent Letter" The above research methodology was employed among the people of Madiri Puram village. But such scientific study will become meaningful only if we consider the provincial and cultural setting of the village.

Chapter 3

MADIRI PURAM VILLAGE SETTING

Madiri Puram, my research village, is one of twenty villages in Waddepally Mandal (Province) in Mahabubnagar district of Andhra Pradesh, South India. Waddepally (Shantinagar) is one of the 64 Mandals in Mahabubnagar district. Mahabubnagar is one of the 23 districts in Andhra Pradesh[1]. Mahabubnagar district has 18,432 sq km of land.

Provincial Setting

According to 1999 estimations, 31 million people make their home in Mahabubnager District (Nageswarao and Rambabu 2002, 149). The name Waddepally is the name in government records. But Shantinagar is the new settlement of the village on the interstate road between Karnataka and Andhra Pradesh, where all provincial government offices like revenue, agriculture, education, medical, banking, vegetable, civil and veterinary offices are located. Business transactions intersect in this town.

What Is a Mandal?

A Mandal is a pro-poor administrative arrangement that N. T. Rama Rao, one of our former chief ministers, inaugurated this system. He defined it as:

> Mandal is the Government method to stand at poor man's door, and knock to learn of his sorrows and joys, and to resolve them immediately. It is an institution introduced to serve the society, to ensure the wellbeing of six crore (sixty million)[2] population, and to enhance an all-round development of the state. (N.T. Rama Rao quoted in *Mandal Gananka Darshini* 1985 [Census Report], front cover).

---

[1] Andhra Pradesh is 276,754 km wide with 80 million people living. The State consists of 29,379 villages. Apart from other communities there are 56,000 *harijans* (children of god, [Dalits hereafter]) and 15,000 tribal people.

[2] Today (2008), the State of Andhra Pradesh has 80 million people.

A background to Waddepally Mandalam will serve as a platform to understand the social, religious and political background to Madiri Puram village, my research village.

Geographic Boundaries of Waddepally Mandal

The Tungabhadra River forms the border in the south of Waddepally Mandal. This river flows from west to east. It separates the Telangana region from the Rayalaseema region within Andhra Pradesh. Telangana was ruled by Muslim rulers called Nizams, while Rayalaseema was under the British Raj governed from Chennai (Madras). Itikyal Mandal is to the north, Ieej Mandal to the west and Manopad Mandal to the east. The Interstate road between Andhra Pradesh and Karnataka runs through Waddepally Mandal. The geographic map of the Mandal is in order here.

Figure 1: Map of Waddepally Mandal— Political Background

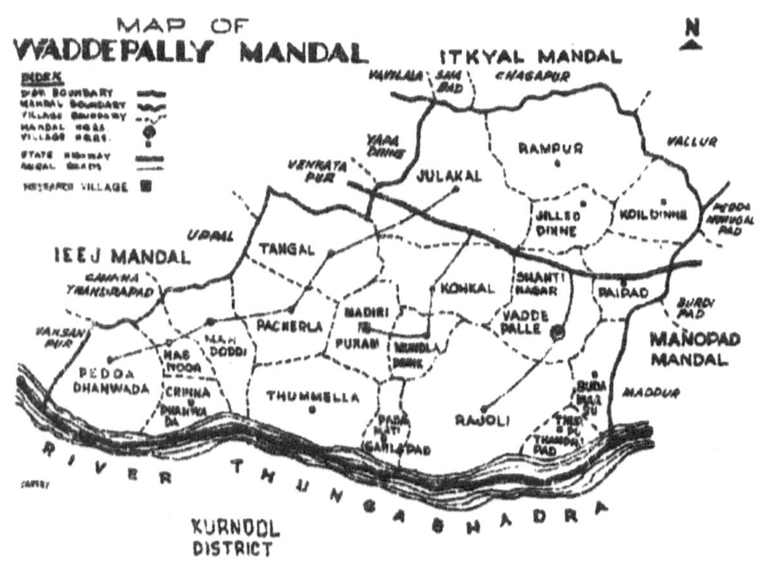

(Source: Waddepally Mandal Revenue Office 2005)

According to the information displayed at the Mandal Revenue office, Waddepally Mandal consists of a total geographic area of 6,53,4605 square acres. There are 20 villages, 3 revenue centres, 19 Panchayats and 31 Fair Price shops. The number of ration cardholders is 10,586 (6,756 white cards, 3,830 rose cards). The ration card is held by the male head of the family (e.g. the father). The ration card is a family's civil supply identity card. It speaks of a family's economic status; so the quota of government supply of essential commodities like rice and kerosene is recorded on the card. The card is the basis on which one counts the number in the family and, as such, the adult number is used for the voters' list.

The next question we will concern ourselves with is about the literacy rate. The literacy rate in Waddepally Mandal is just 16.69 per cent. Out of a total population of 75,326, only 12, 576[3] know how to read and write. This raises the concern that people are ignorant of government programmes, policies and benefits. The 2001 census report presents us with the demographic picture of the twenty villages in the Mandal.

Table 1: The 2001 Census Report of Waddepally Mandal
(M-male, F-female, T-total)

Name of the Village	Total Population as per 2001 Census			Scheduled Caste Population			Scheduled Tribe Population		
	M	F	T	M	F	T	M	F	T
Pedda Dhanwada	1282	1219	2501	0	0	0	6	6	12
Chinna Dhanwada	667	612	12792	50	228	478	0	0	0
Nasanur	622	608	12301	02	94	196	0	0	0
Mandoddi	1926	1924	38505	27	490	1017	10	7	17
Pacharla	1563	1521	30844	20	409	829	0	0	0
Tanagala	1757	1709	34665	52	527	1079	10	14	24
Julekal	1349	1323	26722	36	250	486	32	31	63
Ramapuram	2318	2222	45404	99	429	928	0	0	0
Koildinne	567	545	1112	89	66	155	0	0	0
Paipad	1305	1285	25903	03	281	584	30	29	59
Jillelidinne	364	353	717	83	89	172	0	0	0
Waddepalle	4693	4579	92727	61	733	1494	15	15	30
Konkala	1975	1936	39113	23	317	640	7	6	13

---

[3] Caste people 61,840; Scheduled Castes 13,169; and STs 317 = 75,326.

Contd., **Table 1**: The 2001 Census Report of Waddepally Mandal

Name of the Village	Total Population as per 2001 Census			Scheduled Caste Population			Scheduled Tribe Population		
	M	F	T	M	F	T	M	F	T
Mundladinne	857	861	17182	50	269	519	0	0	0
Madiri Puram	1760	1661	34215	66	538	11046		4	10
Thummilla	1112	1075	21873	23	296	619	0	0	0
P.Garlapad	131	119	250	100	92	19200		0	0
Rajoli	5883	5734	11617	958	905	1863	49	37	86
Budamorsu	850	842	16922	30	230	460	2	1	3
Thurpu Garalapad	365	366	731	174	180	354	0	0	0
Total	31346	30494	61840	6746	6423	13169	167	150	317

(Source: Assistant Statistics Officer,
Waddepally Mandal Revenue Office, 13 September 2005)

(Note: The research village demographics are shown in bold type)

Census Inaccuracies

In the above census report, the Scheduled Caste and Scheduled Tribe populations are shown separately, and are not included in the total population of the Mandal. Hereafter, these Scheduled Castes and Scheduled Tribes will be referred to as "Dalits" (oppressed people for over 3,500 years by the Hindu caste hierarchy). Christians of Madiri Puram come from Dalit background.

The total population minus Dalit totals comes to 61,840 (see the top headings column 3 to the right). The Dalit numbers are shown separately from the Hindu population. It amounts to an official discrimination against the low castes. If we add up the Dalit numbers to the total population of the Mandal the census numbers increase to 75,326 people. Dalits of Buddhist, Sikh and Hindu religious background are entitled by the Constitution of India for economic, employment and political benefits, such as a set quota for admission into government higher and technical education institutions. In contrast, Christian Dalits are eligible for just 1 per cent of such facility alleging that they are backward class, while they remain deprived of social, economic and religious freedom.

It may also be noted that the numbers for Dalits are not available for Pedda Dhanwada village. That should not be taken to mean that Dalits do not exist in the village; it simply means for some reason the numbers were not available at the time of census enumeration. According to the assistant census statistician Chinna Dhanwada (Sl. No. 2 above), Nasanur (No. 3), Pacharla (Sl. No 5), Ramapuram (Sl. No 8), Koildinne (No. 9), Jilledidinne (No. 11), Thummilla (No.16), P. Garlapad (No.17) and Thurpu Garlapad (No. 20) have no Scheduled Tribe inhabitants. Scheduled Tribes may be taken here as either transitory residents or wandering groups and are therefore not recorded.

Male and Female Population

There are only 30, 494 women for 31,346 men among the high Castes (852 less). There are 6,423 females for 6,746 men among Scheduled Castes (323 less), and 150 females for 167 males among the Scheduled Tribes (17 less). It appears there is a general aversion towards the girl child. In Hindu religion, boys are preferred to girls for progeny and ancestry rituals. A girl is married away. Thus, she is a burden.

Drought and Migration Effects

Waddepally Mandal received above-average rainfall (in centimetres) during 2000-2005, except for 2004-2005. However, in difference to the *Directorate of Economics and Statistics Department*, people of Madiri Puram village report that the monsoon failed them for two years in succession, in 2003 and 2004. The village is 11 km south-west of Waddepally Mandal headquarters. It is possible that other areas in the province received rains but not Madiri Puram. The year 2005, in the beginning of third year of no rains, the researcher was present, and I will expand this theme in the section "Peasant Theology of Prayer (see chapter 6). The yearly rainfall in Mandal for 2000-2005 is as follows:

Table 2: Yearly Rainfall 2000-2005 (in centimetres)

Monsoon Year	Normal	Actual
2000-2001	544.3	662.7
2001-2002	544.3	635.0
2002-2003	544.3	560.7
2003-2004	544.3	560.3
2004-2005	544.3	485.2

(Source: Directorate of Economics and Statistics, 2000-2005, AP. Hyderabad)

During the drought years, crops failed and living conditions worsened. Famine situations bring chaos to the rich and the poor alike; but it is the poor who receive the brunt. Droughts force husbands to leave their spouses and children at home to find a job in urban areas. Families are separated, and holistic growth of children is at stake since only one parent rears them. Separation can increase tensions within wedded life or cause bad habits like drinking. Culturally, it is observed that men are more prone to extra-marital relations than women when away from home. On the other hand, some migrants earn better incomes and have invested in lands or have built better houses. Their economic and social status has shot up. However, among the Christian Dalits of Madiri Puram only 21.94 per cent out of the 13,169 people migrate on a seasonal basis. Temporary migrants return to their village during sowing, reaping and festival times, such as Christmas and Easter.

Political Scenario of the Mandal

Political leadership plays a great role in managing general calamities like drought or economic challenges in the province. The 2001 census report brings to fore the administrative arrangements and village level *Panchayat* (the traditional council of five elders) and the power networks that exist. The following table outlines the state administrative system, which is based on democratic principles.

Table 3: Mandal Praja Parishad—List of Honorary Members (2001-2005)[4]

As per the information displayed on the wall notice
at the Mandal office as on 23 September 2005.

1.	Shri R. Shreedhar Goud	President-MPP	Ramapuram
2.	Shri C. Venkataram Reddy	Member of Legislative Assembly (M.L.A.)	Alampur
3.	Smt. H. Sugunamma	ZPTC Member	Rajoli
4.	Shri. D. Vithal Rao	Member of Parliament (M.P.)	Mahabubnagar

[4] As per the information displayed on the wall notice at the Mandal office as on 23 September 2005.

Contd., **Table 3**: Mandal Praja Parishad —
List of Honorary Members (2001-2005)

5.	Smt. G. Lakshmi Kumari	Vice President MPTC	Konkala
6.	Shri Madhusudan Reddy	MPTC	Paipadu
7.	Shri M. Saibaba	MPTC	Waddepally - I
8.	Smt. Shesha Ratanam	MPTC	Waddepally - II
9.	Shri. Kistanna	MPTC	Rajoli-I
10.	Smt. Gorukal Somamma	MPTC	Rajoli-II
11.	Smt. C. Sarojamma	MPTC	Rajoli-III
12.	Shri. Golla Ramakrishna	MPTC	Julekailu
13.	Shri.Singam Kukkanna	MPTC	Madiri Puram
14.	Shri. Sudhakar	MPTC	Tanagala
15.	Smt. Ramulamma	MPTC	Paccharla
16.	Shri. Kurva Sunkanna	MPTC	Mandoddi
17.	Shri. H.Eeshwarayya	MPTC	Chinnadhanwada
18.	Shri. Ramudu	MPTC	Peddadhanwada
19.	Shri. Nazeer Ahmed	MPTC	Co-opted Member

(Source: Mandal Praja Parishad Office, Waddepally)

The Mandal Parishad Territorial Committee (MPTC) members represent Mandal concerns to the Mandal President. The Zilla Parishad (district council) Territorial Committee (ZPTC) members bring district concerns to the overall headship of the Member of Parliament and the Member of Legislative Assembly. The Mandal President is the presiding officer in all official meetings.

All *sarpanches* (village heads) are members of the Mandal Council. The welfare of the village depends on their ability. A *sarpanch* is in office for five years. The *sarpanches* of Waddepally Mandal for 2001-2005 are listed below.

Table 4: Sarpanches for 2001-2005

S.No	Name of the Sarpanch	Name of the Village
01.	N. Sreenivasulu	Waddepally
02.	Smt. Sugunamma	Rajoli
03.	Sanjanna**	Turpu Garalpadu
04.	K. Linganna	Budamarusu
05.	K. Jayanna	Paipadu
06.	Smt. D. Nirmalamma	Koyaldinne
07	Vinod Kumar	Ramapuram
08.	Venkatram Reddy	Jillela dinne
09.	K. Linganna	Julakallu
10.	Smt. Gokharamma	Konkala
11.	M. Laxmanna*	Mundladinne
12.	N. Sreeramulu	Madiri Puram
13.	S. Paulayya*	Tummilla
14.	Naganna*	Tanagala
15.	Smt. Sujanamma*	Paccharla
16.	Smt. B. Govindamma	Mandoddi
17.	Smt. K. Rameswari	Nasanoor
18.	A. Mohan Reddy	Chinna dhanwada
19.	Pedda Keshanna	Peddadhanwada

(Source: Mandal Praja Parishad Office, Waddepally)

Key: ** a seat reserved for Dalits but general category
(i.e., Scheduled Caste or Scheduled Tribe).

* A Dalit candidate elected in the Scheduled Caste category.

A Dalit sarpanch receives a government allowance of Rs 800 per month, while a B. C. (Backward Caste) sarpanch receives Rs 600 per month. Sarpanches from Christian backgrounds who claim Dalit status testify to caste discrimination in the allocation of development funds at the provincial council. High-caste sarpanches get priority as they form the majority in a Mandal Council.

Education and Child Labour

A professing Christian Dalit sarpanch of Tummilla village says that one of his responsibilities is to represent the concern of his village school to the Mandal (provincial) Education Officer or to higher-ups at the district level. There are 5 Zilla Parishad (district) High Schools, 4, 23 Upper Primary Schools and 4 Primary Schools in the Mandal (province). To cater to the needs of students, the government runs 2 Scheduled Caste, 1 Backward Caste (Christian and others like Moslems) and 2 Scheduled Tribes Social Welfare Hostels. Waddepally also has a Private Junior College called, Laxmi Nagireddy Junior College.

The 11 Mandal schools lack adequate teaching staff. Their distance from Mandal Headquarters, together with allotted posts and vacant situations at each school is shown below.

Table 5: Schools with Vacant Teaching Posts

Name of School	Distance from Mandal (province) HQs In Kilometres	Total Posts	Vacant Posts
UPS-Pedda Dhanwada	28	5	3
PS-Chinna Dhanwada	24	4	3
PS-Nasanoor	23	5	4
UPS-Mandoddi	21	4	2
UPS-Paccharla	18	3	2
PS-Thummilla	18	4	3
PS-Ashok Nagar	15	2	1
Madiri Puram	13	5	2
PS-Chintala Camp	14	1	1
PS-Jakkireddypally	11	3	2
PS-P.Garlapadu	11	2	1

(Source: Mahabubnagar District Teachers Federation
[Status in November 2005]

Key: UPS=Upper Primary School, PS=Primary School)

It is hoped that with the 2003 District Selection Commission (Scheduled Caste) recruitments effected in 2005, most of the vacancies will be filled, resulting in better education conditions for students. In Chintala Camp (Table 5), there is no government teacher. It is observed that there are two voluntary teachers working, but the service of voluntary teachers is not as effective as education service provided by the government.

In most cases, schools have a bare minimum number of teachers; for example, Primary School (PS) at Chinna Dhanwada lacks three teachers out of four, Nasanoor lacks four out of five, Pacharla lacks two out of three and Thummilla lacks three out of four teachers. These figures add up to a 63.15 per cent deficiency in staffing. The effect is poor educational future for the student and a bad reputation for the school. The solution to this problem lies in the determination of government and local administrators. Another solution is for voluntary organisations to take up the challenge of educating people through adult education and night schools.

Another challenge that schools face is "school dropouts." The Mandal Educational Officer admits to a drop in attendance during the male-female flower pollination season of commercial crops such as cotton, a season of three to four months. A child is a preferred worker for his or her tender hands and fast movement. A rich "Rytu" (farmer) advances daily wage money to parents, two to three months in advance, so that they send their children to work. A superstitious worldview adds to the child labour problem. The belief is the tender touch of the girls in the field is a blessing to the crop, and the touch of the women with monthly periods pollute [reduce] the yield. Thus, school dropout rates rise from July to September. Poor families are compelled to drop their children out of school temporarily, resulting in poor attendance, loss of lessons and not doing homework. This results in poor performance in exams and grasp of the subjects. It is also found that dropping out of school causes disinterest and stress in students later.

Health Care

Due to the above realities, it is possible that young people grow with stress, raising the question of what is available for treatment. Waddepally is a Mandal with 75,326 people. It needs more than one civil hospital as well as private clinics with training and experience. The lack of adequate staff is a major reason for poor health care; as seen on December 28, 2005 the health care staff position was as shown below. The other reason is that doctors in general avoid working in rural areas. Instead, they prefer urban centers.

Table 6: Primary Health Centre

Name of the Post	Total Posts	In Position	Vacant Post
Community Health Officer	1	-	
Civil Assistant Surgeon	1	1	-
Staff Nurse	1	1	-
Senior Assistant	1	1	
MPHS (Male)	3	FW 1 NMEP 1	1
MPHA (Female)	11	FW 9 MCD 1 OP -	21[5]
Attender	1	1	-

(Source: Mahabubnagar District Medical Department—2005)

Key:

M.P. H.S   –   Multi Purpose Health Supervisor (Male/Female)

M.P. H.A.   –   Multi Purpose Health Assistant (Male/Female)

F.W.   –   Family Welfare Programme

N.M. E. P. –   National Malaria Eradication Programme

M.C. D.   –   Mother and Child Development

O.P.   –   Out Patient

The total vacant posts are four. But as noted above, as a growing agriculture sector, Waddepally Mandal needs more than one Primary Health centre run by the government.

The Agriculture Scene

Agriculture is the primary industry in the Mandal. There is no other industry of note. Rajulabanda Diversion Scheme (Rajulabanda Diversion Scheme) has supplied canal water to all the twenty villages in the Mandal since 1958. The list of the main crops and total acres under irrigation and other information is given hereunder.

---

[5] A post vacant at Rajoli village.

Table 7: Irrigation and Related Information

Total villages irrigated	20
Total acres under irrigation	21,067[6]
Important crops	Cotton, Paddy, Ground nuts, Sun flower and Millet
Police Stations (PS)	2
Veterinary Hospitals	2
Overhead drinking water Tanks	8
Pensions	Old age -627, Widows – 82
Banks	4
Important industry	Agriculture
Agriculture Co-operative Societies	5

Source: Waddepally Mandal Revenue Office—2005

Brief History of the Rajulabanda Diversion Scheme Canal

The Rajulabanda Diversion Scheme has brought life to the region. A brief history of the Rajulabanda Diversion Scheme Canal is in order including the injustice done in releasing the allocated thousand million cubic (TMC) feet of water. Rajulabanda Diversion Scheme is an interstate project of Karnataka and Andhra Pradesh states, consisting of an *anicut* (an ogee type masonry structure or a dam) built across the Tungabhadra River for diverting 24.07 cumecs (=850 cusecs, a cusec is one cubic feet of water flow per second) of water into the 143 km long Rajulabanda Diversion Scheme Canal to benefit the drought-affected area of 15 villages in Raichur Taluka of Karnataka State, 8 villages in Gadwal Taluka, 67 villages in Alampur Taluka and 4 villages in Kurnool Taluka. The work was started by the Nizam Government of Hyderabad in 1947. The construction of the head work was completed in 1958 and the main canal in 1960.

Due to the reorganisation of states in 1956, the head works *anicut*, 42.60 km length of Rajulabanda Diversion Scheme main canal along with its distributaries 1 to 12 covering a localised *ayacut* (irrigated area) of 2,379 *ha* (5,879 acres) have gone to Karnataka.

Out of the 6,53,4605 square acres of land in the Mandal, only 21,067 acres is irrigated. So, in general, the province is prone to poverty. However, most of the land in Madiri Puram receives the Rajulabanda Diversion Scheme canal water.

The remaining length of Rajulabanda Diversion Scheme main canal, from 42.60 km to 43.00 km, along with distributaries D/12A to D/40 covering a localised *ayacut* of 35,410 *ha* (87,500 acres) have come into the territory of Andhra Pradesh.

The development of *ayacut* is significant from 1966-67 onward. The maximum *ayacut* developed so far is 2,230 *ha* (55423 acres) of which 9,662 *ha* (23873 acres) covers *Khariff* or wet area farmlands and 12,768 *ha* (31,550 acres) covers *Rabi* or Irrigated but dry area farmlands (Executive Engineer 2005, 1).

What is important to point out is how much of the water was released to the Andhra part of Rajulabanda Diversion Scheme Canal and what are some of the present struggles in realising the allocated thousand million cubic feet of water?

Foul Play in Allocation of Canal Water (1975-2004)

The allocated 11.9 thousand million cubic feet water was released just for ten years to Mahabubnagar District (1975-1984). Then it was diverted per musclemen belonging to Rayalaseema and Karnataka regions. Within about two decades (1987 - 2004) there has been a reduction of 5.34 thousand million cubic feet of water from the initial 11.9 thousand million cubic feet. Moreover, the original intent to supply 17.2 thousand million cubic feet of water to the Telangana region (Gadwal and Alampur Taluks) has never been materialised. R. Jakarayya, a Christian Dalit social activist and one of the affected farmers in Madiri Puram village, gives four major reasons for this injustice:

1. Construction of a below-capacity canal for a required 17.2 thousand million cubic feet Rajulabanda Diversion Scheme; thus officials gave into political pressures or have worked for selfish gains

2. Lack of advocacy for Telangana cause (e.g. no engineers from the region)

3. Rayalaseema *goondas* (musclemen) divert water by unjust means

4. Lack of political will among concerned Andhra legislators (MLAs), e.g. infighting for shares from allocated funds for renovation of canal (Jakarayya 2005, 5).

The table given below points to a gradual decrease in the allocation of canal water.

Table 8: Water utilisation since 1975 -2004 under Rajulabanda Diversion Scheme (representative years)

Year	Area Irrigated in Acres			Water Utilised in TMC[7]			Remarks
	Khariff[8]	Rabi[9]	Total	Khariff River flow	Rabi	Total TMC	
1	2	3	4	5	6	7	8
1975-1976	26680	27697	54577	6.92	6.85	13.77	50,624 acres were irrigated during 1975-1984, with arelease of 11.99 TMC feet ofwater
1976-1977	26072	0	20072	7.33	1.43	8.76	
1977-1978	22642	24653	47295	7.09	7.07	14.16	
1978-1979	22175	27001	49175	6.39	6.57	12.96	
1979-1980	22587	32155	54743	6.92	6.71	13.63	
1999-2000	18500	16686	35186	3.569	3.101	6.67	But by 2000-2004 acres irrigated dropped down to 37,990 with theshort supply of 5.34TMC of water dueto manipulations.
2000-2001	19223	21650	40873	4.125	2.715	6.84	
2001-2002	21335	0	21335	4.14	0	4.14	
2002-2003	11935	0	11935	3.38	0	3.38	
2003-2004	20272	12664	32936	3.08	1.144	4.227	

(Source: Mahabubnagerv District Gazette 1990, 73)

[7] TMC= thousand million cubic feet of water flow.

[8] Khariff=crops like rice/paddy, which need regular supply of water. Dam or reservoir is full of water during the rainy season (June to September).

[9] Rabi=crops like peanut, which need only occasional water supply. Crops like these are also called dry but irrigated crops. Rabi is also an indication of season (December- April).

It is important to point out which villages in Waddepally Mandal got Rajulabanda Diversion Scheme Canal water. The entire twenty villages in the Mandal enjoy Rajulabanda Diversion Scheme canal water. The Mahabubnagar Collector has noted the following statistics for 1990 (P. Krishnaiah, Collector & Magistrate- *Mahabubnagar 1990*, 74 -75). His statement gives the names of the villages with wet and dry crops, land survey numbers, and the total acres irrigated during that year. Madiri Puram gets water through distributary canal number 25.

**Table 9: Wet and dry irrigation statistics - 1990
for Waddepally Mandal Province**

ABSTRACT

Name of the Village	Distributary No.	Wet	I. D[10]	Total
(1)	(2)	(3)	(4)	(5)
Thummilla	25	802-15	–	802-15
Mundladinne	25 26	390-15 230-22	–	620-37
Ramapur	27/A	61-31	–	61-31
Koildinne	28 27	127-37	– 61-00	188-37
Jilledinne	27/A 27	29-27	207-16	236-43
P. Garlapad	25	–	513-13	513-13
Rajoli	26 25	914-31 –	– 1823-18	2737-49
Waddepally	26 26 27	20-08	– 1351-38 610-07	1981-53
C. Dhanwada	17		318-33	318-33
Nasanoor	18		640-01	640-01
Julekal	25/A 26/A 26	244-06 156-07 –	178-37	578-50
T. Garlapad	26	–	–	Nil
Paipad	27 28 27	253-39 420-17	– 554-16	1227-72

---

[10] I.D. = Irrigated but dry crop acres

Contd., **Table 9: Wet and dry irrigation statistics -
1990 for Waddepally Mandal**

Name of the Village	Distributary No.	Wet	I. D[10]	Total
(1)	(2)	(3)	(4)	(5)
Budamarsu	27	190-10		152-19
	27		62-09	
P. Dhanwada	17	262-17	799-27	1061-44
	17			
Mandoddi	19	77-26	—	2305-10
	22	339-39	—	
	18	--	677-15	
	23		1211-30	
Tanagala	25	126-06	139-06	265-12
	24			
Pacharla	25	357-02	708-29	1065-31
	23	-		
Madiri Puram	**25**	**450-20**	**·**	**450-20**
Konkal	25	45-33	·	938-55
	25/A	450-19		
	26		443-03	
Total		**5946-27**	**10296-98**	**16243-25**

(Source: Mahabubnagar District Gazette 1990, 74 -75)

The above chart depicts the situation in1990. A few factors are noted:

1. Except T. Garlapad village (Table 9) the rest of the 19 villages benefit from the Rajulabanda Diversion Scheme canal.

2. Thirteen Distributaries 17-19, 22-28 supply irrigation water to Waddepally Mandal.

3. In addition to the water from Rajulabanda Diversion Scheme canal, now there is the possibility of utilising the Priyadarshini Jurala Project Dam[11] water with a link to the Rajulabanda Diversion Scheme canal. The existing Rajulabanda Diversion

---

[11] Priyadarshini Jurala Project Dam is built across Krishna River in Atmakur Mandal and supplies water to Gadwal, Alampur and Kolhapur Taluka (provinces) in the district.

Scheme canal has been re-graded and linked from 116.048 km to 126.705 km to benefit the tail end ayacut about 30,000 acres of Rajulabanda Diversion Scheme canal vide G.O (Government Order) Ms No. 77 dated 15-04-1999.[12] So, the MB churches in this region are rich compared to churches in other regions, such as Kalvakurthy in the same district.

The Need to Modernise the Rajulabanda Diversion Scheme Canal

According to R. Jakarayya, the proposed measurement of the canals was tampered by the influential politicians. The Bachawat Water Tribunal Award (1944) ordered Rajulabanda Diversion Scheme to supply water to irrigate one million acres for each region in the Telangana region of Andhra Pradesh and to Kurnool-Cuddapah districts in the Rayalaseema area. However, the Telangana region did not get its share due to political manipulation. One worry is that the construction solution vents (temporary earth dams to divert the flow of the water to build the concrete dam) were never closed at Rajulabanda village, despite the completion of the dam. Truck loads of protesters from the Telangana region went bare-handed to the dam site in 2004 to arrest this problem, but the Rayalaseema *goondas* (muscle men) came with *lathis* (clubs) and bombs. The protest to implement Government Order No. 109, i.e., to close the construction vents, has failed. Mr. Baireddy Rajashekara Reddy, a Telugu Desham Party Member of Legislative Assembly, led a group of musclemen in 2004 to blast the Rajulabanda Diversion Scheme dam unless his unjust demands to benefit Rayalaseema region were met. Fortunately, a dam guard informed the police of Mr. Baireddy's intentions and he was stopped. Accumulated silt has also not been cleared for many years now. The canal should carry 17.2 thousand million cubic feet of water, but it cannot, as its capacity is smaller. The Kurnool-Cuddapah districts' canal capacity was increased from one million to three million acres, while the Rajulabanda Diversion Scheme canal's capacity was reduced from 87,500 acres to 37,990 acres (Executive Engineer 2005.1) as of 2004-2005.

This disparity calls for social justice between states. If this is the background in Waddepally Mandal, it can be concluded that the situation is equally problematic in Madiri Puram.

---

[12] Refer to a joint declaration by the Executive Engineer of Rajulabanda Diversion Scheme Division at Uppal and the Project Administrator & Superintending Engineer at *Priya Darshini Jurala Project Circle*, Gadwal. 2005, 1.

Summary

We have covered the general background to Waddepally Mandal. Political, educational and agricultural challenges and benefits have been mapped out. We have noted the very low literacy rate in the Mandal. In the census details, we found that the Dalits (Scheduled Castes and Scheduled Tribes) make up only 17.90 per cent of the total population. Scheduled Tribes seem to be mostly a wandering group. The monsoon failure for two years in a row caused poor people in Madiri Puram village to migrate to urban centres, with either the families being adversely affected or their economic status being improved.

But it was just 24.91 per cent migrated and that too it is a seasonal migration. The political scenario relates the Mandal both to Zilla and regional issues under the chairmanship of the Mandal president. *Sarpanches* rule the villages by consensus. Village heads from low-caste background feel bypassed when it comes to majority say regarding development funds. We have also found that schools suffer deficient staff and dropout rates. Madiri Puram has two qualified teachers instead of the required five. Eleven schools suffer from a 63.15 per cent lack of staff. The health care system is well staffed, but one PHC is not enough for a population of 75,326 as per the 2001 census.

Finally, we looked at the grim situation with regard to agriculture, the main industry in the Mandal and how the water allocation is tampered with by official and bad elements. The intended 17.2 thousand million cubic feet of water to Telangana has yet to be realised.

With this geographic, political, agricultural, health and educational background, we are ready to consider the cultural setting prior to the coming of Christian Missions in Madiri Puram village.

Cultural Setting

Figure 2: Map of Madiri Puram Village in South India

MADIRI PURAM

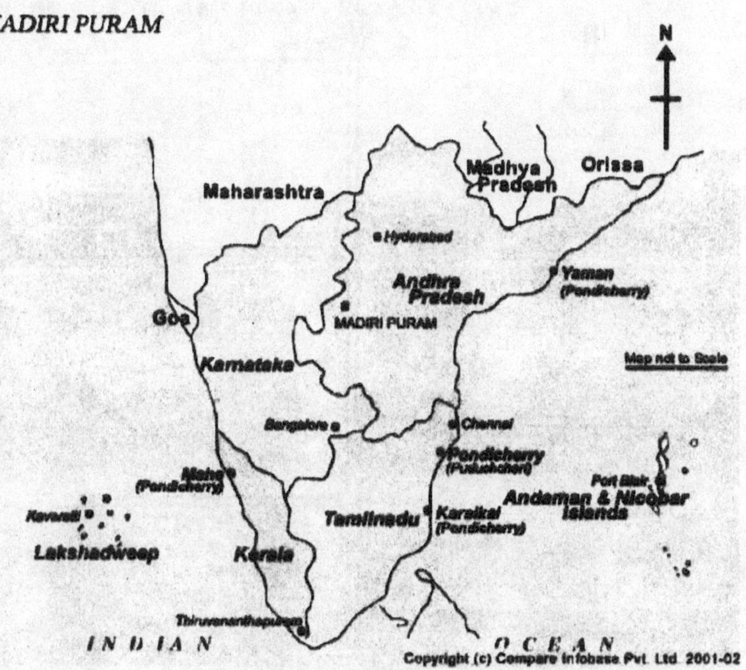

Source: Compare Infobase 2001-02

Figure 3: Map of Madiri Puram Village Panchayath and Hamlets

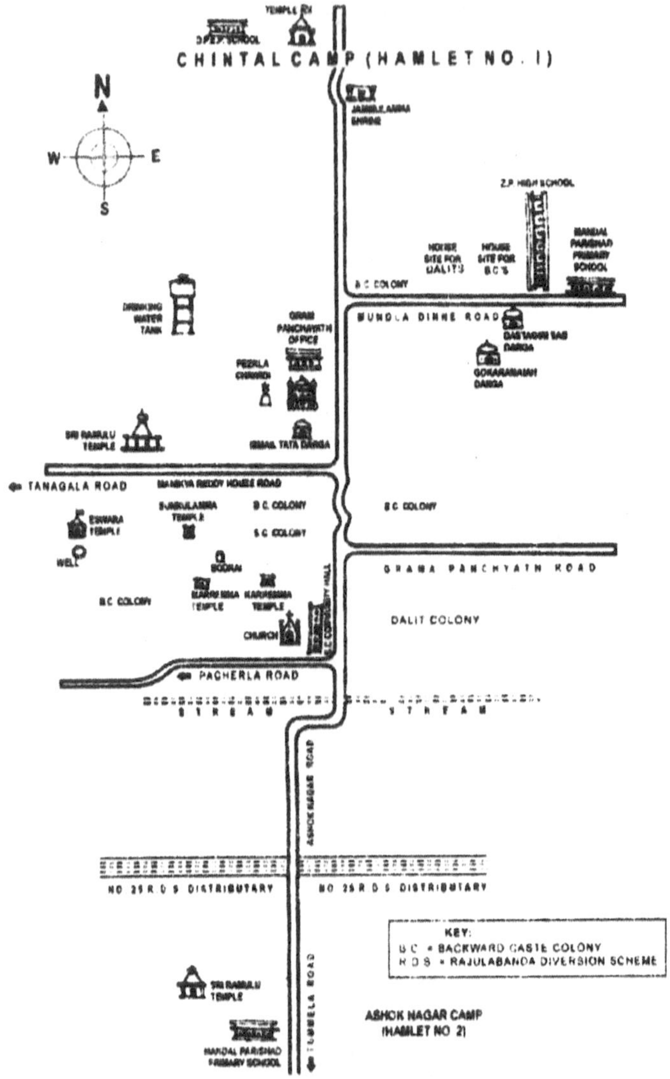

Source:Drawn by Balagari 2005

Introduction

We have looked at the general background to Waddepally Mandal in Mahabubnagar District of Andhra Pradesh. We surveyed the region's geographic, political, agricultural, educational and health care systems.

This section is about the cultural setting of Madiri Puram, the main research village. It is one of the 20 peasant villages in Waddepally Mandal of Mahabubnagar District.

The study focuses on Madiri Puram village, but half of the key informants hail from four neighbouring villages, namely Mundladinne, Julekal, Shantinagar and Waddepally. The design is to compare the data from Madiri Puram village with that of four neighboring villages. I was not able to make an ethnographic study of four villages, but had qualitative interviews with some of the villagers. The inhabitants of the four villages are mostly non-Christian Dalits. Their opinions serve as contrasts to the views of Christians from Madiri Puram village. Both Christian and non-Christian worldviews are included below. All the four villages are also agrarian by occupation. The distances in kilometres to the four villages from the main research village are as follows: Mundladinne 2 km; Julekal 10 km; Shantinagar 13 km; and Waddepally 15 km.

The introduction to the village is presented in three parts: A Walk through Madiri Puram, Daily Life in Madiri Puram village and Religion, Caste and Worldviews. This description is done with the primary aim of understanding the Dalit situation in its cultural context.

Christian and non-Christian Dalits in and around Madiri Puram village are the chief subject of this research. Their life is described with special attention to religion, caste, political connections and worldviews. The perspective is to look at change and continuity in their lives in these important areas.

Madiri Puram is second to the last village on the south side of the Tungabhadra River. Pacharla village is to the west of Madiri Puram, and Tanagala village is to the northwest. Konkala village forms its northeast border. Mundladinne village is on the east.

As we enter the village from the east, from Shantinagar via Mundladinne village, we find Zilla Parishad High School and Upper Primary School to the right. The roof of the Upper Primary School has been pulled down, pending renovation. Opposite to Zilla Parishad High School are three Sufi Saint *dargas* (tombs) to the left side of the road. The Gokaramayya tomb is the most famous of the three. Alisab *darga* (tomb) the third is not shown on the village map.

Proceeding a quarter kilometre westward and turning left onto the main road, we see the Panchayat Office and Nooran-E-Masjid (the mosque), one after the other on the right side of the main road. The Panchayat premises house a *doora vaani kendramu* (telephone exchange). Near the telephone exchange are two hair dressing salons and a bicycle-repair shop. Beyond the Telephone Exchange is a tall drinking water tank, not in use anymore. The village is supplied with Tungabhadra river drinking water from Rajoli Filter Station since 2007.

Ishmael Tata Dargah

Nooran-E-Mosque is to the left of the panchayat office. Ishmael Tata *darga* (grand father tomb) and *Peerla cavidi* (an open house containing large human shape brass images) of Hassan and Hussain are next to the mosque. *Peerla* brass images are in memory of Hassan and Hussain, the grandsons of Prophet Mohammad, who died as martyrs in a religious war. Ishmael Tata *darga* (a Sufi saint tomb) is a live religious site near the mosque. Moslems and Hindus pay homage to Ishmael Tata in the evenings. Orthodox Muslims in the village give glory only to Allah and do not attach importance to saint tombs. However, most folk Muslims believe in the power of Sufi saints. Sufi families take yearly turns to officiate as mullahs (priests) at Ishmael Tata and Gokaramayya dargas. In villages, people from all faith backgrounds celebrate *urs* or reunion of a moslem saint with his god upon his death. People of all faiths pray to these saints on their death anniversary for healing and fulfillment of life wishes.[13] Ishmael Tata Darga is one such Sufi saint tomb in Madiri Puram. Reddamma (patroness) helped keep up these shrines. It is said that in 1958, 130 sheep and goats were sacrificed at Ishmael Tata tomb. It is Adi Sheshi Reddy who entertained Ishmael Tata,

---

[13] John Bowker defines "urs" as follows: The death of a saint is regarded as a time of reunion with his Lord and therefore considered a happy occasion. . . . Each Sufi order celebrates its particular annual 'urs' programme. Ideally, the 'urs' should take place at the shrine of the saint, but it can be celebrated anywhere...In England, 'urs' dates have become an important social event in Muslim communities. Men, women, and children travel to other cities in order to participate and share the *baraka (blessing) of the 'urs' (such as the healing of sickness and the fulfillment of wishes). The 'urs' ceremony generally has three stages: (i) Qur'an recital, prayers, and a sermon on the saint; (ii) *sama (musical audition), when the whole congregation listens to qawwals (singers and musicians) reciting Sufi poems (when some devotees may lapse into ecstatic states, *wajd). At the conclusion of the sama, the Sufi order's litany is recited, and this leads to (iii) a feast. Though the 'urs' has been condemned as negative innovation by the puritanical *Wahhabis and the * Ahl-al-Hadith, it still has strong support amongst orthodox believers (The Oxford Dictionary of World Religions 1997, 1009).

an immigrant to the village. Reasons for faith in Sufi saints will be given in the next sèction.

Peerla *Cavidi*

Peerla *cavidi* (a folk Moslem religious hall) is another popular location for social integration, in memory of Hassan and Hussain, the grandsons of Prophet Mohammad, the village has developed *alam*, a cultural dance, for nine nights. Peerla *Masjid* (mosque) is the site where this used to go on. Hindu dancers even come in *Pandava*[14] attire to dance. For example, Bheemudu, the second older of the five brothers was the best wrestler of the *Mahabharata* epic. So a dancer would come as Bheema in a wrestler dress. Christian Dalits used to beat the *tappeta* (percussion drum) amplifying rhythmic dances. For some, this is thought to be the right place to take revenge by stepping on the toes of the rival in the guise of dance. Some dancers go into a trance and run to a nearby well, jump in, swim and return to play. Once a dancer had a dagger in his waistband, which pierced him in the well by accident or design. So Manikya Reddy ordered a full stop to *dhulai* (the dance). In folk Islam, some claim faith in Jesus. A Muslim could be touched by a Christian healer. Thus rural India faiths are plural expressions. All this shows that gods and saints are not bound to their primary religions, but are called upon to meet the human in need.

Reddy Residences

Taking a right turn at the Ishmael Tata dargah, we walk on a cement road towards the Manikya Reddy bungalow, a former patron-ruler in the village. Sita Ramanjaneya Temple is to the right. This is the largest Hindu temple in the village. Opposite to the temple is the Kattameedi Maremma shrine. Moving south, one comes to the residence of P.Adi Sheshi Reddy. The Reddy is considered second in rank in the caste hierarchy in this village, the first being the Brahmans. We will look at caste statuses later. Near Kattameedi Maremma is Adi Sheshi Reddy's dilapidated cattle shed. The cowshed is used now only to preserve animal feed (*gaddi vaamu*).

---

[14] Pandavas were the five brother heroes of one mother "Kunti" in the epic *Mahabharata*, namely Dharma Raju, Bheemudu, Arjunudu, Nakuludu and Sahadevudu. Kunti had another son but he joined Duryodhanudu, their opponent and cousin brother's camp Duryodhana represented "Kauravas", or the hundred princely siblings against five cousin brothers to do evil.

Adi Sheshi Reddy's residence and his ruined cowshed employ Norman architecture. Norman architecture is three or four capital "U" upside down shapes. The architecture was copied by the local church for its porches for theological and cultural identity. Adi Sheshi Reddy was known for his twelve-year fight to secure 205 acres of government land for Dalits. The belief is that his motives were many-sided. He wanted to prove to Mahabubnagar district his benevolence to the poor Dalits, as well as show his political acumen against other Reddys in the region. This has cemented inseparable bonds between the local Reddys and Christian Dalits. As a result, major church disputes are settled by the ruling Reddy, himself a non-Christian.

The residence of Manikya Reddy (a cousin to Adi Sheshi Reddy) is the last house in the west part of the village. The road to Tangala village passes in front of his house. To date, the Manikya Reddy residence is the most beautiful house in the village. Manikya Reddy built his house in the style of regional Reddy houses. The grandparents of Adi Sheshi Reddy and his cousin Manikya Reddy migrated to this village from the Rayalaseema region beyond Tungabhadra River. People believe that these Reddys belong to Pakanati *Rajulu* (princes). Both Adi Sheshi Reddy and Manikya Reddy residences are looked after by their *Jeetagaallu* (servants) now.

Lingamanna and Chennakeshava Shrines

Going a little beyond the Manikya Reddy house we find a bridge over the brook that separates the village from its fields on the west. Crossing the bridge and taking a left turn, we come across two holy sites, those of deities Lingamanna and Chenna Keshavudu. Their stone images lie in the midst of growing crops. In recognition of services of the priest and in honor of Chennekeshava god, Chintala Camp is a site gifted by the ruler of the village to the priest family of Chenna Keshavudu. About fifteen acres in size, the camp is 1 km away to the north of the village.

On return, past the Manikya Reddy residence, we see on the right the house of Damodara Rao, now eighty years old. He served the village as the long-term *Karnam* (Revenue Officer). This lone Brahman house is the largest in the village. From the top of this house, one can view the entire village.

Eshwaralayamu: The Ancient Structure

Sunkulamma Gudi (shrine) is a three-minute walk from *Karnam's (revenue collector)* house. Her shrine is within the shepherd (Sudra) caste community; she is their clan goddess. Past that area, we find a big Eshwaralayamu or the temple of Shiva with a huge *gopuramu* (spire). Eshwaralayamu is the most ancient structure in the village. It has *sthala purana* (sacred space myth) attached to it. It is believed that Janamejayudu, the grandson of Arjuna, established this ancient structure in *Dwapara Yugam* (or Age, c. 500 B. C.E to 400 CE).[15] The phallic symbol of Shiva represents the belief in active creation. Shiva is also the god of destruction. The temple faces West, a unique feature in the history of Shiva temples. This temple is second only to another temple facing West in Gurujala village of Yemmiganoor taluka (a sub-region) in Kurnool district. A temple facing West is contrary to *Vastu* (starry combination) regulations. But this is an exception. Thus exceptions, even contradictions, are part of India's plurality of faiths.

Bodrayi: The Leader Stone of the Village

Moving east from Shiva temple, we spot a stone buried in the middle of a *veedhi* (street). It is *Bodrayi* (the navel stone) of the village. It is one foot above the ground and about two feet deep in the ground. It looks like a *lingam* (a phallic-shaped stone) related to Shiva worship, but not so. *Bodrayi* has its historical value. It is the mythical leader and centre of the village. It is said that a village without a *Bodrayi* is like a human without a head, without direction. People hesitate to entertain marriage alliances with such a village. Life protection and safety from pestilences is attributed to this navel stone. Moving further east, we come out on to the main road. Here we find *Komati* (trades caste) houses with their *kirana* (general) stores. There are some petty shops and hotels, as well as a medical clinic run by a Registered Medical Practicenor (RMP). The RMP visits patients even in Christian Dalit palem.

Low-caste Areas

Turning south, we sight two older and younger sister shrines, Maremma and Karremma shrines, one after the other and are located adjacent to the main road. Karremma has a simple shrine made of

---

[15] Alf Hiltebeitel, "Mahabharata , in Mircea Eliade (Editor in Chief). *The Encyclopedia of Religion* (LIU-MITH). Vol.9. London: Macmillan Publishing Company. 1987:118-119. Cf. Washburn E. Hopkins, "Mahabharata in James Hastings (ed).*Encyclopedia of Religions and Ethics*. Vol.VIII (Life-Mulla).Edinburgh: T & T Clark, 1915: 325-327. Hopkins dates *Mahabharata* epic as late as 5th to 9th century A. D.

three stones. Maremma, the older sister was the chief deity of the Dalits. The Dalits build big temple in honour of Maremma in Mahabubnágar district. But the Maremma temple in this village has been in ruins since the coming of Christianity in the 1920s.[16] R. Jakarayya, my key informant, says that the Maremma temple was once the centre of the Dalit [his] community. The area from here to the end of the village is covered with Christian Dalit houses. This is traditionally called *Harijan Wada* (Children of god Street). Caste hierarchy is a reality in the village.

Church: The Centre of Christian Dalit Life

The Gilgal India Mennonite Brethren Church, the only church in the village, is located on the same side of the road as Maremma and Karremma shrines, to the west. The church building is the largest structure in the entire village. The Church premises and parsonage put together are three times bigger than the Sri Sita Ramanjaneya temple and its precincts. Christian houses are located to the west and south of the church grounds and to the east of the main road. The Church is the centre of the Dalits. The Christian Dalit colony forms the single largest caste population in the village. Unlike in most villages, the Dalits of Madiri Puram hold land adjacent to the village, especially to the east and south. The church is a live community with Sunday morning and night worship services, Friday women's meeting, Saturday intercessory session and daily *Edugantla prardhana* (evening 7 o'clock devotion and prayer time for the youth). Making our way towards the south end of the village, we find the Dalit Community hall under construction. It is going to be one of the largest buildings in the village. Walls are raised but work has stopped due to some *Panchayat* (village council) mismanagement of funds. Upon completion, the community hall will add another attraction to the Dalit section of the village, besides the church. The community hall will be used for social functions like marriages and community festivals. The surroundings of community hall are now covered with thorny bushes. Women use the area to attend nature's calls.

---

[16] Some say that Maremma had Dalit respects until the 1970s; then as their Christian faith grew, she was left an orphan. But one of their households continues to be her priest.

Moyiddin Kirana Store

Beyond the Christian Dalit housing section and traveling towards Mundladinne village, we come to Moyiddin's house cum Kirana (grocery) store. Moyiddin's business depends mostly on the Christian colony. He and four of his siblings maintain cordial relations with Christians. One of the reasons could be that they are migrants from Rajoli, a former Fort Township and a former Hindu vassal state. Moslems are hard-working and good at business. Prior to receiving Rajulabanda Diversion Scheme Canal water, poor people in Madiri Puram village used to depend on Rajoli Township for their livelihood and business. Grandparents of Gilgal MB Church members used to sell firewood and buy groceries in Rajoli. Rajoli handloom is quite famous in Andhra Pradesh.

Boyas and Naiks

Past the Dalit section and Moyiddin house, the Boya and Naik (Sudra caste) houses begin and continue until one reaches Zilla Parishad High School on the left side of the main road.

Summary

The above sections complete our walk through Madiri Puram. The structures important to our study are Christian Church, Kattameedi Maremma shrine and P. Adi Sheshi Reddy residence and cattle shed. Areas where continuity is most apparent are open-ended beliefs and practices. For instance, some Christian Dalits continue to worship Maremma their ancient deity. Change is seen mostly in animist Dalits embracing Christian faith. Their worldview has changed from animism to Trinitarian monotheism. The change is also projected in Christian Dalits borrowing Norman architecture from the Reddy premises. The walk through the village leads us to consider what daily life is like in the village. The Madiri Puram village life has remained the same for hundreds of years. However, significant changes have taken place in the last ninety years.

Panchayat (Elders' Council) Way of Rule

All societies require social order. Whether a palem (colony) or a village embraces change or not, maintaining order in the village is most important. For ages the Panchayat way of rule has been functioning well. The accepted procedure is to ensure consensus rather than voting to defeat the other person. Even today social boycott is the method by which a person is chastised. Of course, the jealousies and dominances of caste, class or clan networks show their might. In addition, modern India has introduced Panchayat elections and candidatures based on caste. This is one step forward and two steps backward, because once caste is made the base, then communalism creeps in, disturbing social integration. People make selfish gains out of politics. In a democracy, social representation is managed when there is a weak Sarpanch (village head) from low caste. High caste people are generally rich and manipulative in villages. Manipulation of money, muscle or intimidation is at work. To drain someone's chances of winning the panchayat election, high-caste people encourage low-caste people to file their nominations. They can split the votes if the low caste political contestant does not oblige to their whims and wishes. They see to it that a nominal Sarpanch is elected. My research looks at the political aspects of Madiri Puram village from the perspective of Reddy- Dalit Christian relations. Christian Dalits and Reddys have worked hands-in-gloves for political and social security reasons. *Puliki malavasaramu-malaku pulavasaramu* ("Tiger and Bushes need each other") is a proverb employed to describe their bond. In Madiri Puram, Reddy and Dalits form the dominant class. The Panchayat is the mode by which not only the village, but also the church runs, resulting in a new kind of social order in which the Reddy is the judge and low castes are the judged and loyal subjects.

Economic Status

Any political arrangement is dependent on the economic status of the village. A walk through Madiri Puram village is incomplete without considering the economic status of the people in pre- and post-Independence eras. What people eat or have to wear and where they live are of concern to our study of Dalit life. Jakarayya, my 64-year-old informant, recalls the "unbearable economic conditions" of the Dalit community in pre-independence India (Interview with R. Jakarayya, 13 August 2005). He says that, during the 1940s, Christian Dalits were so hungry that they ate carrion. Our people used to cook meat in clay pots and eat from clay plates. Some hungry people frisked away boiling meat from the vessels; they were labeled as "ghosts." Another way to quench their hunger was to eat raw or boiled wild date nuts. The nut is the tender top part of a plant. Once the nut is axed, the tree dies off. In summer, people used to collect date nuts, dry them, preserve them in big earthen jars, eat them now and then and drink water to fill their belly.

Having nothing to wear, they used to live naked except for a *gosi batta* (small piece of cloth around the loins).[17] In later years, Jakarayya recalls wearing a *chelladamu* (knee-length shorts for men).

In olden days, men used to cut firewood and carry head loads or take cart loads to Rajoli, the headquarters of their vassal kingdom, where they would sell the wood and buy provisions. Their mothers or grandmothers waited at home thinking what food to prepare for their children upon the men's return.

In the 1940s, daily wage rates were a way to measure the economic status of a person. Men were paid four *anaas* (4 cents) and women two *anaas* (2 cents) per head as daily wages.

In the early twentieth century, there were about 100 Dalit families. Harijans had no land of their own except for a few people as follows:

Table 10: Exception to landless Dalits

S. No	Name	Land in Acres
01	R. Jakarayya S% Buddanna	30
02	David S% Kanneppa	15
03	Timmanna S% Tekuru Naganna	15

The land that the Dalits owned was mostly arid. There was no Rajulabanda Diversion Scheme canal water until 1958.

Another way to gauge poverty is to describe living conditions. According to a former pastor, living conditions of the people even during 1993-1994 were not so good: 25 per cent had brick housing and 75 per cent had hutments (Interview with M. A. Isaac, 13 September 2005). A "hutment" was usually a 20 by 10 feet house built with mud walls, or with unhewn stones. Straight or crooked rafters formed the roofs, upon which reed bundles or paddy straw bundles were spread. Most of the houses had wild date palm leaves to cover the roof. Because the palm leaves worn out, every summer they needed to replace the roof cover. In most cases, hutments were one-room houses. Couples had no privacy, as children and their families and their grandchildren all lived under one roof.

---

[17] Jakarayya testifies him wearing just a loin cloth (*gosi batta*) in his childhood.

.Poor people would drink water from their own well. Water pots were filled drawn from the bottom of the well. Unhygienic surroundings invited lots of pests like flies inviting cholera, yellow fever and malaria. Marrying cross cousins is a custom even today. During summers, all the people slept in the open yards of their houses.

The Situation Today (2005)

Economic conditions have improved. Instead of peasants in loin cloths, we see well-dressed and well-mannered people. Today, each Christian Dalit family has at least an acre of land because of the Land Ceiling Act passed during Indira Gandhi's time. Most of the residences are brick houses. People have enough to wear. Some of the Christians'clothing is in no way inferior to that of caste Hindus. They say the Gospel has blessed them.

Influences of Change

As I see it, Madiri Puram and the neighbouring villages are being changed by various influences, one of them being modernity. M. N. Srinivas prefers the term "westernisation" to modernity. He defines westernisation as the changes brought about in Indian society and culture as a result of over 150 years of British rule. The term subsumes changes occurring at different levels technology, institutions, ideology, values (Srinivas 1969, 47). Modernity has raised questions about the *jajmani* (patron client) system. Modernity is what ensured that the Indian Republic would become a secular nation. Of course, secularism in India is Hindu, Christian and Muslim in flavor. For example, Nehru was a secular Hindu. Today, we have Sonia Gandhi, a Christian who has a big influence on the government. Communism, Naxalism and Andhra Pradesh Civil Liberties Movements have helped people rethink about their lot. Secular movements like Ambedkar Youth Association and Dalit Dandora impact Dalit groups. Education is another influence for change. Education of the lower castes by missionary schools and the government systems has enhanced their status. Most of the Dalits have become teachers, clerics, doctors, nurses and officers. In some cases, they have become District Collectors. As children are sent to residential schools in Achampet, or elsewhere, and are exposed to information technology, they in turn talk differently with their parents and playmates. Whether this growth enhances the health of the church or not is a concern for this research.

Technology also forces change. For example, widespread use of livestock to plow has been reduced by individual farmers; and where necessary, they too employ tractors to transplant, sow or harvest and even spray pesticides. However, the reduction in labour intensity has yet to affect the size of families. Dalits in the village still think having many children is a blessing. On average, a family has three to four children.

Yet another factor for change is new forms of transportation. Andhra Pradesh transportation services run buses to every nook and corner of the district. The State's road transportation system is one of the best in the nation. Traveling on buses or trains facilitates social mingling. Rubbing shoulders with high castes or noting the attractions of the opposite sex is routine. Meeting freely with others in the village inspires people to changes in lifestyle while they remain country folk in nature and dress code. For example, a *dhoti-wearing* farmer may adopt trousers for convenience.

Things That Do Not Change

With all this said, there are elements of continuity with the past. The village has not changed from its dependence on the land's produce. Farming remains the basic means of livelihood. As such, inquiry about an auspicious day and time for sowing and reaping is common. With regards to decisions such as marriage alliances, a Brahman future teller is approached first followed by the local pastor. The church in this area is ruled by the elders' council. Individualities are checked in view of social bonds. A woman is expected to be secondary in decision making.

Religion, Caste and Worldviews in Madiri Puram

During a walk-through, it becomes clear that the village people matter more than soci-structural changes or continuities. Worldviews are what make people live their lives meaningfully. As is recognised by missiologists (Hiebert et al. 1999; Hiebert and Meneses 1995, 121-122; cf. 1996, 195), worldviews are basic to understanding people and their many-sided lives. Martin Marty defines worldview as "the mental furnished apartment in which one lives" (quoted in Hiebert and Meneses 1995, 41). A change in worldview affects relationships, language, health and environment.

Worldviews vary in focus. They are means to see, judge and live meaningful lives. For example, a ruler's view of his subjects is harsher than a mother's compassion for her straying child.

Worldviews are static; they could be open-ended as well. They are informed, modified and even refused. Worldviews in Madiri Puram are pluralistic. *The Oxford English Reference Dictionary* (1996, 1115) offers several meanings of "pluralism." The literal meaning is "more than one in number." In philosophy of religion, the term is taken to mean a system that recognises more than one ultimate principle or kind of being (the opposite of Monism). In moral philosophy, the theory of pluralism means that there is more than one value and that they cannot be reconciled to one another.

Religious beliefs are the essence of folk worldview. Four related but different religions exist in the village: Hinduism, Christianity, Islam and Animism. For the folk people in Madiri Puram village, pluralism means a number of things:

- That Hinduism, Islam, Christianity and Animism exist side by side harmoniously

- That plural spiritual or moral worldviews and values exist open-ended in the village so that one can freely embrace and incorporate the beliefs and practices of more than one faith

- That this open-ended belief system relates to continuity and change within one's own primary faith. For example, one can find Hindu-Christians,[18] or Sufi- Christians[19] or Christian Dalits.[20]

This two-tiered life is exhibited in rituals or certain practices, as will become clear later in this dissertation

As in every village, high and low gods, goddesses, holy sites and saints exist in Madiri Puram. A list of gods, goddesses and holy places of these four religions is given follows:

---

[18] We may find a Christian in the region who would feel comfortable revering Hanuman as well being active in a Church. See H. Farmer, "Honor to Christian and Hindu rites and practices," interviewed on 31 March 2005.

[19] A Sufi Christian, a Moslem, can be a priest at a Sufi saint tomb but a secret follower of Christ. He is Moslem by primary faith but pluralistic in practice.

[20] The research finds a distinction between a Christian Dalit and a Dalit Christian. The terms "Dalit" and "Christian" are two worldviews complementing each other. The first term refers to one's primary focus. For example by Dalit Christian I mean that one may have had his marriage done in the church but still continue to be a priest of Maremma, the spiritual power.

Table 11: Religions, God/s, Goddesses and Holy Places

HINDUISM		ISLAM		ANIMISM		CHRISTIANITY	
Gods/ goddesses	Holy Places	Gods/ goddesses	Holy Places	Gods/ goddesses	Holy Place/s	Gods/ goddesses	Holy Place/s
High Religion/ Gods	Eshwaralayamu	Allah	Nooran-E-Masjid			Jesus (Trinity)	Church
Eshwara Rama	Ramanjaneya temple						
Low Religion/ Gods	Mini-temple Shrine	Ishmael Tata dargah	Sufi tomb	Maremma Kattameedi-Maremma	Mini temple Shrine		Parsonage!
Anjaneya Swamy, Lingamanna, Bodrayi, Chennakeshava Swami, Sunkulamma, Peddamma, Kattameedi – Maremma	" " "	Gokaramaiah dargah	Sufi tomb	Karremma, Jamulamma Peddamma etc			

According to a survey conducted in this village, Hinduism has two high gods with two temples, seven lesser gods with a mini-temple (Anjaneya Swami) and six other shrines. Islam has one high God, one mosque and two Sufi saint tombs.[21] Animism has five goddesses and an equal number of shrines. Note that all Dalit gods are female. Maremma alone has a mini-temple, the rest are satisfied with a simple structure. In general Dalits claim that they are not Hindu by faith (see Ilaiah 2007). Christianity has Jesus, but people could argue about the trinity—we will just state that the Bible projects a triune form of God. Interestingly, some of the Christians in the village consider the parsonage as holy apart from the church. For example, these Christians might feel they must guard their speech when in the parsonage.

High Gods and their temples have not been open to Dalits for centuries, though there may be exceptions. Brahmana, Kshatriya and Vaisyas worship high gods. They may also worship others because pluralism allows the low gods of Hinduism to be worshiped by Sudras and even high castes sometimes. For example, Kattameedi Maremma is worshiped by both low and high castes.

In-Betweener Gods and Goddesses, Saints and Shrines

The worship of Kattameedi Maremma by Sudra castes brings to our attention the 'in-betweener gods and saints. They are worshiped by the Hindus and Animists (Dalits). Syncretistic Christians and Islamists pay respects to some of the demi-gods and saints. Some of these demi-gods and spirits are mean in nature; for example, Narsappa is a tormentor spirit.

There are three reasons for faith in Sufi saints. First, Sufis contextualise Islam. For instance, darghas encourage breaking of a coconut and applying of ashes to the chin and throat of the devotees by the mullah. This is similar to what happens at Hindu temples, but is also dissimilar in that ashes are not used for worship in Hinduism. People prostrate themselves at Gokaramayya *durgah* wishing health to their sick children. Mothers even ask the mullah to touch their sick infant's forehead to the saint's tomb.

Second, Sufi saints' miracles impressed the Hindus like the influential Reddy. So, he invited Ishmael *Tata* (grandfather), a Sufi saint, to migrate to his village. Third, Sufism is a way of propagating Islam in India. Apart from syncretistic Sufism, Islam is spread also

---

[21] In fact Muslims have four Sufi tombs in the village.

through force, such as the brute force in 1948 of Razakars, the militant wing of Nizam the emperor.

The respect given by Christians to living and dead saints is not considered worship by people of Madiri Puram, but recognition of their healing or intercessory powers along with their presence and guidance in times of need. This two-layered life is prevalent in rural India as well as in urban centres (see Hiebert and Meneses 1995).

Table 12: In-betweener Gods, Goddesses, Saints and Shrines

Hindu	Islam	Animist	Christian (saints)
Kattameedi Maremma	Peerla Cavidi	Peddamma	St. Mary and Joseph
	Ishmael Tata darga	Kattameedi Maremma	
Singamma Avva	Gokaramaiah darga		Sadhu Yosepu
Naga devata		Singamma Avva	Gutti Healing Center
Peddamma		Naga devata Narsappa	

Epic Heroes: Madiri Puram in Epic History

Epic heroes such as Arjun and Abhimanyu recall *Kurukshetra*, a war between the wicked Kauravas and the righteous Pandavas. The myth supports the Shiva Temple origin. They say this temple was established by righteous Janamejayudu (son of Abhimanyu). Thus, Madiri Puram credits itself with historic, antique and *dharmic* (duty, rule and righteousness) connections. By this story the village claims pre-existence to *Mahabharata* (one of the greatest epics of India) or, at least, to Mahabharata times.

However, the village does not in fact trace its name to Mahabharata, despite its claim to antiquity. Shiva temple is in the middle of the village and has the tallest of spire. This temple is in the high-caste locality and faces west unlike elsewhere. *Mahabharata* is a Vishnu sect story. Krishna is one of the ten *avataras* (incarnations) in Hindu mythology. But a character from Vishnu belief founding Shiva temple in this village speaks to living happily with sectarian differences. Further, *Mahabharata* is said to have originated in North India. But Janamejayudu visiting South India speaks to the importance of the *Akhanda Bharat* (Greater India) theory propounded these days by Hindu extremists like the Rastriya Swayam Sevak Sangh (RSS).

Caste and Worldview

Some gods, goddesses and saints are shared by all religions. While that is the case, caste is a major worldview that determines which god belongs to which caste. As noted earlier, caste is a reality in the village. As per the 2001 census report, 4,535 people live in Madiri Puram. Of this number, 3,421 are from high castes, 1,104 from Scheduled Castes (Scheduled Caste), and 10 from Scheduled Tribes (ST). Scheduled Castes and Scheduled Tribes together make up 24.35 per cent of the population. There is one migrant Mala family. Most Dalits of the village are considered Mennonite Brethren Christians. Ten of the Scheduled Tribes are from Dakkali sub-caste. Dakkalis beg their food from Dalits. They reside in the Dalit section of the village. Dakkalis are also known as Erukulas.[22] A majority of Dakkalis are Christians. There is one police constable from this community. The Brahman, Kshatriya, Vaishya and Sudra castes and their roles in village life will be discussed in the pages to come.

Madiri Puram Panchayat has two hamlets under it: Chintala Camp and Ashoknagar Camp. Migrant farmers from Coastal Andhra dominate these camps. The high-caste population numbers given above include Kamma (Sudra) castes from these hamlets.

What is a caste? Where did it originate and with what assumptions? Caste is a social work division based on hierarchy ascribed by birth. The chart below lists Castes and their social status in Madiri Puram village, in descending order. Scheduled Caste is at the lowest rung of village society.

Table 13: Caste Hierarchy in Madiri Puram

Hierarchy Status	Caste
1.	Brahman
2.	Pakanati Reddy
3.	Komati, Kammari, Kummari, Kamma

---

[22] Dakkalis are Swine herders. Mrs. Subbamma, age 65, says that her parents migrated to Madiri Puram from Devarakadra, a province in Mahabubnagar district. Traditionally, they used to beg for money and food from the Dalits. They number about thirty people today.

Contd., **Table 13**: Caste Hierarchy in Madiri Puram

Hierarchy Status	Caste
4.	Jangamollu,
5.	Munnuru kapu, Naiks, Chetti balija
6.	Boyas, Kuruva, Golla, Mangali, Cakali, Musti, Oil Pressers
7.	Moslems, Pinjari
8.	Mala, Magida (Dalits)
9.	Dakkali (sub-Dalit)

Key: Nos.1-3 pure castes, 4-7 sudrulu, 8-9 untouchables

Origin of Caste

Eminent scholars have reduced the origin of caste into three helpful theories: religious, racial and occupational.

Religious Origin

Proponents of this theory believe that Brahma (god) created castes— Brahmans or priests from his head, therefore, the brain of India; Kshatriya, the warriors, from his arms to take care of security needs; Vaishya from his thighs to trade and do agriculture; and finally, the Sudras from his feet for menial work. The assumption is that only Brahmans can rule the nation and relate people to God. The first three castes are called twice born (i.e., pure by birth and rites). The Sudras are meant to serve, not rule. M. N. Srinivas, the noted 'social anthropologist in India, argues that caste hierarchy based on caste (*Varna*) is "immutable" (1967, 3). The *Varna* (colour) *principle* is the key to Sanskritisation a process by which a "low" Hindu caste or tribal or other group changes its customs, ritual, ideology and way of life in the direction of a high and frequently "twice-born" caste. However, according to M. N. Srinivas, the positions in one's caste may change but *varna* (caste) hierarchy remains intact. Crucial to immutable *varna* is ritual purity headed by Brahmans and supported by Kshatriya and Vaishya castes. For example, contact with a Harijan pollutes the four castes. How do *varnas* (castes) keep their hierarchy immutable? Srinivas offers a four-fold answer:

(1) There is a single all–India hierarchy without any variations between one region and another; (2) there are only four *varnas*, or if the Harijans, who are literally "beyond the pale" of caste, are included, five; (3) the hierarchy is clear; and (4) it is immutable. (1967, 3)

Caste hierarchy was developed in the post-Vedic period (600 B. C. to AD 300). It simply means the supremacy of the Brahmans. Srinivas writes that a Sudra landlord with his caste's numerical strength may over-rule the Brahman in the village. Along with land and numerical calculations, prestige is important in rural India. However, everyone will agree that ritually speaking the Brahman is top in rank though he may be poor. It is troublesome that eternal glories are exclusive to pure castes and eternal doom is reserved for the lowest castes. The assumed method to be used against any philosophy that disregards Brahmin dominion, especially in the low castes, is a "crush."[23]

The three lower castes (Sudra, Scheduled Caste and Schedules Tribes) can never rise above the Brahmans. If they try, they will be

---

[23] Srinivas (1967) documents three guardians of caste hierarchy: (a) the elders of a dominant caste in a village take the responsibility to safeguard the plurality of culture. For example, Srinivas mentions that in 1930 the Kallar [dominant caste] in Ramnad district of Tamil Nadu imposed eight prohibitions against Harijans' disregard of caste, which led to violent suppression. Harijans in Tamil Nadu are called Adi-Dravidas. The below were the prohibitions:

(1) That the Adi-Dravidas shall not wear ornaments of gold and silver;
(2) That the males should not be allowed to wear their clothes above the hips;
(3) That their males should not wear coats or shirts or *baniyans*;
(4) No Adi -Dravida shall be allowed to have his hair cropped;
(5) That the Adi -Dravidas should not use other than earthenware vessels in their houses;
(6) Their women shall not be allowed to cover the upper portion of their bodies by clothes or *ravukais* [blouses] or *thavanis* [upper cloths worn like togas];
(7) Their women shall not be allowed to use flowers or saffron paste;
(8) Their men shall not use umbrellas for protection against sun and rain, nor shall they wear sandals (p.16).

(b) Brahmans, though a minority, have ritual superiority over the rest of the majority caste people. They hold to caste hierarchy. Srinivas agrees with Ghurye (*Caste and Class in India* 1950, 71) who writes that even within Jainism and Buddhism it was the dominant Kshatriya caste monks that called the shots (p. 23). There is conflict between the Kshatriya and Brahman castes for supremacy. So *varna* (caste) is a reality. Another reality that Srinivas accepts is that "the sacred literature of the Hindus" (p. 24), which is largely a creation of the Brahmans, led the way to the supremacy of the caste. (c) Further, the centres of pilgrimage, such as monasteries, also enhance Sanskritisation (p. 22). Such were the conditions before the British and missionary education came to many villages, including Madiri Puram.

violently suppressed. Buddhism is a case in point (see Kancha Ilaiah. *God as Political Philosopher: Buddha's Challenge to Brahmanism* 2003, 83, 92, 102, 213). Untouchables are outside the pale of caste category. Ambedkar has done thorough research on caste and concludes how these Dalits (broken people) came to be treated as untouchables. Present research is concerned with one of these broken peoples, Christian Dalits and non-Christian Dalits. Dalits as a concept includes all broken peoples like the Malas, the Dalits and the Kurumas (shepherd caste), etc. My study concerns the Dalits. Kancha Ilaiah calls all these people Dalit *Bahujans* (many Dalit peoples). For Ambedkar, caste discrimination originated in the Hindu religion, rather than in colour or Aryan race or occupation. He goes on to designate two roots for untouchability:

(a) Contempt or hatred of the Broken Men, as of Buddhists, by the Brahmans;

(b) Continuation of beef-eating by the Broken Men after it had been given up by others. (Ambedkar 1948, iv-v)

Racial Theory

Risley, Dutt, Gait, Hutton and others offer etymological explanations to the origin of caste. The word "caste" was first employed by the Portuguese (*casta* to mean breed). *Jathi* is its Sanskrit equivalent. The racial theory assumes pride because of colour and race through blood. There have been two major invasions and migrations into India, one by Dravidians and the other by Aryans (George Menachery 1982, 3). Menachery rightly points out that invasions and migrations are universal, but never did racism take sanction from religion as in India.

Occupation Theory

A third theory talks of occupational necessities as the root of the caste system. The assumption in this case is that Aryan invaders, upon arrival to India and out of necessity to fight the well-settled and civilised Dravidian races had to set apart some as warriors, others as priests and yet others as servants. Naturally, the conquered people formed the lowest caste. This social category is quite intelligent on one hand and repressive on the other, in that subjects are treated as non-humans.

Caste discrimination bears on the issue of human dignity. Most Hindus believe in the caste system, and the people in the research village experience it throughout their lives. I as a researcher, a Christian Dalit by origin, was made to stand for two long hours while interviewing the eighty-year-old head of the lone Brahman family in Madiri Puram village. This was despite there being enough room and arrangements to sit. His is the largest house by size. The fact was that even this old Brahman stood for those two hours.

Caste discrimination is such a cruel reality for Dalit people in Madiri Puram. This discrimination has even put on a new garb in the form of bureaucracy: government officials ensure that only non-practicing Christians receive reservation benefits.

Conclusion

The introduction to Madiri Puram village is presented in three steps. The first section has taken us through the village. It pointed out to geographic locations of different caste sections, temples, churches, mosques and dargahs (Sufi tombs). The location of educational institutions, such as Panchayat office, telephone exchange and Reddy residence, are also noted. Eswaralayamu (temple) is thought to be the oldest structure in the entire village. The Church has been presented as the center to the local Christian Dalit life.

The second section was concerned with the Panchayat way of administration. In the 1940s, the Dalits were very poor. Most of them were landless labourers. However, today, Dalits have enough to wear compared with their traditional loin clothing. There are a number of influences that played a role in ushering change and continuity. For example, modernity, education and transportation are some elements that have created change. Dalit Rights movements have also had an impact on the poor masses.

The third section pointed out that the key to peoples' change or continuity with the past has to do with their worldviews. Worldviews determine beliefs and practices. People are pluralistic in their worldviews. For example, villagers have plural and open-ended faith life. They hold on to a primary faith (e.g., Christian) along with cultural practices that may be Hindu in essence. Christians worship a trinitarian monotheist God, while at the same time they respect animistic goddesses like Kattameedi Maremma. High religion and low religion exist hands in gloves. One of the chief worldviews that keep the village in order and that create social tension is caste hierarchy. Caste is thought to be detrimental to human dignity. The dominant class is formed with the combination of the Reddy colony with that of the Christian Dalit colony.

The concepts of continuity and change concepts are found in the architecture of Church porches and with that of the P.Adi Sheshi Reddy cowshed. The dominant class network between the Reddy and the Christian Dalits is new but the Reddy caste hierarchy is kept intact. We would also find a Hindu-Christian or a Sufi-Christian in these villages.

Coming of Christianity

Change also came in another form. The coming of Christianity to this area presented the villagers with a new worldview. This is the subject of the next chapter. People believed or refused the gospel on the grounds of its claims, its content, or the methods of presentation. The good news of the gospel is that God created all humans as equal; sin entered as part of their rebellion, but there is a remedy offered in Lord Jesus Christ. The gospel is egalitarian in its core. To accept the gospel means changing both beliefs and lifestyle. Change is resisted by both the Dalits and caste Hindus; yet some accepted it. From here on, I will address four research questions and demonstrate how change and continuity are the reality among the Christian Dalits of Madiri Puram village. This tension can be traced in adopting the Reddy architecture for church porches. Thus, art and architecture are our next concern.

Chapter 4

CHANGE AND CONTINUITY IN ART AND ARCHITECTURE OF THE CHURCH

This chapter presents an analysis of my ethnographic data from Madiri Puram village. It addresses my first research question: "How are change and continuity exhibited in the religious symbols of Madiri Puram village and how does this define their Christian identity?"

The church has borrowed Norman architecture from P.Adi Sheshi Reddy's cattle shed and residence. This is labeled as cultural adaptation. But the continuity element is equally present. In that the church used Bible verses written on the walls, like Ten Commandments in line with the neighbouring churches. This chapter explains an insight I had one day while engaged in the research process. The insight springs from my participant observation but is sufficiently supported by ethnographic data. It reveals how I observed "continuity and change" in the art and architecture adapted for the Church porches at Madiri Puram village. Putting aside available Hindu, Islamic and Harijan forms and designs, the Church chose to imitate Norman architecture from the local Reddy premises, especially that of his "cattle-shed" and residence. The questions are: Why did they do so? What does this indicate of social kinships or differences? How does this project Christian respect for God through art and architecture?

One day, the most effective key informant and I went around the main village[1] to take pictures of "holy and important sites."In my thinking, the sites would be the temples, mosque and *dargahs* (tombs for Sufi saints) and Harijan shrines. But it so happened that my key informant pointed me to the house and cowshed of late

---

[1] Madiri Puram, the Research Village has two hamlets: Chintala Camp and Ashoknagar Camp.

P.Adi Sheshi Reddy. Reddys are landlords and rulers of the village. Neither the late Adi Sheshi Reddy residence nor his dilapidated cattle-shed impressed me. His residence has first floor. Not knowing the significance of the Reddy structures, I took snapshots. The rest of the houses in the village have just a ground floor. In comparison, the Brahman house is largest in the village in square feet but has no architectural importance. Adi Sheshi Reddy is believed to be from *Pakanati Redlu*, the rulers of Gadwal Vassal State. According to the caste system, princes are second in hierarchy only to the Brahmans. They are form the warrior caste.

Adi Sheshi Reddy's cattle shed is much larger than his residence and appeals to the eye, though it is not in use and is in ruins. The number of livestock one owned indicated his riches in those days (1960s). One's prestige increased based on the number of plow pairs one owned. The Reddy maintained the best oxen for his *buggy bandi* (ox cart or car), as this was the best mode of transportation for a rich man. Cows were meant for breeding, as a source of milk and ghee, and even for making income from sales proceeds. On his official tours, his Ox cart was usually accompanied by 30-40 Christian Dalit security men. He would feed them, pay for their travel on the train and keep them at his command. They would never deceive nor desert him. Adi Sheshi Reddy is said to have challenged his rivals, "If you can divert a single Dalit and make him join your camp, and call me Adi Sheshamma (female form of Adi Sheshi Reddy)."

A casual comparison of the picture of church building with that of the Reddy's cattle shed caught my attention. I was caught with the "visible expressions" of Christian and Reddy beliefs. They speak of continuity and change. There is a similarity between the architecture of the church porches and the Reddy cattle-shed. Who copied whom and why? Upon investigation, I found the church copied the Reddy cattle shed and residence porch models with modification. I checked with the treasurer (at that time), and he confirmed that the church porches is modeled after the Reddy sites. The treasurer is one of the best carpenters in the area. The wood pillar designs of his house are worthy of study and appreciation. It is natural that the treasurer and other members on the Construction Committee opted to decorate the sanctuary with the best architecture available. They testify to investigating several church and other structures in and around Mahabubnagar and Kurnool districts.

Finally, they adopted that which is readily available in the village. Why would they refuse other forms in the village and district regions? They copied from a Reddy who used to be one of their masters of "bond-labour." Why would the architectural styles that he used appeal to them?

Theoretical Framework

The theory for this chapter is that "the lower borrow the art and architecture from their social superiors (others)." The belief is that people try to pay the highest respect to God in building a holy structure for Him. Humans are more apt to replicate forms that are egalitarian in heart and liberating in practice. This may amount to a kind of "cultural-imitation." Imitation is meant to honour almighty God and raise the community image of the people. In this case, it speaks of their creativity in contextualising the gospel and their participation in facilitating social harmony.

In this instance, the Reddy was the protector and advocate of Christian Dalits right to life and their welfare. Adi Sheshi Reddy may have felt drawn to relate to the church and its premises since the porch emulated his architecture. On the whole, it appears that the architecture of the Christian church is a mixture of pure poetics and an attempt to cement social bonds. So the dynamics of change and continuity among Christians has stability (porches) and is conditioned by a sustained relationship with their social superior. But the porch is not the only beautiful feature that the church maintains; other Christian forms are also present.

Brief History to Church Structure

The Gilgal MB Church sanctuary was built in 1973 in Madiri Puram village. It is 53.8 feet in length and 23.9 feet in width on the outer side including the porch area.[2] The Church's front porch is adorned with Norman architecture. Norman architecture is present with three upside down "U" joint shapes forming open entrances. The tops of the inverted "U" shapes are round, like the bottom of capital letter "U" (See figure 4).

---

[2] On the inside, the porch yard measures 19.6 feet in length and 7.10 feet in width, while inside the sanctuary measures 39.7 feet in length and 19.6 feet in width.

Figure 4: Gilgal Mennonite Brethren Church

The above leads me to consider the historical development of the church building in the village. The gospel of the Lord Jesus Christ reached the village more than nine decades ago (c.1915 CE). People started to worship at the house of the "pastor-teacher." Then they moved to a thatched roof sanctuary to praise God. A large hut served both as the residence of the pastor as well as the worship place. During festive occasions like Christmas, Good Friday and Easter, they used to put up a large "pandal" made with poles and bamboo sheet walls. The roof was covered with green branches like the mango. Today, they rent-out *shamiyaanaas* (tents) from Shantinagaram, their Mandal headquarters.

The passion to have a sanctuary materialised after about sixty years of practicing faith. Except for the roof (anglers and asbestos sheets), all of the contributions came from the local believers. The roof is a contribution from the Church Conference. They take pride in saying that they did not appeal to neighbouring churches for donations." It is their own. They had taken loan from the Reddy but paid it, in total, on time. There were stringent rules that every family pay a target amount a couple of times. As a result, a large and beautiful structure has come into existence.

The Christian community has grown so large[3] that even the present structure accommodates just 50 percent of the congregation, most of them women (why do women come in large numbers, not men, is a study in itself). Expansion of the present building or building a new structure is on the thinking. Whatever the future plans, the quality art and architecture of Gilgal Church have provided a model to neighbouring village churches. By art, I mean the text on the wall, blinking lights, the photo taken with Sadhu Yosepu and the Decalogue hung on the back wall. Sadhu Yosepu conducted healing campaigns. For example, to welcome the worshippers inside, one of the Bible verses written in large letters reads, "*Come you who are blessed by the Lord,* he said. *Why are you standing out here?*" (Gen 24:31). All these speak of Christian Dalits' faith, doctrine, history and orientation to life and a taste of change from time to time.

Models in View

When the peasant church wishes to construct a sanctuary, what blue prints would it consider? Would they be secular in nature or religious in thought, or a mix of both? What convictions would the people have concerning replication? Would they strive for cultural assimilation or distance? Are there any worldviews at the root of their decisions?

The task before us is to examine the ways that such replication continues or discontinues the community's past and present modes of honouring God. They are facing now an almighty God and constructing a temple for Him. In contrast, their previous goddesses Maremma and her sister Karremma among others were mere local goddesses.

Dalit Houses, Goddesses and Art and Architecture

An examination of Dalit models of art and architecture begins with their residences. Economically poor Dalits had no time to think about architecture since they were bond-slaves all through their lives for ages. So their residences were bland in design. Their former houses were built of mud, without much ventilation. They did not contain any poetics worthy of note. Sometimes they were just huts made of raised mud walls and palm leaf, reed or jowar hay-bundle roofs. Mud houses are, at the most 20 by 40 feet, with small windows

---

[3] Christians number about 600 households whereas the present church building has room just for 300.

on the sides and with a *gavasi* (opening on the roof). The rooftop
is used for drying grain, etc. Stone steps are built into the sidewall
and serve as a ladder. Their houses usually comprised of a single
room. Privacy for couples is difficult. Children and grand children
grow under one roof. In other cases, huts were 6-10 feet in width
with pole walls and thatched roofs. They, too, were mostly one-
room houses. Dalits of Madiri Puram worshipped Maremma, the
main goddess, among others. Maremma has six wooden images in
the village shrine. They are "4 x 2" feet in width. Today her hands
and feet are worn out. This is what their tradition affords them.
Karremma, Maremma's sister, is a triangle stone. It seems Dalits in
India seldom had manufactured gods. All their gods and goddesses
were human in birth, but their heroic works lifted them to the
status of gods. Dalits are spirit worshippers. Some of their deities
are spiritual powers. Their gods are rarely male (Timmappa of
Tanagala village is an example of a male deity). Today, Madiri
Puram Dalits have just a few goddesses, including Maremma,
Karremma and Kattameedi Maremma, plus spiritual powers like
Narsappa.

Figure 5: Maremma Temple

Maremma

Dalits worshipped *Shakties* (spiritual powers) prior to their coming
to know Christ. They were animists. Maremma, the chief deity
among six others, is known for her ferocity. She was at the centre

of their life. Every village in Alampur Taluk has a temple for her. The present male priest of Maremma says about her origin. Jambavanthudu, the first man on earth, had seven daughters. They were powerful women, namely:

- Maremma
- Mankalamma
- Sunkulamma
- Karremma
- Eedamma
- Peddamma and
- Jamulamma

Maremma is a *Shakti* (a powerful spirit). That is the reason why Reddy and Sudra castes worship her on (1) *Eronka Punnamu*[4] and (2) *Ugadi*.[5] Every morning toddy[6] tapers (3) offer the drink to Maremma and her sister Karremma in pots placed near them" (Pentanna, Tolla 2006, 4).

The priest goes on to illustrate an encounter between Jesus and the *Shakti*. Maremma once opposed Jesus; she even won over forty of his people. Killed a few of his group, then Jesus threatened her with dire consequences, since then she fears Jesus" (Pentanna, Tolla *Ibid.*).

She demanded the highest respects. Her worshippers used to offer a male water buffalo to her once in every two to five years. Her temple, "25 x 15" feet, was left to ruins (the size of the temple and the images may differ from place to place, e.g., the one at Mundladinne village is smaller). Maremma is composed of six wooden images: "4 x 2" feet high and of palm size in width. She is not as beautiful as *Laxmi* or *Parvati* of the Hindus. Seldom can we speak of woodwork in her case. Today, she has strong stone temples and bigger wood images in nearby villages (e.g. Tummilla village). But in Madiri Puram her temple has fallen, the images are half worn out and lie on ground. The only people who respect these images

---

[4] April-May in a year, when there is no agriculture work in the fields.

[5] Ugadi is the Telugu New Year's day.

[6] "Toddy" is the sap of a kind of palm tree, fermented to produce arrack (see *Oxford English Reference Dictionary* [New York: Oxford University Press, 1996:1514].

are the toddy traders. They offer "toddy" in an earthen pot every morning at nine.

Maremma was deserted by Christians about three decades ago. Some of the Christians continued to celebrate her festival until a decade or so ago. The truth is a couple of Christian Dalit families continue to operate as priests to her and her younger sister Karremma. I had difficulty being able to interview the main male priest. My key informants evaded the question to reveal the priest's name earlier, and introduce him to me. The families who live close to these deities function as priests and there is more. Maremma is sanskritised![7]

Maremma is adapted by high-caste people of the village because she is a ferocious goddess and can strike the village with pestilences like cholera. At her high caste shrine she sits on a raised platform and has increased her beauty and size. She leans now against the trunk of a neem tree. Usually, she should be enthroned on a new cart made for her. But one day fire from incense sticks burnt her cart. So she is made to lean until the next big festival in two to five years is come.

But since Kattameedi Maremma is Sanskritised, no Dalit can touch even the rectangle platform where the deity is located. According to M. N. Srinivas, "Sanskritization is a process by which a 'lower' Hindu caste, or tribal or other group, changes its customs, ritual, ideology, and way of life in the direction of a high, and frequently, 'twice–born' caste" (Srinivas 1967, 6). As such, positional changes may occur in individual caste but never a structural change to the *varna* (hierarchy on the basis of colour) principle.

Sanskritisation here means an elevation in Maremma's social and ritual status. In general, Sanskritisation requires (1) that a claim is brought forth by a community; for example, a carpenter caste claims Brahman status (Here the claimant is the most powerful Reddy in the entire district.); (2) that the person (community) in question become vegetarian; and (3) that a Brahman preside over their ritual functions.

---

[7] Usually means mobility in ritual status. See M. N. Srinivas 1996, 75; cf. Dumont 1998, 192.

Kattameedi Maremma- Maremma Sanskritised

The Reddies and the Sudras wanted to appease the ferocious Maremma and give her a "face-lift" or "status–lift." Maremma was promoted to Kattameedi Maremma. She is contained in three wooden images, larger in size to those that are in the original shrine in the Dalit section of the village. She is of "6 x 2" width. See Figure 6 below. As local gossip would have it, the ruler Reddy was a womaniser and might have had a Madiga mistress. He may have adopted Maremma to please his concubine.

Figure 6: Kattameedi Maremma Shrine

Her status was also raised from being a Dalit goddess to being a middle ground *devata* (goddess) in between Dalit and high-caste gods. As I took snapshots, the key informant stood at a distance, perhaps unsure of touching the platform. By virtue of my having higher education and being a researcher and non-local stranger, I could touch the platform. Caste people who were on the platform were happy, of course, for a photograph. In fact, a lady asked for a snapshot when developed.

Unlike her original shrine, there is no *kallu munta* (toddy container pot) kept for the deity. Caste people do not pour toddy to her. Nor is a blood sacrifice made in honour of her at this section of the village. It is telling how a deity is Sanskritised and gets a higher rank through vegetarianism. The irony is that Maremma makes her inroads into the high caste section of the village through (1) her ferocity but (2) in this form (*avatar*) she has deserted her sons, daughters and grandchildren in Christian Dalit *vada* (street).

That is the power of assuming caste hierarchy. Kattameedi Maremma, though somewhat crude in form yet could not help climbing the higher ladder.

Maremma is ancient as compared to Adi Sheshi Reddy. But the most powerful Reddy, his family and friends, are led now to worship a sanskritised form of Maremma. There are at least three realities here: (1) in and through his sexual gratifications, the Reddy and the Christian Dalit (woman) have become allies; (2) blood relatives of the both sides are prone now to worship each other's gods or are at least to tolerate each other; and (3) it is most likely that the woman's family comes under the protective umbrella of the influential man. She may be respected even by high castes, lest they face Reddy's anger. Reddy's political power and resilience have shaken even some of the most powerful Reddys in the Alampur taluq. If the concubine begets children through this man, they will be *chandalas* (Untouchables, or non-caste). At best, they may officially have the status of the Woman's (Scheduled or Backward) caste. The children of mixed blood may secretly identify with their father's social status.

This is indicative of irksome change and continuity. The Reddys and Sudra castes continue to worship their high gods like *Balaji* or *Rama*. But in discontinuity with such a list, they added Kattameedi Maremma to their Pantheon. Perhaps this is due to open-ended religion such as Hinduism. Hinduism is an ocean of many cultures or gods. Is the caste system that stands on ritual purity, contradicting itself in admitting a Dalit goddess? Such admission of Dalit goddess may not apply to other villages, but it did happen in the Madiri Puram village.

The Dalit woman in question enjoys certain freedoms from her own kith and kin, owing to her relations with the Reddy. We may not call hers a ritual mobility. But in the case of Kattameedi Maremma, her religious status has changed. It may be called "appeaser ritual mobility." For Maremma has moved to higher spaces discontinuous with her lower status section of the village. Interestingly, a Dalit person is allowed to officiate at the Kattameedi Maremma shrine, though only for "name sake" (Pentanna, Tolla 2006, 4). The priest simply sits down on the rectangular platform where Kattameedi Maremma is seated. The continuity for this priest is that he is still treated as an untouchable. Social mobility means very little to him and his Christian Dalit palem.

What I sense is that the kinsmen and women in these families are open to plural values in day-to-day life. The popular notion in the village is that an immoral person's children do not make to the next generation. Some people serve as examples of the consequences of the extramarital relations. As is the saying, a couple of Christian Dalit males tried concubinary imitating the Reddy, only to ruin their lives and future of their families.

So far I have reflected on how low morals can influence one's adaptation or refusal of certain forms of art and architecture. Kattameedi Maremm's Sanskritised image (larger in size, beautiful in *saris* and painted colours) did not seem to qualify as a model for the porches of the Church. In fact, she lost her right to have a temple and respect from her original children. She lives as a "stranger" in her new locality and thus has lost her "self-respect." But there is no turning back. She is in between her new and old natures. There is no question of art and architecture in honour of her among the Kshatriyas. By nature, she does not require rich art and architecture for her shrine.

What about Karremma, the younger sister of Maremma?

Figure 7: Karremma Shrine

Karremma — Art and Architecture

It is needless to delve into the possibility of Karremma becoming a model for the church's beauty in art and architecture. She is just a triangle stone deity without an image. She sits in a three-sided stonewall touching the ground on the large bottom side of the triangle. She can be worshipped in a bending or sitting position. Cow dung water is spread around her site. The reason I mention this is to point out that her form has no sense of aesthetics.

Griha Devata — Inti Lasmamma

Inti Lasmamma used to be the "house deity" of the Christian Dalits. She is worshiped prior to monsoon each year, so that the year may be a safe one. She is a palm-sized wooden image sitting in a wall at a reachable height. My maternal grandmother used to worship her. A small *goodu* (cave-like section) is a foot-and-a half square window closed by the wall on the backside, but open faced to the north. The deity is covered with a white cloth. Scorpions make their houses in this small shrine and their bites are common. The oldest woman in the house is her *pujari* (priest).

In Madiri Puram, people used to sacrifice a lamb or goat at midnight, roast the flesh and eat it entirely by daybreak. All of the remains, like bones, skin and waste parts are buried in the floor of the house. Griha devata, or its shrine, is not worthy of adoption for church architecture. So the former deities of the Dalits: *Maremma, Kattameedi Maremma, Karremma* and *Inti lasmamma*[8] did not provide models for art and architecture for the church.

If the villager's traditional deities and their sanctuaries did not provide a model for church porches, could it be that Hindu or Muslim architecture provides beauty for the church? I will limit myself to a brief overview of Hindu temples and Muslim structures in the village and then see if Christians have considered any of their art and architecture. A reason is Christians have abandoned their gods and goddesses for a God of the whole universe.

Hindu Sanctuaries

There are two kinds of Hindu temples in the village — temples of high religion and low religion. They manifest differences in architecture. The twice born castes (Brahman, Kshatriya and Vaishya) worship in (i) *Shri Sita Ramaanjaneeya Swami temple* or at (ii) *Shivalayam*. The rest, the Sudras (Boyas, Naiks, Chakali, Mangali and Gouda), worship demi-gods, including the above two.

---

[8] *Inti Lasmamma* may look as colloquial for Laxmi of twice-born castes. Laxmi is the wife of Vishnu. But the nature of Laxmi and *Inti lasmamma* would never match. They are different, though both are worshipped for the well-being of the family.

High Religion

The high religious temples have sculptured *murthies* (idols) in the
Sri *Ramanjaneya Swami* temple. The pillars inside the temple and *gaja
stambhamu* (pilot pillar) at the *varanda* (outer space) contain one of
the best sculptures in the village. It also has the *Swastika* sign. *Rama
Linga Swami devalayamu* [Shivaalaymu] has phallic and snake stone
symbols. *Om* (ancient or eternal voice) is written above its spire in
Sanskrit. An orange flag is hoisted on top of these temples.
Shivaalayam has the tallest *gopuram* (spire) in the village. Dalits
have no entrance into Hindu temples.[9]

Figure 8: Ramanjaneya Swami Temple

Shivalayam also pictures adult male and female genitals in position.
A papal tree grew over a neem tree trunk. The neem trunk is cut
to depict an erect male penis and then dried out. The pipal tree
(vagina) is alive but the neem tree log is dead by design. The erect,
but dead, trunk imitates a stone phallic image of the Hindu god
Shiva. The neem trunk is black in colour. The supposition is that the
trunk was mildly burnt on purpose. This is one of the high forms
of Hindu religion. The picture is that Shiva lingam stands for

---

[9] It is reported that the lone Mala family is allowed into Hindu temple. But to date,
no Dalit [Madiga] is allowed in Madiri Puram village.

reproductive power. Thus, it may be that Shivaalayam's art and architectural forms are unthinkable for a church adaptation.

Figure 9: Shivalayam (Shiva Temple)

Village Christians do not venerate reproductive organs, but rather the giver of sex organs. In fact, their traditional Dalit gods and goddesses were seldom vulgar and related better to common people. None of their traditional deities were considered for the church porches. But before elaborating on Dalit deities, let us look at why the lesser gods of Hinduism, their art and architecture were not considered.

Low Religion: Shudra Gods and Goddesses

The lowest of the gods in Hinduism is Anjaneya, the monkey form of deity. The monkey or *hanuman* god temple is located at Chintala camp, a hamlet north of the Madiri Puram village. Some of the Christian "mason-sculptors" were hired for the *garbha gudi* (the holy of the holies) of this temple. Anjaneeya is an obedient servant of Rama who defeated Ravana, an evil king of (Sri) Lanka. I visited the inside of the temple and saw some of the beautiful flowers, arrows and garlands sculpted into the stone pillars. Christian Dalits did not copy these beautiful figures.

The rest of the architecture is that of the small gods of Sudras. They include *Chennakeshavudu* (a three-foot by seven-inch cream color stone), *Lingamanna* (a semi-round, black stone that is a foot in diameter), *Bodraayi* (a palm-sized brown naval stone above the ground), *Singamma avva* shrine (a Boya caste village border goddess- a small stone), *Sunkulamma* (a shepherd caste goddess—an arm length and six-inch wide stone) and a *Nagula Panchami* stone (a snake couplet, flat 2 ½ foot stone). Though all would be worthy, they did not come into the purview of the Christian sanctuary builders.

The construction in-charge elders of that time have surveyed the church architectures in Kurnool, their neighbouring district, and Mahabubnager, their district. Kurnool has one of the most beautiful Baptist sculptured churches in Andhra Pradesh. Unlike the Baptists in the region, the Mennonite Brethren Mission did not emphasise rich church structures. Baptist and Mennonite Brethren churches are mostly cross-shaped, either with entrances on three sides or if in villages with two entrances. The Madiri Puram church is not cross-shaped, but is like a big "godown" (larger in length and shorter in width, with asbestos sheets as roof put on anglers).

So, which art and architecture appealed to them? Apparently, it is the Norman architecture at the Reddy cattle shed and his residence. Norman architecture was adapted for church porches, apart from writings on the walls copied from Mennonite Brethren and Baptist traditions, including the "Decalogue." The Ten Commandments are written in Telugu on the wall behind the pulpit.

Figure 10: P. Adi Sheshi Reddy Cattle Shed

Norman Architecture at P.Adi Sheshi Reddy Cattle Shed

Norman architecture uses an upside down "U" shape. There are three such shapes making open entry points into the church. It is perhaps Persian or Moghul in origin. Persian or Moghul religions uphold God as creating all people as equal. It is not the origin of this architecture for the porches at the church, but why was it copied — that needs exposition.

Why would they copy Norman architecture while they had other forms to choose from and while the Reddy agreeably had low morals? A couple of reasons may be advanced. The foremost reason is relationships: (1) The late Adi Sheshi Reddy fought for 205 acres of government land and distributed it among Christian Dalits free of charges. The Reddy single-handedly fought the legal battle for 12 long years (1949-1961) to secure this land. It cost him about Rs. 70,000.

The Sudras, along with the Brahmans and other Reddies in Alampur taluq, were against the local Reddy, but he fought successfully. He could pursue the case even at the Supreme Court level.

Figure 11: P. Adi Sheshi Reddy Residence

A proverb comes to the elders of this church: *Puliki malavasaramu-Malaku pulavasaramu* (the tiger and the thicket need each other). Mutual dependence is at the core. It is "unusual" for a Reddy to fight for the rights of the Dalit community, but Adi Sheshi Reddy did.

(2) A male key informant said, Pakanati Adi Sheshi Reddy was of "royal origin"[10] (Danam 2005, 20). If royal people help the helpless, respect is due to them. In fact, Adi Sheshi Reddy was a migrant from across the Tungabhadra river; I will not go into that. His victory at the Apex Court created an "affinity" between the Reddy and the Christian church. Christians were earnestly praying for victory over this matter for twelve years.

Upon judgment in favour of him, the Reddy went on pilgrimage to fulfill his vow and offer his long hair to Tirupati Venkateswara Swami. It was just before Christmas time. Christian Dalit spirits were raised high, but the liberator, Reddy, asked the Christians to downplay their Christmas celebration. He instructed them to wait for him to join them for the New Year's festival. The Church obliged. They received him with the traditional *dappu* (percussion instrument), garlands and much joy. Of course, this unusual relationship has created what is called "Reddy-Christians" with a couple of impacts, in that Reddy has a final say in major disputes of the church. The danger is that he may not respect biblical principles. On the other hand, it has led Christians to continue as vote banks for the Reddy. This is what I would call "continuity" in a new form. Yet another limitation is that the caste hierarchy is not critiqued.

In summary, the Reddy-Christian architecture connection emphasises the personal relationship between the Dalits and the most powerful human in the village. More so, adopting the Reddy architectural form was not related to idolatry. It shows their honour to God.

Table 14: Norman Architecture—Person, Reasons and Result

Person (Reddy)	Reasons	Result
Race (Royal blood)	Neutral architecture	Honour to God
Ruler	Non-idolatrous	Reddy-Christian Bonds
Poetics	Lesser evil (non-caste)	Social Harmony
Name (fame)	Love for poetics	A model for neighbour Churches

---

[10] Pakanati *Redlu* (Reddys) ruled Gadwal *Samstanam* (Vassal State). Pedda Somanadri was one of the famous kings at Gadwal. Adi Sheshi Reddy is thought to come from this family. See Figure 11: P.Adi Sheshi Reddy's Residence

Discontinuity

The discontinuity of this adaptation of architecture is limited to the porch part of the church. The church adapted only three porches out of four from the cattle shed of Adi Sheshi Reddy. This reflects the triune God (Father, Son and the Holy Spirit). On the other hand, Adi Sheshi Reddy had four porches, which may indicate plural religions or, simply, may have better facilitated the movement of his cattle. Porches are the index of the church. The walls carry Scripture verses of life importance. Why three porches not more and not less? The then treasurer of church construction (1973) said:

> We have travelled two districts, Kurnool and Mahabubnager to survey on architecture models for adaptation. We were satisfied with none, but in our village Adi Sheshi Reddy cattle shed and his house provided us with enough ideas. And we adapted just three of the porch ideas to represent our belief in *tandri–kumara–parishuddhatma devudu* [triune God: Father-Son-Holy Spirit] (Paras 2005, 1).

The rest of the church is synagogue type. The walls carry Scripture verses of life importance. On the inside wall, in the east direction, hangs a photo of Sadhu Yosepu taken on 29 July 1962.

Figure 12: Sadhu Yosepu Visit (1962)

Sadhu Yosepu is a Church of South India itinerant evangelist and "healer-saint." He is revered even today. People go on pilgrimage to receive his *deevena* (blessing), near Guntur. The back wall displays the Decalogue (Eoxd. 20:2-17) written in large letters. Like some synagogues, the Gilgal IMB Church has an upper room[11] with part

---

[11] The Upper room seats around 30 people.

of it functioning as a balcony. The wooden staircase is one of the efficient arrangements. Fasting prayers, said for yearly monsoon rains, are held in the upper room. The upper room of the church served as a granary until a parsonage was built with enough room for grain storage.

Summary

This chapter argued that Christian Dalits borrow art and architecture from their social superiors. In this case, it was Norman architecture from the late P. Adi Sheshi Reddy premises, his cattle shed and his residence for the front porches. The front view of the church has the beauty of the structure. It is not from any religion in the village. It has also borrowed from Baptist or Mennonite church structures, such as design, length and width. It has art expressed through Scripture verses on the walls. Art is found even in a hanging of a photo of Sadhu Yosepu on the east wall. Yosepu is a church of South India healer-saint. So, poetics in the church have no claim to one tradition. It is a mix of three major traditions. Thus, this is a case for social harmony and, more so, for projecting continuity and discontinuity in worldviews.

Analysis: Inculturation, De-Sanskritisation and Social Integration

I have explained why Christian Dalits of Madiri Puram village copied Norman architecture, abandoning several other examples available, though not that it is the only architecture the church possesses. I suggested that a primary reason was that the Dalits wanted a form that was egalitarian in essence and non-religious (Hindu) in nature. Norman architecture is present now in the Reddy premises as well as in a modified form at the church precincts. What themes spring out of the above description? What does it mean? What do scholars have to say? These are some of the questions the following section is concerned with. Three major themes of crucial importance emerge out of the above description. Who indigenises the gospel—the western mother Church or the governing body of the national church or the local community of believers? In this case, it is the Madiri Puram peasant church who borrowed the Norman architecture for its porches. The issue to grapple with here is the surrounding *inculturation*. The second theme to wrestle with is what "parameters" come into play for the Reddy and Sudra caste people to *de-Sanskritise* Kattameedi Maremma, the chief goddess of Dalits? A third inquiry relates to an unusual bond between the Reddy and Christian Dalits. The Christian Dalit contribution to social integration in the village is the concern. Let us consider these themes.

Christian Dalit Inculturation of Architecture

Our first discussion with regard to Christian Dalits accommodating[12] Norman architecture from the Reddy premises for their church porches is about "inculturation." The Christian Medical Journal of India focuses on architecture as one of the great features of India. N. M. Wadia Hospital at Pune is adorned with Norman Architecture. Wadia Hospital was started by a Swedish mission.[13] However, this is not to say that the late P. Adi Sheshi Reddy borrowed Christian architecture and, therefore, Madiri Puram Christian Dalits from his. As far as we can trace, there is no link between the two. And for the purposes of this book, the origin of the porches matters little, but, rather, how it was adapted after considering several forms in the region.

Contextual theology has two faces to it, one is inculturation and the other is socio-economic concern (e.g. liberation theology). Our interest is both the aspects. Etymologically, "inculturation" means the insertion of new values into one's heritage and worldview and it tries honestly "to make Christ and his liberative message better understood by people of every culture, locality and time" (John Waligo 1991, 506).

A brief overview of inculturation from the perspective of Christian missions would lay the groundwork and for what we are up to, especially the ramifications of such concern. David Bosch, in his magisterial work *Transforming Mission* (1995, 447-456), has a fine way of summarising "mission as inculturation" from a historical perspective. The two terms he clarifies are "inculturation" and "indigenisation." The former term is common to Catholic missions,

---

[12] Matteo Ricci (1552-1610), a Jesuit scholar-bishop supplied a programme of "accommodation" as a bridge building tool with the Chinese. Ricci was a learned scholar. He wrote *Elements of Geometry*. He talked of friendship and human relationships as bridges to preach the gospel. See Ralph R Covell with contributions from Jean-Paul Wiest and the China group in Scott W. Sunquist eds., A *Dictionary of Asian Christianity* 2001, 703-705.

[13] See Sundar Rao, PSS. Dr. "Medical Missionary Association–A Firm Foundation." In *CM J I* (Christian Medical Journal of India)–A Quarterly Journal of Christian Medical Association of India. Vol. 20 & 21. No. 4 (Oct - Dec 2005) and No. 1 (Jan - Mar 2006): 21.

the later to Protestant missiologists. Both the terms mean the same thing. Bosch thinks that for Protestants, the term is limited to events such as "incarnation." This research finds inculturation in Madiri Puram to be beyond eventualities. It is an ongoing reality — a process. It is continuous with its own (Baptist/Mennonite) church tradition as well discontinuous with it.

The ramifications of inculturation[14] are noteworthy. David Bosch's review is the best that we can rely on. He is right in saying that "the Christian faith never exists except as 'translated' into a culture (1995, 447). The review of Bosch points to eight factors that western missiologists developed with regard to their understanding of inculturation. According to Bosch:

> First that accommodation never included modifying the 'prefabricated' Western theology. Second, it was actually understood as a concession that the Third-World Christians would now be allowed to use some elements of their culture in order to give expression to their new faith. Third, only those elements which were manifestly 'neutral' and naturally good, that is, not 'contaminated' by pagan religious values, could be employed (cf Thauren 1927, 25-33; Luzbetak 1988, 67). Fourth, the word 'elements' further implied that cultures were not regarded as invisible wholes but, in Enlightenment fashion, as separate components that could be put together or disassembled at will; it would thus be perfectly in order if one were to isolate some components and employ them in the service of the Christian church. Fifth, it went without saying that indigenization or accommodation was a problem only for the "young" churches ... (Bosch 1995, 448-449).

Bosch's eight ramifications may be summarised in four points. Firstly, that inculturation is the problem of younger churches (e.g., India) and not of Western (mother) churches. Secondly, it identifies a separation between the "kernel" (essentials) and "husk" (non-essentials) of the gospel. The kernel is supposed to remain intact, though adapted to local forms. The husk may be changed. Thirdly, inculturation is thought to be a concession in the former missionary mindset by those who want the younger churches to remain in their pristine form, remaining theologically in tune and growing within their control.

But Madiri Puram church is ninety years old and not a younger church. Its relationship with the western church is very negligible.

---

[14] "Inculturation" as a concept was present even before the Jesuits piloted it. It was P. Arrupe, a Jesuit superior, who introduced it to the synod of bishops in 1977. Since then the Protestant circles also accepted the concept. It is a term widely used both in anthropology and missiology. See Bosch 1995, 447.

Its links to the national church are also marginal. It is a full-fledged local church, above the three-self attributes in the Henry Venn definition. It has lived out contextualising the gospel (however, it is observed that among the three Venn selves—self-support, administration and propagation—we find the Madiri Puram Church weak in the self-propagating aspect). Fourthly, the kernel and husk are in creative tension in this village and cannot be separated from each other. For example, the kernel (Trinity) is qualified by the three porches but limited by excluding the fourth porch from the Reddy cattle shed. The husk I point to is the present Reddy–Christian Dalit relationship.

The gospel is the kernel, but its differing contextual practices are taken as husk. In other words, essentials[15] remain intact while non-essentials of the gospel are negotiable or altered. The kernel is sometimes reduced to denominational distinctives (e.g. Catholic or Protestant).[16] An editorial in *International Bulletin of Missionary Research* considers these concepts and defines the Gospel as:

> Good News is that Jesus the Christ, who both engages and transcends human time and culture, freely offers to unlock the potential of persons, families, and communities so that God's kingdom can come and God's will can be done on earth, as it is in heaven. Such a hope is Good News indeed! (Editorial, *IBMR* Vol.30.No.1 (January 2006): 1, 2)

While no definition is complete, the above one satisfies our need (cf. I Cor 15:2-5). The impact of inculturation is to ensure an ongoing "new creation." Pedro Aruppe describes inculturation as follows: It is "a principle that animates, directs, and unifies the culture, transforming it and remaking it so as to bring about a 'new creation' (Aruppe recited in Bosch 1995, 455)." Inculturation in a comprehensive way, but at the local level, should consider several things. For Bosch, "it involves the entire context: social, economic, political, religious, educational, etc" (Bosch, 453).

The Kernel-Husk Issue at Madiri Puram

The Christian Dalits of Madiri Puram have gone beyond inculturation. In that they copied the architecture from the late P. Adi Sheshi

---

[15] Essentials of the gospel may be stated thus: belief in the God of Israel, the trust in the Scriptures, Salvation by grace through faith in Jesus Christ, the leading of the Holy Spirit and the Second Coming of Christ. Non-essentials may include rites such as modes of baptism, Eucharist, dress codes, etc. See walls 2004: 23-24.

[16] Traditionally, one could refer to the Nicene Creed as the essence of the gospel.

Reddy premises. But it is clear that these Dalits were fully conscious of what to adapt and how much to adapt. We have noted above that they adapted three porches from the four on the Reddy architecture. I must then suppose that they followed certain parameters. The parameters were: that the Christian Trinity provide the norm and limit, that the Trinity be crowned by the cross of Jesus Christ, that adaptation[17] be egalitarian in worldview for copying a model, that it relates to the highest power structure—the Reddy, that it embraces with the Reddy against the Sudra opponents over socio-economic issues, and that they form a new type of class called "Reddy-Christian." The fact that they borrowed three porches instead of four from the Reddy premises makes one ask, why not four or more or less? The question is to be refined here because not just the porches were adapted, but also the Baptist/Mennonite church art forms from the neighboring churches, apart from Dalits' own Maremma model. The answer is not as simple as the supposition that only three porches fit the size of the sanctuary. The builders carefully studied (phenomena) the church models before deciding on the porch design, the porch being the index of the church. We suppose that the fourth porch was not copied for two reasons. One was their doctrinal orientation to monotheism. The other reason was that the concept behind porches was critically contextualised from what was available.[18] They testify to narrowing into the church (Jesus only way) instead of making it a broad way (plural ways). Apparently, the Reddy cattle shed had four porches for the sake of aesthetics and to facilitate ease of movement for the animals, his bond labourers and himself.

The teaching that the Madiri Puram Christian Dalits received for over five decades (1915-1973) on the God-head was (and still is) Trinitarian: God the father, God the Son and the indwelling Holy Spirit. Christ is the focus of this church architecture. As a mark of this emphasis, the middle porch has a mini cross above it and a

---

[17] "Adaptation" is a concept pioneered by Roberto De Nobili (1577-1656) in Madurai of South India. He wanted to redeem the gospel bound to the *parangi* (low caste converts) and become a Hindu to Hindus. He became a *sanyasin* (a monk wearing an orange dress unlike the cassock of a Roman Catholic priest) to reach the Brahmans of that period. He asked his converts to remain Hindu in every possible way (e.g. vegetarianism, or taking holy bath in a river). See H. L. Richard. "De Nobili, Roberto" 2001, 233-234.

[18] See Hiebert 1985, 171-192.

much larger one still above that. Christ is projected among the trinity. The name board has two cross signs on it. The large cross sign is in red on the back wall and is in between the wall texts of the Ten Commandments (Exod 20:2-17) and the beatitudes (Matt 5:2-11), illuminated with spark bulbs. The iron gates of the compound wall are full of cross signs.

The entrance into the sanctuary, however, has three even-sized porches. It appears that the local church has done critical contextualisation with regard to the trinity and has done so by borrowing from the Reddy architecture. What is trinity like? What is God like? This is a critical component of the thinking on the part of the church. In one sense, God is functioning in a triune way, as given in the Bible. The Scriptures supply us with some guidelines as to how to picture God but not make an idol of Him. Judaism, Christianity and Islam (Exod 20:4; Deut 4:15 and 27:15 cf *Qur'an* Surah CXII: At-Tawhid) used to hate equating God with any form or idol. Christianity, and even Islam, by way of Moghuls,[19] started thinking of exhibiting God in some human form. What is God like? He is like humans. After all, did not God say on the sixth day of the creation: "And now we will make human beings; they be like us and resemble us" (Gen 1:26). Jan Qaisar has done fine research on how artists gradually began to depict God in anthropomorphic forms:

> Very soon, God the *Unknowable*, became a *personified* object evolving through metaphors and symbols to a 'concrete form.' Some hold that the doctrine of Trinity (God the Father, Son= Jesus and the Holy Ghost or Spirit in one God head) contained the germ of anthropomorphism. Christ's assumption of human nature gave him the status of a being 'half-divine and half-man.' This was exploited by the artists in the first place to project him alone in human form. Later, when the fear of idolatry vanished, the artists started representing God in human form. But this did not happen all of a sudden. First, the artists experimented with the depiction of the 'Hand of God' — only the right hand of God, to be precise — to suggest His presence in a particular episode, the gesture being that of divine support (Pl. XXIII b). Afterwards, from the fifteenth century, with the triumph of the doctrine of Trinity, metaphorical

---

[19] Influenced by European artists like (e.g., Michelangelo) Moghul emperors like Akbar had artist Basawan in his court. Bichitr the artist was serving in Jahangir and continued through Shah Jahan's reign. They depicted the emperors being blessed by God the father with angels in the skies. For example, the Holy Spirit descended on Jesus in the form of Holy Spirit so taking clue Bichitr replaced Shah Jahan in place of Jesus. See Jan Qaisar 1993, 86.

> or allegorical allusions to God were abandoned and in its place emerged.
> God's portrayal in full-fledged human form (Pl. XXIC a-b). This can be
> noticed in many paintings where the concept of Trinity was delineated,
> especially with reference to the episode of Crucifixion; where God is
> shown sitting on the 'Throne of Justice' behind the Crucified Christ, and
> the Holy Spirit is exhibited as a dove. (Pl XXV a-b, see Jan Qaisar 1993,
> 85)

Our proposal is that the even-sized porches at the church depict the character of God the Trinity. They are equal in substance and function. They are the same but not the same, yet one. Even size speaks of equality of humans who enter to worship. There is no difference between high and low castes, the rich and the poor, or the able and disabled persons. Perhaps this stresses equality over disparity.

However, these three porches at the church have also created limitations or discontinuity for Dalit art forms. It limits them from modifying the architecture as long as this structure stays. They left out the fourth porch, perhaps to avoid having more than were needed for their faith position and or to avoid pluralism like in Hinduism. But the very fact that they have copied this architectural design shows they are dependent on other forms to understand their God and, more so, to express His incarnation for them. Porches closed on the top side for us limit God's "otherness or transience." The researcher agrees with Clifford Geertz, when he adjudges cultural symbols (such as art in our case) as essentials to understand humans and vice versa:

> Such symbols are thus not mere expressions, instrumentalities, or
> correlates of our biological, psychological, and social existence; they are
> prerequisites of it. Without men, no culture, certainly; but equally, and
> more significantly, without culture, no men." (Geertz 1973, 49)

Cultures are human creations. They limit God in some ways. Therefore, any culture is prone to sin and under the wrath of God (see Hiebert 1994, 102).

Summary

We have just finished considering the first theme, "inculturation of architecture," which arose from our description. The Madiri Puram Church has critically analysed and borrowed only three porches to preserve the kernel (the Trinity) of the gospel but not deviate from scriptural mandates or Anabaptist community hermeneutics. The residence of the Reddy has just three porches, while the centre porch serves as the entrance and the two on either side are for aesthetics.

The next concern is a reversal of the previous discussion, that is, the Reddy and Sudra castes *Sanskritising* Kattameedi Maremma. Inculturation goes two ways and is open ended. At this time, high-caste people have adapted Maremma, the chief Dalit *devata* (goddess) and her wooden images. Only she could be elevated upon a name change from Maremma to Kattameedi Maremma. Her image is bigger, more colourful, and gorgeous in expensive *saris* (dress for woman). This means that low-caste spiritual powers can be adapted with certain ritual procedures. On the contrary, Christian Dalits and non-Christian Dalits remain untouchables, while a higher or purer status is attributed to their goddess. Caste people can add deities to their pantheon, but do not accept an untouchable priest.

There is limit within which caste Hindus can assimilate Dalit gods. It is noteworthy that only a female goddess like Maremma could make it to the list of Madiri Puram Hindu divinities. Why is there such inhuman treatment of Dalit peoples? In order to understand the seriousness of our topic, we will need to look briefly at what the caste system is and how Dalits are outside the pale of the caste system. Caste discrimination is cruel, while the higher the caste the better the "sacred" image, so people strive to Sanskritise (ritually move up the ladder). But when it comes to Dalit people, they are put into the "profane" category.

Kattameedi Maremma Sanskritised but Her Priest and People De-Sanskritised

Maremma, the chief goddess of the Dalits is Sanskritised (face-lifted). She has been moved to higher spaces in the village. But her priest or priestess, a Dalit, remains an untouchable along with the Dalit people. Social anthropologists like M.N. Srinivas (1967) and McKim Marriot call this de-Sanskritisation. Any goddess or human when their status is lifted up their nomenclature usually changes. Name change is tied to character change. Kattameedi Maremma (or elevated Maremma) is a prime example of this trend, "De-Sanskritisation." De-Sanskritisation as a concept demands a brief overview of caste, the dynamics of Sanskritisation (social mobility) and its relation to De-Sanskritisation.

India is a land of the caste system.[20] The caste system is thought to be one of the best social stratification methods in the world, or so say its advocates. It classifies people on the basis of their birth into a certain caste (e.g. Brahmans). Such classification is thought to be sanctioned by Hindu religion. The belief is that Brahma (God) created humans from the beginning with a particular occupation in view. Brahmans emanated from his head to be the brain of society and a mouthpiece to God when it comes to worship. They are the purest of the pure in blood. The ruler caste (*kshatriya*) is the second. They came from·the shoulders of God and are assigned to rule people. Vaishya, the third category, is meant to do trade and agriculture. Vaishyas are born of the thighs of Brahma. Sudra, the final caste, is created to serve the above three castes.

The Brahman, Kshatriya, Sudra and Vaishya castes are considered as *dwija* (twice born). Twice born are (1) pure in blood as well as (2) eligible for religious initiation (Dumont 1996, 50, 67,363). Kshatriya and Sudra castes can initiate sacrifices to a deity but only the Brahman can perform it. Therefore, it is with the primacy of the Brahman that the caste system works.

Caste stratification necessitates the category called non-castes or untouchables. Untouchables are generally black in *varna* (colour). In summary, caste is based on colour, birth, occupation and religious unction. One either has a social rank or is devoid of such status. A person is pure or impure based on his or her birth. Social and ritual hierarchy is the essence of this worldview. Dalits, the subjects of this research, are non-castes and in most cases, are treated as inhuman. Caste rigidities governed exploitation, class conflicts, oppression, poverty and slavery. As a response, the Indian Constitution has forbidden the practice of "Untouchability" in all its forms (Article 17, see George Menacheri, Vol.1. 1982:3).

A twentieth century example of caste cruelty will suffice for laying the foundation on the state of affairs of the Dalit status. Srinivas mentions that in 1930, the Kallar (dominant caste) in the Ramnad district of Tamil Nadu, imposed eight prohibitions against the Harijans; a disregard of them led to violent suppression. The eight prohibitions were:

---

[20] Hindu countries like Nepal also live by caste stratification.

1. That the Adi-Dravidas shall not wear ornaments of gold and silver

2. That the males should not be allowed to wear their clothes above the hips

3. That their males should not wear coats or shirts or *baniyans*

4. No Adi-Dravida shall be allowed to have his hair cropped

5. That the Adi-Dravidas should not use other than earthenware vessels in their houses

6. Their women shall not be allowed to cover the upper portion of their bodies by clothes or *ravukais* (blouses) or *thavanis* (upper cloths worn like togas)

7. Their women shall not be allowed to use flowers or saffron paste

8. The men shall not use umbrellas for protection against sun and rain, nor shall they wear sandals (Srinivas 1967, 16)

Such things happen even today. For example, the researcher, a second generation Christian and a Dalit by origin, was made to stand for two long hours while interviewing the head (70 years of age) of the lone Brahmin family in the Madiri Puram village, despite the fact that there was enough grounds to be seated. The fact was that even this old man stood for that many hours. At another time, the researcher was lucky to get a tour of the man's house top. The motivation may have been to show that theirs is the largest house in the village. This aged person served the village for 29 years as Karnam (revenue collector). Caste discrimination is a reality for Dalit people. There are other factors of change and continuity.

The key here is the Brahman's ritual superiority over the rest of the people. Brahmans hold to caste hierarchy. Srinivas agrees with Ghurye who writes that even within Jainism and Buddhism there were the dominant Kshatriya caste monks who called the shots (G. S. Ghurye quoted in Srinivas 1967, 23). Since one's caste determines one's image in society, people try to make a concerted effort to move up the ladder. Srinivas has labeled this universal trend as "Sanskritisation." His definition of the term is as follows:

> ... as the process by which a 'low-caste' or tribe or other group takes over the customs, ritual, beliefs, ideology and style of life of a high and in particular, a *dwija* (twice-born) caste. Sanskritization of a group has usually the effect of improving its position in the local caste hierarchy. It normally presupposes either an improvement in the economic or

> political position of the group concerned or a high group self-consciousness
> resulting from its contact with a source of the Great Tradition of
> Hinduism such as a pilgrim centre or a monastery or a proselytizing sect
> (Srinivas 1998, 88).

A tribe or a group may try to move up the caste ladder, but the position of the Brahman cannot be exceeded by anyone of any caste. This is the essence of caste the system in practice. The *varna* (colour) principle is the key to Sanskritisation. According to M. N. Srinivas, the positions in one's caste may change, but the *varna* hierarchy remains intact. He calls *varna* dharma as immutable. Crucial to immutable *varna* is ritual purity headed by Brahmans and supported by the Kshatriya and Vaishya castes. For example, contact with a Harijan pollutes the four castes. How does *varna* keep its face immutable? Srinivas offers a broad four-fold answer:

1. There is a single all-India hierarchy without any variations between one region and another

2. There are only four *varnas*, or if the Harijans, who are literally "beyond the pale" of caste, are included, five

3. The hierarchy is clear

4. It is immutable (Srinivas 1967, 3)

It is plain that the Dalits are non-caste people. As such, apart from land and numerical calculations, prestige in rural India is also important. However, all will agree that, ritually speaking, the Brahman is at the top in rank though he may be poor.

De-Sanskritisation of Dalit Priests and People

If Sanskritisation means mobilisation to higher spaces in caste, what does de- Sanskritisation mean? While the Christian Dalit embracing Reddy architecture may be identified as a sign of Sanskritisation, the opposite is also happening. The high Castes also opt to Sanskritise Maremma, the chief goddess of the Dalits. Srinivas (1967) in agreement with McKim Marriot (1950) sees this "de-Sanskritisation" as limiting the impact of Sanskritisation. This localising of Sanskritisation is also called "parochialisation." What Marriot means by this term is that while a host of castes within the *varna* system strive to move up the hierarchy, there is also the reduction of this element.

In what ways is De-Sanskritisation a concern for our study of the Madiri Puram region? We find that Sanskritisation is not only a process exercised by the lower strata, but that even the higher castes in Madiri Puram have engaged in Sanskritising Maremma, the chief goddess of the Dalits. But there is a difference, in that Maremma is Sanskritised to the status of Kattameedi Maremma (elevated Maremma); she is elevated from the untouchable section of the village to that of the touchable caste section.

Kattameedi Maremma is now large in size and gorgeous in colourful attire and in best paints. She has gained reverence among the Brahman, Reddy (warrior) and Sudra (hunter, hair dresser and washerman) castes. She seems to enjoy this ritual and social hierarchy while having abandoned her Dalit children long ago.

Interestingly, the high castes also retain Dalit priests for Kattameedi Maremma. This is where Sanskritisation (mobility) and de-Sanskritisation (de-mobility) have critical tensions. The past and present Dalit priests[21] are allowed to officiate at the Reddy section of the village but never allowed to say prayers or perform rituals on the platform. At the most, the priest may sweep the premises and tidy up the idols, but he cannot touch the high caste-people at the shrine. The high-caste people themselves break a coconut or offer a personal wish and then share half of the offering in the basket; for example, a sweet cake offering (*bhakshalu*) to the priest. He or she shall be seated near the entrance steps to Kattameedi Maremma, not near the deity on the platform.

Pure and impure boundaries are broken with regard to the *devata* (goddess), but are never with regard to her priest and her children in the Dalit colony. She can never rise to the status of an *ista devata* (preferred or personal goddess) of a high-caste family. This is unique, but painful de-Sanskritisation. It asserts rigid caste mentalities.

Sanskritisation is possible for the goddess, but not for the low-caste priest and low-caste people. The treatment of a Dalit priest is similar to that of a Christian Dalit pastor. The pastor is respected for his education and clean habits but never embraced by high caste-people.

The Sacred and the Profane: Theoretical Understanding

What is happening here is a value judgment against humanity. Humans earn worth if born into a high caste, otherwise they are

---

[21] Except for the present one, all the previous priests were women.

lesser than animals. Practices like these are bound by worldviews. How can we understand this schizophrenic de-Sanskritisation? The ideas of the sacred and the profane come into play to help us understand the relationship between God, divinities, humans and things.

The sacred and the profane are two paradigms that both complement as well as contradict each other. We have evidence from our key informants that Kattameedi Maremma is considered sacred by high-caste people in the village, but high-caste people contradict themselves by not recognising the Dalit priest who performs the rituals on behalf of them. The question then arises, if the priest is the medium through which one reaches the deity, will the high-caste peoples' prayers and ablutions be accepted by the goddess if they do not also embrace the Dalit priest? Appeasing the priest does not seem to be a concern to high-caste people. Another way to look at the elevated position of Kattameedi Maremma is simply to pacify her. But what is going on here?

Carsten Colpe helps us understand the schizophrenic attitudes concerning the Kattameedi Maremma shrine. We need to remember that the adoption of a Dalit goddess by an entire caste people (Brahman to Sudra) may not happen in other villages, but it has happened in Madiri Puram. Colpe unravels the puzzle by helping us understand two concepts "Sacred and Profane" (Carsten Colpe 1987, 511-526), basically through their Latin roots. He thinks that modern language scholarship is indebted to Latin for these terms. He writes:

> To the Roman, *sacrum* meant what belonged to the gods or was in their power; yet when referring to *sacrum* one was not obliged to mention a god's name, for it was clear that one was thinking of cult ritual and its location, or was primarily concerned with the temple and the rites performed in and around it. *Profanum* was what was "in front to the temple precinct"; in its earlier usage, the term was always applied solely to places. Originally, *profanare* meant "to bring out" the offering "before the temple precinct (the *fanum*)," in which a sacrifice was performed. *Sacer* and *profanus* were therefore linked to specific and quite distinct locations; one of these, a spot referred to as *sacer*, was either walled off or otherwise set apart—that is to say, *sanctum*—within the other, surrounding space available for profane use. This purely spatial connotation adheres to the two terms to this day, and implies that it represents a definition of them, or at least of their more important features. (Colpe 1987, 511)

The sacred and profane often exist side by side many a time (e.g. a church besides a town hall). In case of the Madiri Puram village, it is Kattameedi Maremma and her Dalit priest who are in close proximity within the shrine precincts. "The relationship between the sacred and the profane can be understood either abstractly as a mutual exclusion of spheres of reality, or cognitively, as a way of distinguishing between two aspects of that reality" (Colpe *Ibid.*).

Why would high-caste people respect Kattameedi Maremma? The answer is: She is one of the *grama devatas* (village goddesses). She is, in a symbolic way and in reality, appeased. In this sense, the divine is accepted, but not the human (Dalit priest). He cannot even perform the *puja* (ritual/worship) for high-caste people. Therefore, the rituals at Kattameedi Maremma are both sacred and profane. She is "venerated yet sinister, holy and accursed" (Colpe *Ibid.*, 513).

Elevated Maremma is released but that demeans her own children (Dalits and Christian Dalits). They are further fixed into their non-caste box. The key to this is that high-caste people cannot perform rituals in a polluted section of the village. Therefore, a middle ground is broken to bring the deity closer, but bring the human public disgrace. Sensitive Christian Dalits hate the present priest (a nominal Christian) officiating at this shrine and bringing disrepute to them in a modern age. But he would not listen to their counsel owing to his family tradition and worldview. The other thing is that since the rest of the Dalits claim more or less strict adherence to the Christian faith that the priest would benefit from all the offerings, such as sweet cakes, coconuts, or money offerings. Further, he gets to drink the toddy offered to his devatas, Maremma and Karremma. So there is a profit motive, apart from the profane social pressure from high-caste people, that motivates his family to continue the priesthood.

We will benefit from an understanding of the biblical, Hebrew concepts of sacred and profane. Colpe explains the two biblical terms, namely *qadosh* and *herem*. The all-important concept in the Hebrew Bible is *qadosh*. It comes from the root *qd* ("to set apart"). Its fundamental meaning is like that of the Roman *sacer*. "But it is also possible that its root is *qdsh*, as in Akkadian *qadashu* ('to become pure'), which would point to a cultic connection. Nothing is *qadosh* by nature; however, things only become *qadosh* by being declared so for, or by, Yahveh Elohim"(Colpe *Ibid.*,515). Colpe goes on to describe that all of creation, persons, animals, temples and things are eligible to be set apart for holy use. The opposite of "use," is "useless." The Hebrew term *herem* serves the opposite of *qadosh*, i.e., "the banned object."

Here, at Kattameedi Maremma, two elements come into play. Maremma is face-lifted, but the Dalit priest is put aside as "damned" (*herem*) for destruction. There is continuity in the respect for Maremma that is exercised by high-caste people. It is understood as change by rituals and the art forms of her. But the human is not counted as equal to his own deity. The unseen spiritual power of Maremma is feared by high-caste people, while economically, hygienically and by blood, the poor and culpable Dalit loses his image further. He is made an instrument of social disintegration. So the Sanskritisation of Maremma by upper-caste people does not improve the human status of the Christian and non-Christian Dalits in Madiri Puram village.

Summary

The two key terms considered in the above section are: "Sanskritisation" of Maremma and "de-Sanskritisation" of the Dalit priests and her people. Sanskritisation is a concept facilitating the ritual mobility of a particular (Kshatriya, Vaishya and Sudra) caste of people. In the process of this mobility, the superior status of the Brahman is unchallenged. Brahmanism remains the topmost rung of the Sanskritisation ladder.

The irony in the Madiri Puram village is that Maremma, the Dalit goddess, is Sanskritised, but her children, the Dalits, are not. They were "De-Sanskritised." This is where we have seen the worldviews concerning "Sacred and Profane" (Colpe 1987, 511-526) playing their influence. The result is that even Kattameedi Maremma herself is "helpless", while her children are publicly disgraced.

Religious mobility has definite limitations. Limitations are set by caste rigidities. No ritual procedure can redeem the "de-human" situations of the Dalit community in Madiri Puram and its surrounding villages.

The above situation raises certain genuine questions. If caste rigidities dehumanise the Dalits, what happens to social harmony in the village? Thus, social integration is our next theme for comment. In what ways do Christian Dalits contribute to communal harmony? How can the dominant castes facilitate or frustrate such efforts? Is there a dominant class that emerges and governs social life? If so, how would hierarchy spin around such an existence?

Christian Dalit Contribution to Social Integration

Social harmony is a reality in the Madiri Puram village, but harmony is worked out continuously; therefore, it is fluid. There are concrete examples of art and architecture that reflect an agreement to maintain social bonds between dominant and opponent castes and classes. This research has determined that three types of social "glue" function in the village: (1) ritual- or caste-wise integration, (2) poetic integration and (3) political integration. All three may or may not include the element of contesting moral integration, which will become clear as we proceed.

Ritual or Caste-related Integration

Christian Dalits are considered ritually impure within the Hindu caste system. Though Jesus Christ has become their superior God, their belief has not raised their religious status in the context that was discussed earlier. One example of that is the distancing of the Dalit priest from officiating at the Kattameedi Maremma shrine because Maremma and her original children are labeled as "profane" persons.

First, the Christian Dalit's role in maintaining social integration is critical. In one sense, they continue to accept a subordinate position, in that they would never venture to live in a high-caste locality. Community living matters most to peasant people. It forms their social identity. Similarly, high-caste people do not move to reside in a Harijan colony. The low- and high-caste people keep to their boundaries with regard to space and worldviews. Caste-ridden existence is pressed into service. In this sense, any trespassing from both sides will be checked and violently suppressed if need be. Caste-based social structure, in general, works for social integration, though it is de-humanising to the Dalits. It is de-humanising because social integration is aggressive and hierarchical. Hierarchy is not easily worked out. It takes willingness, majority mores and long-term experiences. Hierarchy is power. Religious hierarchy is arrogance. It has a crushing effect on the "have-nots." However, village people have continued to live together for ages. Living together is thought through and such statuses are maintained. The high castes' superiority over the former bond slaves is an active mindset. Such statuses are maintained.

Our second but primary interest is to view social integration from the perspective of adapting art and architecture. Social integration is a process. It is sensitive, and transforming. In transforming, it asserts itself from the perspective of higher morals, such as the "equality" of all humans. Christian Dalits expressed this through the art forms and architecture that they adapted. Art and architecture carry "didactic significance" (C.R. Jones 1981, 56). For example, Hindu temple art and architecture projects its values and ethos. The society around a temple shall abide by the accepted ethos, even though some of them are not eternal (like the schooling only high caste pupils).

In his comprehensive coverage of the importance of "iconography" in churches, Samuel Rayan thinks that art can symbolise revolt. He quotes Samuel Laeuchli who is convinced "that visual art can be a carrier of rebellion" and a "tool of revolt." Figurative art is a threat to power, be this power religious, political, intellectual or ethical. Paintings and sculptures address us directly, without any need of "explanation" (Samuel Laeuchli quoted in Samuel Rayan 1996, 32).

The photograph of Sadhu Yosepu, which includes a section of the church and the village people taken on July 29, 1962, hangs on the east inside wall as another sign of art. Yosepu is a living healer-saint. This photograph is revolutionaryto general iconography, which usually depicts the diseased saints. It, among other symbols (like multiple crosses), projects a living God and his immediate care through saints like Sadhu Yosepu.

The Gilgal India Mennonite Brethren Church has adapted three shapes of Norman Architecture from the Reddy premises, apart from synagogue and Baptist/Mennonite forms. It appears to be rebellious in its presentation of the equality of all humans through the "crosses." Except for their silent, but continuous, protest against caste disintegration, Christian Dalits have not voiced their protest save the *Ambedkar Yuva Jana Sanghalu* and *Dalit Rights Porata Samiti*, which are working to ban discrimination, particularly in the case of low-caste people being served in separate cups at tea-stalls in the village. Caste-prone disintegration is linked to the nation's weakness. In this sense, social integration is workable, transforming and functional in the village.

Chapter 5

TWO NAMES FOR ONE CHILD: FAITH AND SOCIO-ECONOMIC STATUS IN CREATIVE TENSION

Tailor Prashanth is one of the tallest persons in the Christian palem (colony). He is a reputed dressmaker. The entire village, the palem Christians in general and his friends in particular, like to chat with him and take his advice on life issues. People also come to his house to make pay-phone calls. People exchange ideas and news. Prashanth is the only one in Harijanwada who has a television set—an additional reason why his friends congregate at his house.

Introduction: A Child with Two Names

School-going children run to his residence to get their new school outfits during the reopening of schools in the middle of June every year. One time, a six-year-old boy came to collect his clothes. The conversation began:

Prashanth: Little fellow, what is your name?

Child: Which name do you want, the name at my school or the one at church? I am Vikas (enlightened) at school but Visvas (believer) in church.[1]

Prashanth was dumbfounded for a moment at the response of the lad, but then burst into laughter at his shrewd but innocent answer. This brief, but telling, event raises several complex questions of continuity and change among Christian Dalits of Madiri Puram village. Why two names for one child? Obviously, Visvas did not choose the names. One was given to him at his christening ceremony and the other was supplied to satisfy school requirements.

The above child is innocent as far as his two names are concerned. But his Christian Dalit parents and his palem are concerned for his

---

[1] Telugu Transliteration: *Eperu seppale, badiloda? gudiloda? gudilo naa peru "Visvas", badilo naa peru "Vikas".*

future. A Christian parent choosing two names for a child means that the parent will produce a document of the child's Scheduled Caste origin from the Mandal Revenue Office.

For government records, such parents and children are non-Christian and Scheduled Caste people. Waddepally Mandal officials often make certain that a Scheduled Caste certificate holder is not a practicing Christian. They ask several other critical questions before issuing such documents.

There are four occasions when a Mandal certificate is required to claim Scheduled Caste benefits: (1) education, (2) agriculture or home loans, (3) employment and (4) contesting Panchayat or Assembly elections on the seat reserved for the Scheduled Caste.

But for all practical purposes, in the Gadwal Mennonite Brethren Field area, "Madiga" is a synonym for "Christian Dalit" and vice versa. The question for Christian Dalits is how to take advantage of reservation benefits. It is said that even some pastors make use of Scheduled Caste benefits.

The Scheduled Caste status paves the way for free professional education and a 15 per cent reservation chance for employment in government institutions. Claiming backward class status (B. C. "C") or Christian parentage reduces the chance of reservation for jobs and even political positions to 1 per cent.

The issue is complex, mainly because the core caste system has not changed in modern India. There are only four castes—Brahman, Kshatriya, Vaishya and Sudra. The rest of the people are untouchables. To uplift their socio-economic conditions, the British government labeled the untouchables Scheduled Castes, or Scheduled Tribes.[2]

Social sanctions in the entire Christian palem hamper individuals from seeking reservation benefits. Christian Dalits have been struggling to be included as Scheduled Caste beneficiaries, on par with converts to Buddhism and Sikhism who are from low castes. All the national governments so far, including the Congress government, have shed crocodile tears over this social justice issue. Of course, the Bharatiya Janata Party (BJP) and other nationalist forces vehemently oppose extending reservation benefits to Christian

---

[2] Scheduled Castes are generally the Mala and Madiga communities. These Dalits [Madigas] are the majority in the Gadwal area compared to that of Mala.

Dalits. The simple reason is that they are moving forward in education and health. They are alleged to have embraced Western religion. I also see fear as a reason—fear that the Dalits would turn to Christian faith in great numbers if the 15 per cent reservation doors were open. Thus, religious and socio-economic exploitation is going on in the Gadwal area, as elsewhere in India.

The 2001 census found a total of 1,104 Scheduled Caste people and 10 Scheduled Tribes people in Madiri Puram village. The census listing has only these two categories; it does not have room for "Christian" as a category. It may be said that 90 per cent of the entire Mandal Scheduled Caste and ST communities are Christian Dalits; so there is the necessity to show "Christian" as a separate column. But it seems that such "columnising" is not preferable to Christians because that could end their right to 15 per cent reservation benefits. That is why this chapter concerns itself with change and continuity in the religious and soci0- economic status of Christians in Madiri Puram village.

Life Orientation of the Child

Visvas begins to understand that he should learn to live in two worlds: the world of his church and the world of his school. His understanding unfolds as he responds to his class teacher taking attendance: His name is Vikas. Within the Christian palem, he is known as Visvas. Having two names becomes a routine in life. What does all this mean? There are four possible meanings. My ideas are summarised in the table given below.

Table 15: Life locations: Scheduled Caste and Backward Caste "C" Categories

S. No	Church	School	Work Place	Caste Category
1.	Visvas	Visvas	Visvas	B. C. "C"
2.	Visvas	Vikas	Vikas	Scheduled Caste
3.	Vikas	Vikas	Vikas	B. C. "C"
4.	Visvas	Visvas	Visvas	Scheduled Caste

Category 1: All through life cycles one claims to be a Christian Dalit, i.e., B. C. "C" (Backward Class, "Christian").[3]

Category 2: A person starts as a Christian at birth but ends up as a Dalit, i.e., Scheduled Caste "Dalit"

---

[3] There are other backward classes like Moslems. BC "C" is a category referring to Christians.

Category 3: A person retains the Dalit name though had embraced Christian faith, i.e., "Backward Caste "C"

Category 4: A person retains his Christian name but ends up as a Dalit, i.e., Scheduled Caste

It may be mentioned that these categories overlap and differ in both quality and quantity. Other examples of changing a Christian name in order to maintain the Scheduled Caste status would be Yehoshua (Joshua) to Yeshoshiva (the eminent Shiva[4]), or Suguna (woman of character) to Srijana (woman of creativity).

Scheduled Caste

Two sub-castes, Mala and Madiga ('Dalit' for Madiga hereafter), comprise the Scheduled Caste category. Scheduled Caste people generally live in the villages in the plains[5]. Their lifestyle is different from that of the Scheduled Tribes or Hill People. Malas and Dalits have social and behavioral differences. Malas think they are superior to Dalits. My interest is to study Dalits and Christian Dalits in the Madiri Puram village. Incidentally, there is just one migrant mala family in the village.

Some argue that it was the British who labeled the untouchables as Scheduled Caste and Scheduled Tribes thus assigning them a lower status than the four Hindu castes: Brahman, Kshatriya, Vaishya and Sudra. In one sense, there is now a non-caste category. People who cast the blame on the British administration tend to deny the Aryan invasion of Adi-Dravidian (early Dravidian) cultures and the imposition of their colour superiority on the natives and Adi-Vaasis (early tribals). In broad strokes, India is said to contain two ethnic groups, the Dravidian (South) and Aryans (North) India people. Historians think of both of these races as invaders of primitive India one after the other. Hence, the caste hierarchy that developed after the Aryan invasion. The benefit of the British category is to give the Scheduled Castes certain constitutional safeguards.

---

[4] Shiva is one of the trinity of Hinduism, viz, Brahma, Vishnu and Eshvara or Shiva.

[5] The current research now claims that plains people were once tribes. See *Deccan Chronicle* (The largest circulated English daily published in Andhra Pradesh) Monday 15 January 2007, 1-2. The column in essence says that the caste system may have existed much before the arrival of Aryans c. 3,500 years ago. In one sense, the blame for the Aryan concoction of evil, the caste system, is reduced by this study. The study does not refer to religious sanction of caste discrimination in Hinduism.

Dalits

A second term has come to be used frequently, i.e., "Dalit." The word "Dalit" means people who have been "crushed, exploited, suppressed" for at least 3,000 years. The Dalit movement has been led mostly by Christian liberation theologians like Prof. A. P. Nirmal. Dalit theology works from the perspective of Christians with the Scheduled Caste background. In fact, there is a call to unite Christian and non-Christian Dalits to fight for social justice. Of all terms in this section, this is the one preferred by both Christians and non-Christians. The term expresses their agony and resolve to fight for their human rights. I am using Dalit or Scheduled Caste Dalits to refer to the same group. The "chaturvarna" (four castes) have put the Dalits outside their categories. Mahatma Gandhi, who in the final analysis wished to retain the caste system, criticised Hinduism for its treatment of untouchables. Gandhi wanted to treat them as Harijans (children of God).

Dalitbahujans

Prof. Kancha Ilaiah, Dalit Activist and Professor of Political Science, Osmania University, has a broader argument and strategy to press for the rights of all the oppressed people groups. Ilaiah has coined the term "Dalitbahujans." Ilaiah rightly calls the attention of Dalit theologians to consider other communities that are also treated equally bad by the three dwija or twice-born castes (Brahman, Kshatriya and Vaishya and some wealthy "Sudras"). Ilaiah argues that his native kuruma or shepherd caste is one of the oppressed, as are also the Mangali, Chakali, and all the Sudras. His writings such as *Why I am not a Hindu: A Sudra Critique of Hindutva Philosophy, Culture and Political Economy (1995)* and *The State and Repressive Culture — The Andhra Experience (1989)*, hold up a mirror to discriminatory practices. Strategically, it would be better for all the Dalit groups and Dalitbahujans to join forces to achieve their goals.

Benefits of Scheduled Caste Status

However, the concern of this research is to investigate the Scheduled Caste status in Madiri Puram village and its region, Gadwal and Alampur. There are four areas of help for the Scheduled Caste from government institutions: reservations in education and professional schools, loans for agriculture and housing, job reservations and reserved seats for elections (e.g., for Sarpanch). First, students receive scholarships for education. Even with a minimum percentage of marks in competitive exams, Scheduled Caste college students get 15 per cent of the seats in professional schools, such as engineering or medical schools.

The second benefit is in agriculture. The parents of "Vikas" have been either bond labourers or tenant farmers or small-scale farmers. They are assured of loans for implements, crops and horticulture, and for chicken or animal farms. Christian and non-Christian Scheduled Castes are eligible for loans with a subsidy of up to 50 per cent. This is quite an attractive offer. People from poor backgrounds are likely to depend on government subsidies. The church has not been able to create avenues of help in this area. Agriculture is the main source of livelihood for Madiri Puram village, so naturally people look for economic benefit, without which it is hard for them to make the ends meet.

Traditionally, Dalits have nuclear families and boast of having more than four children. This creates a critical problem. The one-acre ceiling (government) land is insufficient. By the time children are grown up, each one will get a very little share of one acre of land unless the farmer invests in additional land. Prashanth needs to get his children educated and married. This adds to financial stress. Moreover, if the monsoons fail, farmers are forced to consider short-term migration to a city like Hyderabad. The struggle to survive will compel them to teach their children to seek clerical or occupational jobs.

In addition, the Dalits in the Gadwal area practice the dowry system. A dowry of one to three acres of land is gifted to a son-in-law, as well as some cash. Possession of land is necessary for arranging the marriages of daughters. To meet the economic challenges, a number of families, like that of the Tekuri clan, have migrated to Madhya Pradesh as "*Palamoori* laborers." Palamooru is the ancient name of Mahabubnagar, the district headquarters under which Madiri Puram village falls. "Palamoori laborers" is often used as a derogatory remark, because the district had no resources of livelihood except depending on monsoons, which often fail for years in succession.

However, the situation today has changed with the provision of the Rajulabanda Diversion Scheme Canal water coming to this area. If the Rajulabanda reservoir is full, there is every possibility of growing paddy, cotton, sunflowers, seed brinjal, beera and other crops. Most of the crops nowadays are cash crops. But, there again, the constant struggle is with the Rayalaseema *goondas* (musclemen and political thugs) diverting more than their rightful share of Rajulabanda Diversion Scheme water.

Additionally, the Pesticide Companies supply the *rytu* (farmer or tenant farmer) with capital for crops and the pesticides. The yield is measured by international standards. There are farmers who go bankrupt in this endeavour when crops fail or monsoons fail them.

The third benefit is employment. Fifteen percent job reservation for the Scheduled Caste is available. However, except for a few, most Christians of Dalit background have become middle-class people with white-collar jobs, though seldom in executive positions. In fact, they would be prevented from climbing the professional ladder by the inner circle hegemony or lobby of upper-caste officers. It may be that Christians of Dalit origins have fared well compared to their non-Christian Dalit compatriots.

With regard to employment, some Christian Dalits have advanced professionally by claiming the Scheduled Caste status. Some admit that this is done on purpose—for a quick rise in social status. A Mandal Revenue Inspector could be a Christian in disguise who wanted that position. But when it matters to stand for Christ, he or she may not openly come out. People with Scheduled Caste certificates get faster promotions.

Will that assure them job satisfaction? When asked, they answered in the negative. In essence, such officials discourage Christians wanting B. C. "C" certificates. The broader question is why these Christians do not fight for economic help on the basis of their poverty status rather than because of their caste. They say that is not the way the system works. Therefore, we empathise with people in continuing disparity caused by their caste and more so because of the egalitarian demands of the gospel. There is so much hatred and violence against the Dalits and Christian Dalits and attacks on their self-respect.

Fourth, there is the benefit of gaining a political position benefit as person with the Scheduled Caste status. The government has encouraged low-caste individuals to become the *Sarpanch* (head of a village) on a rotation basis. Every five years, elections are held for the village head. The government purposely rotates the reservation system to offer different caste people the opportunity to be selected. One term is declared for Scheduled Castes, in general. The next time it is reserved for B. C. "C", i.e., Christians of the Scheduled Caste origin. Another term is set for forward caste candidates. This is to facilitate shifts in the social paradigm. However, the reality is different. For example, the Sarpanch of Tummilla village is a Christian Dalit. He says:

> Even as a Sarpanch, I hear the complaints of the high caste people, while seated or standing. I know I am a Dalit by caste but a Christian by faith. Christian faith does not mean you assume equality with the high Castes (Patayya, *Field Notes*, October 2005, 64).

The Sarpanch sees the misuse of democracy at the Mandal Council. He says that all the Reddy Sarpanches form a majority voice or vote and snatch away the best part of Mandal development funds. Low-caste Sarpanches, because of their minority in the council, are left with the rest. The officials are hands-in-glove with the majority because they call the shots. So the reservation system of election has changed only the technique, not caste discrimination. Yet Patayya and political leaders from similar backgrounds testify that they do their best to develop the villages compared to other Sarpanches. This quality work attitude is attributed to the effect of the Christian gospel.

Thus, the researcher sees a clear, critical existence between continuity and change. Christian leaders continue to be treated as Scheduled Castes but at the same time, they better represent and aid their village development. Sometimes, they are in a fix to answer whether they are Christian and not Scheduled Caste, which simply means Hindu for government official records — and records are what finally counts in a democracy. If this is the social status quo, will not the Dalits protest?

Dalit movements like Dalit Dandora and Ambedkar Youth Associations protest as explained below. Dalit movements like Dalit Dandora[6] and Ambedkar Yuvajana Sangham[7] use their influence on Christians of Dalit background. These movements encourage Dalits to take pride in identifying themselves as Dalits.

---

[6] Dalit Declaration

[7] Ambedkar Youth Association

The Impact of Madiga Dandora and Madiga Reservation Porata Samiti

A senior pastor of the region reported that Madiga Dandora invokes the self-respect of Dalits. *Tappeta* (a percussion drum) is the instrument that announces their resolve to achieve social justice. Madiga Reservation Porata Samiti (MRPS) is a social rights movement. Their basic philosophy is: "Be proud of your Dalit origin, as a Brahman would be of his." Manda Krishna Madiga, the President of the movement, asks Christian Dalits to feel honoured to add the suffix "Madiga" after their names. For instance, Joseph should add Madiga to his name, thus, being "Joseph Madiga." *Madiga Reservation Porata Samiti* promises reservation benefits to Dalit Christians, provided the churches support their movement under Scheduled Caste terms.

Madiga Dandora youth enter the church and teach Christian young people to fight for their social rights and put a flag in the premises of church building. The Dandora youth teach that "Dalit" and "Christian" are interchangeable words. This is a sign of cultural assimilation. They celebrate Ambedkar *jayanti* (birth anniversary) with cultural dances and beating the *dappu* (another name for percussion instrument). When asked how all this affects the church tradition, a pastor replied:

> Members of this group rarely make it to church worship services. Therefore, they are a stumbling block to the church youth. Ambedkar was a Buddhist, and he did not say to put a flag in the church premises but these people do it anyway. I do accept Ambedkar was a national leader, more so a Dalit liberator. But these youth overact. They blow whistles, apply colors and *kumkuma*.[8] I have seen this in Ieej area (Pradeshi 2005, 18-19).

In general, youth are carried away with secular ideologies without studying the impact on the church. Sometimes this enthusiasm leads them to go overboard on Scriptural instructions or church traditions. Youth involved in such activities are never committed Christians. On the other hand, churches need to answer these questions from the perspective of worldview change. One way to handle it is to provide in service training to the shepherds or have regular disciplining sessions for the youth.

---

[8] "Kumkuma" is red powder applied to the forehead.

Ambedkar Yuvajana Sanghaalu

The second movement that influences Christian Dalit protests is Ambedkar Youth Association. Unlike Dalit Dandora, the Ambedkar *Yuvajana Sanghaalu* (Ambedkar Youth Society) even has some Sudra followers. According to a daughter of a senior pastor, one MB Church contributed Rs. 10,000 to the construction of an Ambedkar statue in their village (Arunodaya, M. I. 2005, 5). The Baba Saheb Society demanded this contribution, saying that Christians are beneficiaries of the struggle of Ambedkar to raise the low caste status.

Therefore, the church was obliged to contribute to the erection of the statue. How shall we assess this puzzling situation? It is not easy. We need to investigate what is happening from the perspective of Mandal officers. Bureaucracy also contributes to the harassment of Christian Dalits. They require pastors to vouch for the non-Christian status of a Christian Dalit.

Mandal Official Asks Local Pastor to Vouch Non-Christian Status

Apart from the poor economic background of Dalit Christians, there are other reasons why pastors of this area authorise the authorities to issue Scheduled Caste certificates to Christian Dalits. The personal files of the longest-serving pastor in the Madiri Puram village reveal that on 13 September 1997, an official from Alampur wrote him a letter (see *G. Devadanam File 1996-1998*) asking him to certify some people as non-Christian by religion. A request like this is unusual when compared to what happens in neighbouring Revenue divisions, such as Narayanpet. Officially, it should be a Village Executive Officer (VEO) or a Sarpanch of the village who should acquire such clarification.

The text of the Officer's letter can be translated as follows:

13 September 1997

Gauravaneeyulu Rajashree (His Excellency Pastor),

Please write to say the below-mentioned persons are not of Christian religion.

Names[9]

    A w% B

    C w% D

---

[9] The original letter is in Telugu. The names have been changed to alphabets.

E w% F

G S% H

I S% J

K S% L

M S% N

O W% P

Yours
Signature

(Vice President)

Almapur ABDR

The letter indicates that the eight Christian Dalits have submitted their applications for Scheduled Caste status certificates and that the matter is pending for verification by the pastor of the church at Madiri Puram. Except for the third and fourth pairs, the spouses have non-Christian names, though the letter does not clarify whether all applicants are Christian in the first place.

The system is painful in that the official does not ask for the candidates' faith status but their religious category; hence their allegiance to and eligibility for Scheduled Caste reservation benefits. For the pastor and many other government servants, there exist just two options: The people are either Scheduled Caste (Hindus) or Christian by religion. Conversion to Christianity is a change of religion. It amounts to discontinuity from their traditional practices. Therefore (by implication), they are not eligible for reservation benefits.

The official seems to be a very civilised man since he is polite with the pastor. He addresses the pastor with highest respects, "Gauravaneeyulu Rajashree." Using the address "His Excellency Pastor...." may be out of respect to priests in the area, or the official might wish to pacify the pastor for seeking a sensitive but undue document from him.

We found later that this unusual request became a tradition in the research area, and pastors were taken to task by the church if they did not vouch for their Dalit status to Mandal officials. The church institutionalised the practice and made it statutory as one of the qualifications in recruiting a pastor. The pastors who refused to comply either resigned from their post or went to another church that did not require such letters. On the other hand, we have no record of whether the pastor in question responded to the letter of the Vice President of Alampur ABDR.

However, we do find some other pastors responding to such official letters. A pastor in Madiri Puram wrote to the Mandal Revenue Officer at Shantinagar concerning a similar request. The letter clarified that the person in question, Mr. Y, had not taken baptism and so belongs to the Scheduled Caste. The research found the date of the letter on the reverse side. The letter also contained the church seal and signature of the pastor.

We can safely conclude that the church is in agreement with the pastor vouching for the applicant as non-Christian Dalit. Therefore, he is not a Christian by religion but a Hindu by implication.

The statement is that "Y" is not a Christian by baptism; he is a Dalit and so Scheduled Caste; therefore, a Hindu by religion. This assumes that baptism is the only criteria for belonging to a faith. Some try to differentiate between faith and religion. Other Christian churches have the incomplete idea that "Christianity is a way, not a religion." Still others say, "Either you are a Hindu or a Christian by religion—there is no middle ground." It is clear that there are conflicting theories about faith and religion. The biggest confusion is about who authorises the pastor to document somebody as non-Christian. If someone is not a Christian, is it not the responsibility of the Sarpanch to say so? Pastors are also pulled into the game of continuing or discontinuing their call to preach and disciple people.

Y's Scheduled Caste status is more attractive than if he were a Christian. The difficulty is the question as to whether the pastor will be required to intimate if Y chooses to follow Christ and become baptised say at his marriage. This may happen after he receives the non-Christian status letter. We entirely agree that the poverty compulsions are there. There is tension among Christian, Scheduled Caste and Hindu statuses. This tension is uncalled for if a poor man is not required to produce a certificate. That is not easy, because if not for education, one is in want of loans for crops.

Pastor's Conditions for Issuing Clearance for Scheduled Caste Certificates

A middle-aged but brilliant pastor worked in the Madiri Puram village from 1984 to 1986. Today he is pastoring another village MB church. The researcher visited him on July 24, 2005. He feels sorry for preachers vouching for Scheduled Caste certificates for Christians. He says it is against one's conscience. Dalit Dandora and Ambedkar Yuva Jana Sanghalu have enforced this view in the churches. The researcher learned from him about the conditions under which pastors write a clearance certificate to a Mandal official. They write, "Mr. X is not baptized. He lives according to non-Christian practices." Does that really mean he was not baptised? The pastor confided they write like that because they are not sure whether Mr. X was baptised or not. So, what will the applicant submit? The person concerned submits in writing that he is not a Christian and that he has no relationship with the church. We take three documents in proof of his contentions:

1. An application addressed to the pastor
2. A copy of his previous caste certificate
3. A Xerox copy of an affidavit from a lawyer

"Based on the above documents we write, Mr. X is not a Christian. Then all the responsibility (curse or blessing) falls upon pastor's head. But this is not a good practice. There is no government order for us to do so" (Pradeshi, L. S. *August 2005, Field Notes*, P. 13).

The pastor went to inquire of a Mandal Revenue Officer (provincial magistrate) why a pastor is required to write such a note to him. The officer said, "To safeguard our jobs we require you to assure us." The government trusts a pastor more than a village executive officer or a Sarpanch. The letter by the pastor absolves both the Hindu village officials as well the government officials from their responsibility. All of them are involved in a matter of "conscience." They take corporate action which safeguards the higher-ups. Pastors feel this is how the officials make "scapegoats" of them. The Christian society also puts pressure on them: if they do not help the members of the church, they are taken to task and there is misunderstanding. Christians blame the pastors for their difficult economic lot. In one way, this is a social justice matter; in another way, it amounts to obeying religions or biblical principles.

While learning the above pastor's views, the researcher checked with the India MB Church Constitution. It says that people who get certificates for "self-benefit" lose permanent membership in the church, hence leadership positions: "If [an MB Christian] gets a certificate for 'self-benefit,' he loses permanent membership in the Church" (R. S. Lemuel. *Mennonite B rethren Local Church and Field Association Statutes- GC.* (Mahabubnagar, 1988. Section vi. 10, 7).

The MB Church regulation does not define what "self-benefit" means. The probable interpretation is that it refers to a Christian Dalit securing a Schedule Caste Certificate. The article does not say what happens if children of church leaders hold Scheduled Caste certificates. The least that can be said about the rule is that Church is not sensitive to the struggles of the rural church.

The researcher asked the pastor how as spiritual *gurus* (teachers) we could understand the issue. The pastor lamented: It is by killing our conscience. We have no escape than to write. But if our Conference leadership can issue a ban on writing such notes we can stop it. We can quote the ban when people ask for it.[10] No pastor is exempt from this risky job in the area.

> The Mandal (province) Revenue Officer, District Collector, and Revenue Divisional Officers refer the matter to the concerned village pastors if a candidate from his palem gets a job on reservation quota. Since we know the candidate and his childhood and of his Scheduled Caste status, we also take that as an advantage and reply with affirming his low caste status. This is a very difficult task. We are bound to kill our conscience and do it. . . we should give account on the Day of Judgment that there is no other way to go (Pradeshi, L.S. *August 2005-Field Notes*, 14-15).

Pradeshi suggests that if all the pastors of the area and MB Church Conference leadership appeal to the District Collector, there can be a solution. The solution should include a continued pressure to extend reservation benefits to poor Christians and, until this happens, instruct the Mandal officials not to require pastors to write letters judging somebody's caste or religion. That is not their job or calling. We should also realise that an appropriate action is needed in a society that is sick with "scapegoat culture." In this sense, democracy is a mob culture that does not do justice to the suffering people. To this effect, recently, MB Christians in Gadwal held a rally and submitted a Memorandum to the Revenue Divisional Officer (RDO). Their demands included among others, freeing pastors from issuing Scheduled Caste certificates.

Effects on Church's Life

These struggles have created an imbalance in the church's life of the Madiri Puram Circuit[11] and Gadwal Revenue Division. One of the

---

[10] We have already pointed to the Conference/ Leadership stand. See footnote 5.

[11] Madiri Puram as a Circuit Centre used to have eleven village Churches under its jurisdiction, namely Julakallu, Konkala, Mundladinne, Paccharla, Paramati Gaarlapaadu, Ramaapuram, Senagapalle, Tummilla, Vayilaala, Venkatapuram and Yapadinne.

results is dislike of pastors who do not want to license a Christian as a Scheduled Caste, which in the end means that the person is a Hindu for Census records. Some MB Churches[12]

> A preacher must write certificates to vouch we are Dalit by caste. He better oblige or else he is considered useless for our interests, he is not supported. Therefore a send off is unwritten law. . . . It is a condition for recruitment. (Itzaaq, M. A. *September 2005 - Field Notes*, 13)

All the village churches in the Gadwal area (including Alampur and Yemmiganur taluks) are self-supported. Laymen have a definite say in the recruitment of a pastor. A few churches with over 800 members become economically attractive to pastors.

Naturally, all do not qualify, even with high theological education and experience. Some pastors are willing to write certificates for monetary benefits by way of a fee for each certificate.

A second effect is that, sometimes, a pastor can side with the ruling group in the church and show "prejudice" (see July 2005-Field Notes, 22) against others. There was a complaint against a pastor accusing him of showing partiality in writing Scheduled Caste Certificates for some and refusing others. The elders of the opposition have written to the Chairman of the Field Association requesting a transfer of their pastor. A copy of this letter is given below:

To
October 23, 1996
The Chairman and Secretary
MB Gadwal Field Association

Dear Sirs,

Subject: Request to transfer pastor "Y"

Please transfer Pastor "Y" from our church. He vouches some members of our church as Schedule Caste but for some others he denies it. This is practicing partiality. Thus creating split in the church. When you send a different pastor, we will recruit him on the grounds that he agrees to our policies.

However, the Circuits are considered outdated as of October 2005. The M B Conference has proposed "Mandalization (provincializing)" of Field Associations, Madiri Puram being one. As such, Gadwal Field will be sub-divided into seven or more Mission Fields.

[12] Like Mandoddi and Maldakal.

Yours in Lord's ministry

MB Bethlehem Church Elders, P-Village [13]

Thirdly, how would a church deal with a Mandal Revenue Officer who refuses Scheduled Caste Certificates to Christian Dalits? They teach him a hard lesson. "CK" village has a large Christian presence. It falls under the Narayanpet Revenue Division of Mahabubnagar. Recently, they built a beautiful church building. One of its leaders served as *Upa Sarpanch* (Vice-President) of the village. Christians were refused Scheduled Caste benefits on the grounds that the "entire palem is converted Christians." They are no longer Dalits. The church leadership pleaded their case with the Mandal Revenue Officer because they continue to be economically poor as a result of ages of exploitation. He would not listen. Sometimes, inexperienced or young Mandal Revenue Officers like to create history. This one tried to do   this. So the Christians planned to teach him a lesson.

A buffalo died in front of the Mandal Revenue Office. Culturally, no high-caste person will touch a dead animal. The Mandal Revenue Officer sent word to the leaders of the Harijan Palem. Low-caste people took this as their chance of teaching the authorities a lesson. They responded by saying, "We are Christian and do not touch a carcass." Two days passed. The rotting carcass was spreading an unbearable stink. The Mandal Revenue Office could not function well. Meanwhile, Christians were united in their fight for social justice. The Mandal Revenue Officer had to recall the Christians of Schedule Caste origin and request them "please arrange to remove the dead animal. I will issue Scheduled Caste certificates to all those in need" (Jayanna, P. J. *August Field Notes*, 25-26).

At another time, Christian Dalit leaders saw that the Mandal Revenue Officer was invited to a house dedication ceremony. Everyone else stood outside while the Mandal Revenue Officer cut the ribbon and entered the house all alone. As arranged, a lady was taking bath in the new house. She was in her bathrobe. The photographer did his job taking photos with the chief guest inside the house, unaware of the drama ahead. The lady shouted "Rape...

---

[13] Name of the village is changed.

rape... rape... rescue me!" A furious mob surrounded the house and made a big hue and cry: "Why did you enter the house with nobody with you?" They saw to it that the picture of his "attempted rape" was published in daily newspapers. As a result, the Mandal Revenue Officer was troubled, ashamed and compelled to seek immediate transfer, and left the place. This is a shrewd way of getting rights.

Principles

1. Caste categories: The Indian bureaucracy works under caste categories. It is supposed to be a secular country but it is run on a democracy governed by caste mentalities.

2. Use of tactics: People use tactics to teach lessons in a society ridden with caste discrimination.

3. End justifies the means: Can the end justify the means? Can Christians in good conscience use un-Christian means to force justice? If Christians resort to such tactics, will the Mandal Revenue Officer and other Hindu officials ever be open to the Christian gospel? The reverse argument is: How else can justice be ensured? In this sense, justice-making is not anti-gospel. Paying the price of injustice is part of the gospel. But could there be a better way to teach officials a lesson?

4. Justice to all people: Perhaps true justice will come only with justice to all communities irrespective of caste backgrounds. For example, there are poor Brahmans.

5. Meaning in administration: Defining all ethnic people with one set category results in poverty in a thinking nation. There must be alternative categories in dealing with human needs. What is meaningful to the Mandal Revenue Office and to the Christians is not following fanatic means, but building the nation with care and compassion for the most needy. In this case, the Scheduled Castes need uplifting through government benefits.

6. The Hindu hierarchy better think twice before using the administrative system to discredit the claims of poor masses.

Scheduled Caste Certificate and Politics

A fourth impact on the Church is that some pastors may suffer imprisonment. It is not just the Scheduled Caste Christians who suffer. There are political parties that drag pastors into issuing two contradictory certificates to one person. *Padiris* (pastors) who are overconfident may end up in jail for a while and pay very dearly for the mistakes committed. But before considering politics, I need to clarify a minor matter here—Scheduled Caste certificates and the pastor's role in other revenue areas.

Prodduturu Christian Malas of Church of South India

Pastor Pradeshi hails from Prodduturu of the Cuddapah district. The Church of South India has done great service to the Dalits in the area. Most of the Christian Dalits in this area come from the Mala, sub-caste background. There the pastors have nothing to do with issuing caste certificates (Pradeshi, *August 2005–Field Notes*, 19). By implication, Pradeshi seems to say that Dalits do not demand their rights, while Malas of Cuddapah do.

Narayanpet Revenue Division

Narayanpet is another Revenue division adjacent to the Gadwal, Mahabubnagar District. Here Christians are mostly from Dalit background. (The researcher's native village falls in this division). Mandal officials harass poor Christians, but a pastor has not been required to issue a Scheduled Caste certificate so far. Thus, what is found in the Gadwal area is a repressive culture, created by officials who are high caste by origin. Churches in the Gadwal area have uncritically accepted this discriminatory tradition as binding. On the other hand, Dalit Christians, whether from Mala or Dalit sub-caste background in Narayanpet of Mahabubnagar district or Prodduturu of Cuddapah district have not forced the pastors to manufacture such documents. Why is this so?

A pastor was pressurised in a village in Narva Mandal of Mahabubnagar, a district, to write a Scheduled-caste certificate to a Christian Mala contestant for a Sarpanch post. The man argued with the pastor vehemently. But the pastor said, "I cannot renounce baptising you, I discipled you for so many years. I exhort you to continue as a disciple of Christ and not deny him for the sake of the village headship." The politically minded Christian secured the Scheduled Caste certificate anyhow and won the election. His spiritual father and pastor never gave up his stand. So the entire region never again went to him for such documents.

Deception—Pastors Caught in Political Feuds

However, this does not mean that leading Christians do not get Scheduled Caste certificates by means other than pastors. Christian

Dalits are easy targets for political retaliation. Panchayati elections are one such time for attacking the low Castes. "Conversion" to the Christian religion is the name of the game here for some BJP workers.

A senior pastor, a junior pastor and a "Dalit" were used as *paavulu* (dice) in the hands of a BJP candidate in a village and the judicial system in Alampur Taluk. It all began when a Dalit was found not to have cast his vote for the BJP candidate. In villages, news is a public affair, including for whom a person has voted. A succession of events followed in which a senior and a junior Mennonite pastor were imprisoned. Let us hear the story from the perspective of the senior pastor.

The Story: Two Contradicting Certificates
(As told by a senior pastor in the Gadwal area)

I lacked wisdom, whether it was right or wrong to write scheduled caste certificates for Christians from Scheduled Caste background. This being the status, an event occurred.

Propaganda for Panchayat elections was in full swing in a village. Low Castes in general prefer the Congress Party. There was a political exchange between Madhu, a Dalit voter, and a Bharatiya Janata Party (Hindu) contestant on the Telugu Desham ticket. Madhu did not cast his vote in favour of the Hindu. The Hindu party abused the Dalit and g ave the untouchable a severe beating.

Mistreatment of a low caste is a grave offence under the Constitution. The Dalit filed a complaint with the magistrate court under human rights violations. As a result, the political leader and his group were arrested and eventually put in a taluk jail.

Irked, the Hindu leadership was united in fighting the case to the end. They collected about Rs 70,000 for this cause. The leaders in the prison sought the advice of an advocate for a way out of this trouble. The judge advised, "Produce a document to the effect that Mr. Madhu is a Christian and you will be freed." "Who issues such certificates?" "A pastor," answered the lawyer. Relatives of the imprisoned man lured my junior pastor in the troubled village. The junior pastor said, I am not eligible to write such a certificate, but my senior is."

One day, Madhu came along with my junior pastor claiming to be a Christian. He said there was a government job in Priyadarshini Jurala Project Office (irrigation department) and it was reserved for·B. C. "C" candidate. He needed my help in writing a certificate to produce at the

Project Office. Moved with compassion, I wrote a certificate to say, "Madhu is a converted Christian," only to find later that it was a trick the aristocrats played.

Fake Madhu and Christian certificate

God knows whether my junior knew the rich people's design. The high castes produced the certificate to the magistrate and secured the release of their friends from jail. The freed people entered the village celebrating their victory. The procession included dance, loud shouts and humiliating taunts against Dalit Madhu, their opponent.

The real Madhu is in trouble now. He works as a watchman in the Priya Darshini Jurala Project. He was employed under the Scheduled Caste category. Now his adversaries have submitted a document to the court that he is a Christian. Loss of his job is at stake for cheating the government.

Realising the danger, the real Madhu rushed to me. He pleaded with me to travel to his village. He took me to his house and exhibited his household gods and all the signs of Dalit practices and said, "Sir, I am not a Christian, I am a Dalit. My political rivals have tricked you. With your letter, I am in danger of losing my job any time. Please protect me by confirming my Dalit status.

I was convinced and wrote a second certificate to say, "I was wrong [earlier] in writing a Christian certificate to Mr. Madhu of X Village. He is not a Christian, but a Dalit" (Itzhaq, September 2005 –Field Notes, 17). The second certificate saved the reputation and the job of the true Madhu.

But the Hindu miscreants turned the case against me and produced both the certificates to the magistrate. Now it was my turn to bear the brunt of the entire issue. In the flow of the events, I was summoned, arrested and eventually jailed.[14]

The Turn of Events

I approached a senior Advocate at Gadwal. He initially advised me to deny writing two certificates to one person and say they were a "forgery." That was the only way out.

I said, "No, if you cannot argue my case, leave me alone. If I wanted to, I could have renounced it before the taluk Session's judge and saved myself from custody, but as a pastor I cannot lie about writing two certificates

---

[14] The Junior Pastor says that he too was jailed.

for one person's name." The senior judge was furious at my non-cooperation, but he took up my case. His intelligence and experience rid me of this sensitive trouble.

The senior pastor had to sell an acre of his paddy land to pay the advocate fee and other incidentals. Finally, this senior pastor offers some advice:

> Therefore, whether Christian, or a preacher or a bishop, ora big leader, whoever we are, either writingthese certificates, or encouraging others to write such certificates, or involvement in such act is not healthful. I say this out of my experience (Itzaaq, September 2005 –Field Notes, 19).

The section on two contradicting Scheduled Caste Certificates and politics has focused on how Panchayat elections and democratic feuds can hurt Dalits and some pastors of Dalit background. As usual, many undercurrents can be seen.

First, pastors' writing contradictory documents for one person is not condoned. Second, political battles in villages are fought between the dominant caste and the weaker caste. Sometimes personal grudges against a Dalit can drag one to court and imprisonment. Third, the story does not indicate whether non-Christian Dalits or the Christian church will come to the rescue of the individuals in trouble. The Christian church in the Gadwal and Alampur area is not united with the poor people in their struggles.

Fourth, political parties like the BJP override the weaker sections in matters involving Scheduled Caste or B. C. "C" certificates. Officials such as the Mandal Revenue Officer manipulate such situations. Fifth, in this case, the senior pastor admitted his mistake and made it clear to the advocate that he would not lie about writing two contradictory documents. This shows Continuity and Discontinuity in the reverse angle. The said pastor discontinued his vocation to preach the gospel but took up advocating social justice for the Christian Dalits without realising Scheduled Caste or the Hindu categories. He later realised what he had done; he stopped doing it.

Conclusion

A Christian Dalit child begins to live with two names: Visvas and Vikas. He starts to live with competing worldviews for life. One is sacred and the other secular. Visvas relates to ritual life and Vikas to existential realties. The Scheduled Caste status of a Christian Dalit increases 15:1 to that of a Christian who claims B. C. "C" category. One's privileges in educational institutions, employment, 50 per cent subsidy in housing and farming loans and opportunities in political arena are all necessities of life. Very few deny these benefits.

Social movements like "Madiga Dandora" and "Ambedkar Yuvajana Sanghalu" raise the Dalit pride in being labeled as such (e.g., Yosepu Madiga). Further, caste-ridden Mandal officials require Christian Dalits to state their detachment to the spiritual activities of the church. This amounts to social injustice.

In Gadwal and Alampur taluks, being low-caste people seem to make them more vulnerable to discrimination compared to those in other revenue divisions like Narayanpet in the Mahabubnagar district and Prodduturu in the Cuddapah District.

Pastors in the Gadwal MB Field Association are the recipients of the brunt of some political vendetta. The Mandal (province) official requires them to ascertain the non-Christian status of his church members. He needs to go against his conscience at times. On the other hand, MB Churches in general state their pastor's willingness to vouch their Dalit status. His call and commitment became secondary to existential questions.

Analysis of the Chapter

We will reflect on three of the issues raised in this chapter, namely competing worldviews, existential struggles and influences of Dalit social movements.

Competing Worldviews

We began this chapter with the story of a young boy named Visvas (believer or faithful one). He is also called *Vikas* (enlightened one). "Visvas" (faithful one) is for religious use and "Vikas" for secular needs in the education system. But these two names represent two competing or collating worldviews in the Christian Dalit colony at Madiri Puram village. Secular and sacred can complement each other but they compete with each other when it comes to Dalit identity. As he grows older, the boy may face another worldview at his workplace.

All humans are born into worldviews. They inherit some and create others. For example, we say that this child is born a Dalit or that girl is born a Brahman. Noted anthropologist Charles H. Kraft thinks that every culture conditions humans to act at two levels:

> Culture consists of two levels: the surface and the deep worldview levels. At the core of culture and, therefore, at the very heart of all human life, lies the structuring of the basic assumptions, values, and allegiances in terms of which people interpret and behave. These assumptions, values, and allegiances we call *worldview* (Kraft 1996, 11).

Paul G. Hiebert and Eloise Hiebert Meneses suggest that worldview is basic to understanding humans better. Martin Marty calls a worldview "the mental furnished apartment in which one lives" (Marty quoted in Hiebert and Meneses 1995, 41). Hiebert and Meneses go on to say, "Like glasses, worldviews shape how we see the world around us. They are what we look with, not what we look at" (*ibid.*). Worldviews are a reality the human encounters. Hiebert and Meneses say, "If our worldview is shaken, we are deeply disturbed because the world no longer makes sense to us." As Clifford Geertz points out, "There is no fear greater than meaninglessness—of not understanding the world in which we live. Even death itself can be endured if it has meaning" (Geertz quoted in Hiebert and Meneses 1995, 42). In fact, our worldview monitors cultural changes, as pointed out by Kraft (Kraft quoted in Hiebert and Meneses 1995, 42).

Worldviews make human life livable or difficult. In the case of the Dalits of India, caste discrimination continues to make their life miserable. The theory and practice of having four castes has reduced the Dalits to untouchables and non-humans. Hindu reform movements like *Rastriya Swayamsevak Sangh* (RSS), *Viswa Hindu Parishad* (VHP) and others promise a change in the worldview of Hindutva[15], while the reality in villages remains discriminatory.

Competing worldviews label people. The bureaucracy helps the Hindu worldview in administering social injustice. The Christian Dalits of the Madiri Puram region are checked before being issued a Scheduled Caste certificate. Visvas and Vikas is a double category created by Christian Dalits to suit the needs of life. Christian Dalits agree to go by *harijan* (children of God) or Scheduled Caste categories to make themselves eligible for economic benefits. This

---

[15] Hindutva is a fanatic form of Hinduism. For them cultural nationalism is their food and god. The other worldviews that challenge theirs are seriously and violently crushed. For example, Graham Stains and his two young sons were burnt alive in the State of Orissa on 22 January 1999.

I call change and continuity in relation to existential demands Existential demands are fierce when people have been economically exploited for ages. But existential questions have their own implications for Dalit Christians.

Existential Struggles and Dalit Christians

Why would Christian Dalits accept double categorisation? A simple answer would be to satisfy their existential questions. Embracing existential categories invites its own limitations. A Christian Dalit is in want of self-identity and economic benefits through the reservation system. Getting a 50 per cent subsidy for loans for agriculture and homes or small-scale industries is quite an attractive option, if one were a non-Christian Dalit. There are also scholarships for higher and technical education. Fifteen percent employment is another possibility. But a Christian Dalit is required to register himself or herself as a Scheduled Caste. Once a Dalit claims that he is a converted Christian, his or her reservation percent drops from 15 to 1 per cent. So a poor person is at a crossroads to decide. The situation worsens since the church in general offers no scholarships for higher education; for example, training for medicine or a Master of Business Administration or to become a District Collector. These are existential questions for Christian Dalits.

Soren Kierkegaard (1813-1855), considered to be the founder of existentialism, defines existentialism and its implications for a human being:

> An existentialist is a philosopher who claims himself as an "existing thinker", that is, a thinker who is always involved in the reality he is thinking about, so that he cannot take up the purely objective attitude of a spectator; also, he is always on his way from one matter to another, so that as long as he exists he never has a complete picture. So existentialism stands opposed to all those grand metaphysical systems that profess to give a comprehensive and objective account of all that is (Kierkegaard cited in John Macquarrie 1987, 222).

An existentialist is always on the move, between two or more subjects in his thinking process, with many concerns and sundry thinking. Metaphysics is not his concern. Being comprehensive is not his aim. He is subjective, as we will explore in the coming pages. Macquarrie adds to the understanding of existentialism in that he moves beyond the philosophical realm, that is, from non-relational "thinking being" to relational person to community life struggles Macquarrie expands the existential categories:

For several centuries, Western philosophy has been deeply influenced by Descartes' famous pronouncement, "I think, therefore I am." The existentialist would claim that this accords too much preeminence to thinking. We are also beings who experience emotion, and our emotions are not just transient inner moods but rather ways of relating to the world and becoming aware of some properties that do not reveal themselves to rational observation. Equally important is the will, we will learn about the world not just by beholding it and reflecting upon it but rather by acting in it and encountering its resistances (Macquarrie, *ibid.*, 223).

Christian Dalits cannot just think in vacuum. Theirs is a life battle. They have emotions to express. They cannot take up "ascetic life modes to detach themselves from their families. They must act upon day-to-day affairs. It is a life-and-death matter for his son or daughter needs education; he cannot afford to support the child's educational expenditures. Therefore, the Christian Dalit community decides together to establish a two-tier Christianity, one for the sacred circles and the other for socio-economic challenges. For them, it is not a matter of orthodoxy, but critical praxis. Suffering from existential realities, the Gadwal area Christian Dalits go public with the declaration:

The high-caste oppressors do not let us enter their temples and prayer houses in exercise of Untouchability. Distanced by such treatment we express our *bhakti* (devotion) to Jesus Christ, and attend church worship for peace of mind. By faith we are Christian but by religion we are Hindus. (Editor.„*Adugaduguna daga padutunna Dalitulu* [Dalits exploited at every step of life] *Vaarta*— A Telugu Daily News Paper, Thursday, 7 November 1996, 10).

The above statement projects three aspects of life existence. Firstly, that the Christian Dalits in the area have no entrance into Hindu temples. Secondly, they worship Jesus Christ for peace of mind. Thirdly, they claim Hindu status. In this sense, Christian worldviews are modified by existential demands of life. A majority of (Hindu) worldviews split personalities and allegiances. The Hindu/Caste hierarchy ensures consistent division in society. Egalitarian demands of the gospel are resisted by the caste order. The truth is that India has a secular but Hindu government at the core of its functions. In such a system, Christian Dalit demands are chained to a log. Freedom of religion means having a free hand in the hegemony of the majority religion or the "haves" against the "have-nots."

The basic assumption of existentialism is human freedom. For Kierkegaard, this freedom to choose can never be absolute, so it leads to the realisation of human *finitude*, to anxiety, thus leading a believer to recognise the *infinite* God. Conversely, if one is an atheist, it leads to "despair" (see Macquarrie 1987, 224). I sense that "survival" is the reason why the Christian Dalits of the Madiri

Puram village region say, "We are Christian by faith but Hindu by religion."

Rudolf Bultmann has applied Heideggerean "existentialia"to demythologise the "spelling out" aspect of the gospel. He hermeneuted that the hidden "myth" in the New Testament is "kerygma" (proclamation), a divine Word addressed to humans. The "kerygma", he believes, sets before us a possibility for which we are summoned to decide (Bultmann reviewed in John Macquarrie 1971, 351). Unfortunately, Bultamann has ruled out the connection between the Jesus of history with Jesus of the "kerygma." Historical Jesus is immaterial to him. This is how Christian Dalits may also describe themselves—as detaching from the demands of the gospel and the existential realities. While the truth of the matter remains, they are exploited even today. The repressive state and the church at large have yet to grapple with the existential concerns of Christian Dalits in India.

The Haul of Social Movements on Christian Dalits

Existential struggles draw Dalit Christians to embrace socially uplifting movements such as "Ambedkar Youth Association" or "Dalit Reservation Porata Samiti" (Dalit Rights Protection Society). Ambedkar is compared to Moses in liberating Dalits from their caste bondage. An example of the impact of these movements on Dalits is to feel proud of their Scheduled Caste origin as a Brahman would feel of his birth. In this venture, Dalit social movements encourage people to suffix Dalit to their Christian name; for example, "Joseph Madiga."

As part of the behaviour, Madiga Dandora, another Dalit social action movement, visits churches and puts Dandora flags within the premises of the church. They do this as part of celebrating the birth anniversary of Dr. B. R. Ambedkar. This is an effect on the mindset of the Dalit. James Massey, a noted Dalit theologian, laments Dalit roots causing Dalit mentalities. Massey quotes M. L. Srikant, a 'Commissioner appointed by the President of India in 1950, who reported on the state of affairs of *Harijans* (children of god):

> By the force of the habit the Harijan has lost his self-respect to such an extent that he regards his work to which his caste is condemned not as a curse from which he should extricate himself but as a privilege or presence, which he must protect. He has not much courage to seek another job in field or factory. He has thus become lazy in mind and body and callous to his own condition; and he will not educate his children (M. L. Srikant quoted in James Massey 1994, 41).

Massey highlights three factors from the statement of Srikant: first, that the Dalits have lost their self-respect. Second, they have become lazy in mind and body and callous to conditions. Such status cannot be simply dealt with by merely passing a resolution or providing economic facility. The Commissioner notes, out of 15 per cent jobs reserved for the Dalits only 2.2 per cent vacancies are filled (Massey 1994:43). Third, against the observation of Srikant, Massey stresses education as a possibility for the social mobility of a Dalit. Of course, education is one sure way to uplift the Dalits.

One could dismiss Srikant's depiction as outdated and a factor from the 1950s. But after 30 years, the Mandal Commission of 1980 also affirms similar situations of exploitation. The Commission records the caste system as the root cause of all kinds of backwardness of the Dalits. The Commission notes:

> The real triumph of Caste system lies not in upholding the supremacy of the Brahman, but in conditioning the consciousness of the lower Castes in accepting their inferior status in the ritual hierarchy as part of the natural order of things (Massey 1994, 45).

The key to the effectiveness of social movements on Dalit Christians is the spirit of the youth. They call the shots in the villages. Naturally, they try to make an impact. The trouble is that they may not completely consider what they are up to.

D. M. Ravi Prasad, a Professor of Kakatiya University at Warangal (District), has done a great study on the Dalit postgraduate and graduate student ethos. Most of the Dalit students experience discrimination from their high-caste classmates. Upper-caste students visiting Dalit homes hardly accept anything to drink or eat. They maintain "social distance" from lower-caste friends. Friendships between them do not last long. So, university education has seldom helped eradicate caste "discriminations" (D. M. Ravi Prasad 1997, 155-156).

As a result, the oppressed sections of the youth, forced either by demeaning culture or by shear enthusiasm, are restless. They have found two alternatives ways to vent their despair—one, by doing whatever they think is right, whether it is "good or bad." For example, erecting the Madiga Dandora flag[16] in the church premises is one such behaviour. Joining Naxal (extremist) movements

---

[16] Madiga Dandora flag contains a cloth flag with a percussion drum symbol on it tied on the top to a pole. This percussion instrument is the symbol of Dalit tradition.

is another way to vent despair among the Dalit youth. They join protest movements such as Dalit Sahitya (Literature) Society. The youth stresses "inter caste marriages" as a solution to establishing egalitarian society. The second way is to assume "silence" and patience. Thus, they develop either "deviant" or "disciplined" behaviour (Prasad, *ibid.*, 54-55).

Chapter 6

MORALITY AND LIFE GUIDANCE

This chapter will delineate the question: "In what ways do Christian Dalits of Madiri Puram Village enact change and continuity in morality and life guidance?" All humans are faced with questions of morality and life guidance. Some events in life project moral heights. For example, David killed Goliath (1 Sam 17). Other life junctures point to institutionalised immorality. Humans seek guidance in life crises and even when they wish to perform better. We are interested in exploring peasants' cry to God when they are faced with famine.

Introduction

To analyse the data in this chapter, I depended on Walter Brueggemann (*Theology of the Old Testament*, 1997). Brueggemann's volume is likened in stature to the works of veteran Old Testament scholars such as G. von Rad and Walther Eichrodt. I am utilising Brueggeman's missiological insights to interpret moral issues such as church land encroachment and sexual immorality. I will also use his ideas in hermeneuting a peasant theology of prayer. The peasant theology of prayer is from a life crisis and an evidence of seeking God's guidance. A second volume that helped me analyse my data is that of Karen Wenell's *Jesus and Land* (2007). She has thoughtful ideas on how land was treated as sacred as well as social space during the second temple Judaism.[1]

Morality, Life and Guidance

In this venture, defining "morality," "life" and "guidance" is important before I journey further. Morality is defined in reference to a life situation. It deals with how a people or society understands their social and religious ethics in their daily life. The Latin root

---

[1] Second Temple Judaism is that of Herod the Great's to that of the destruction of the Temple in in AD 70 by the Romans.

word for morality, *moralitaser*, refers to "manner, character, and proper behavior." It concerns the "principles of right and wrong behavior" (Erickson 2001, 128). I am referring to morality and life guidance in relation to the Christian Dalit community, in which biblical, Dalit and Hindu values intersect with each other at all times. I like the *Wikipedia* definition of morality because it refers to individual conscience, systems of principles and judgments and moral values shared by a culture:

> Morality refers to the concept of human ethics which pertains to matters of right and wrong — also referred to as "good and evil" — used within three contexts: individual conscience, systems of principles and judgments... (*en.wikipedia.org/wiki/Morality, cited in wordnet.princeton.edu/ perl/webwn*).

The next term we need to define is "life guidance." By "life guidance," I mean the appeal to God for favours of wisdom, provision, etc. — all those things that we lack, and that God can provide for us." We will find examples of these controversies in the pages to come to prove that there is change and continuity among Christian Dalits of Madiri Puram village.

Life Setting in Madiri Puram Village in the 1920s

Morality and life guidance is best understood in its social and religious context. R. Dhyryam, a long time Secretary to Madiri Puram Village Church, a prominent Dalit Social Activist and the historian in the village area, records Christian Dalit living conditions prior to the arrival of the gospel,

> Prior to the gospel, our village was subject to worldly traditions and Satan's fetters. The "*Christu bodd*" [the gospel] was being proclaimed in Gadwal and Alampur Talukas (province), under the auspices of American Mennonite Brethren Church, under the supervision of a missionary at Gadwal with the help of a few of his native evangelists. Evangelist Chennipati Yosepu was the first to proclaim the good news to our village on ... [no date mentioned], followed by other evangelists, such as Vayilala Janayya, Kuluru Lukayya, Nandavaramu Ratnamayya, and Pedda Dannada N. R. Samelu and so forth ... (*SV [Minutes] 1951-2005*, 2).

Dhyryam's record does not mention the year of the arrival of the gospel to Madiri Puram village. His minute is contested concerning the pioneer evangelists and the approximate year of the arrival of the gospel to their village. Therefore, he left a gap over the issue of date (see above quotation). But Mr. Paras had a clue that it was "Boyyala Guddam Timmayya" who first preached the good news to their village[2] (Paras 2005; cf. Gattanna, 2005; Nagaraju, 2005). Upon our personal visit to the foremost evangelist's native village and upon verification, we concluded that the gospel came to the village around 1915 through Timmayya[3] and then through Chennipati Yosepu, the second evangelist to the village.

A few of the terms in Dhryam's minutes demand exploration. For example, what is meant by (1) subject to "worldly traditions" and (2) "Satan's fetters"? For sure, the situations in the 1920s were humbling for the Dalits in India. By worldly traditions Dhryam means that, they were bond slaves to *Zamindars* (landlords) and that they were under the oppression of caste hierarchy. They were untouchables. A description by late M. N. Srinivas, the noted social anthropologist of India, would depict the undignified status of Dalits.[4]

Dalits were not allowed to worship Hindu high gods or even dare enter their temples. Dalits were spirit worshippers. They suffered abject poverty, only on rare occsions a few have land. Additionally, the Madiri Puram region was a dry area and was dependent on monsoon rains until the Rajulabanda Diversion Scheme irrigation canal came in 1958.

---

[2] Mr. Paras told me that he heard from his father that it was Boyyala Gudda Timmayya who first preached the Good News to their village. "Sankati" was Timmayya's family name. Timmmayya was also known as "Pani", Timmayya meaning a "cobbler."

[3] Gospel Preacher, Sankati Timmayya, worked in Pulachinta village of Nandavaram Mandal, in Kurnool district. S. Timmayya practiced a twin occupation "preacher-cobbler." There is evidence that Timmayya worked with the American Baptists based in Ieej town. He died in 1935, a year before Gadwal Field was being transferred to the American Mennonite Brethren Mission in 1936. Thus, he must have brought the gospel to Madiri Puram village much earlier to 1935. It may be in his years of good health, at least by the second decade of the 20th century (1901-1915). See The Governing Council of the Mennonite Brethren Church of India.1972. *India Mennonite Brethren Church at Cross Roads*, 87. Mr. Dhyryam, the local pastor, and the researcher paid a visit to Boyyalaguddam village to verify the facts.

[4] M. N. Srinivas, a Brahmin by caste and a noted social anthropologist in India noted eight prohibitions laid down by the Kallar caste (a dominant caste in Ramnad district of Tamil Nadu State), which pretty much describe the inhuman status of the Harijans in the 1930s. Dalits are called Adi-Dravidas in "Tamil Nadu" one of the four States in South India. According to Srinivas, these regulations were imposed since the Adi-Dravidas were questioning caste hierarchy:

1. That the Adi-Dravidas shall not wear ornaments of gold and silver;

2. That the males should not be allowed to wear their clothes above the hips;

3. That their males should not wear coats or shirts or *baniyans*;

Worldly Traditions and Fetters of Satan

What does Dhyryam mean by people being subject to the "fetters of Satan"? Dalit gods were comprised mostly of "human heroes" who died in defending their people. They are never gods but a mere ancestor, says Professor Kancha Ilaiah, a Dalit humanist (Ilaiah 2000). Dalits had divergent views on heaven and hell. The non-Christian Dalits that I interviewed had some sense of good and bad deeds like "jealousy" and "non-helping nature" (Farmer 2006, 2)[5]. A few others were "not sure" whether heaven and hell exist (Suraj 2006, 2).[6] Yet others felt there is judgment on human actions in the form of "cause and effect" (Victoria 2006, 2).[7] Their belief also included that their late mother is *devata* (female deity), since she gifted them with life. Some would even wear a "fetish" of their late mother around their neck and would not let anybody take a snap of it. One thinks that his mother's honour is gone when somebody takes a picture of the fetish (Hussan 2006, 1).

However, the reverse is also true, that Dalits believe in spirits. According to Mr. Vahanam, a middle-aged auto trolley driver, non-Christian Dalits are exposed to evil spirits. For example, an evil spirit called Narsappa possesses men or women to drain off their health. He describes the evil spirit's torment as follows:

> Narsappa will possess a man in the form of a woman and drain his semen entirely by sleeping with him, so much that the possessed becomes a skeleton. When Narsappa possesses a woman in the form of a man, he causes constant monthly periods or hemorrhage, sothat the woman is dried of her strength (Vahanam 2005).

What are some of the worldly traditions? Suez B. H. Truman has done an excellent study on Dalit conversions to Christianity in the

---

4. No Adi-Dravida shall be allowed to have his hair cropped;

5. That the Adi-Dravidas should not use other than earthenware vessels in their houses;

6. Their women shall not be allowed to cover the upper portion of their bodies by clothes or *ravukais* [blouses] or *thavanis* [upper cloths worn like togas];

7. Their women shall not be allowed to use flowers or saffron paste;

8. The men shall not use umbrellas for protection against sun and rain, nor shall they wear sandals (Srinivas, M. N 1967, 16)

This status continued well after Independence in 1947.

[5] Farmer is an Open University discontinued student.

[6] Suraj is a 12th class-fail student and worked as fair price shop owner.

[7] Victoria is an ordinary housewife and non-literate.

Ongole (now renamed as Prakasham) District in Andhra Pradesh. Truman's master's thesis concerns the work of the American Baptists among Dalits in Coastal Andhra Pradesh. His thesis provides us with evidence of Dalit worship of demons. He quotes Frank Kurtz's description of one such heinous practice by hook swinging, which was also practiced in Bengal of William Carey:

> Hooks were inserted in a man's back and he was suspended at the end of a pole attached to a cart, while thus suspended in mid-air the man was drawn around the temple three times. The man upon whom this cruelty was practiced belonged to the shoemaker caste. (Frank Kurtz quoted in Truman 1984, 15; cf. Elmore 1984, 31, 75)

In such bad conditions, the missionaries shared the gospel with low-caste people and made them disciples, changing their lifestyle and appearance.

Signs of Change among Dalits

According to W. F. Strait, prior to conversion, outcaste habitations were of unspeakable filth. But the impact of the gospel has changed the entire palem. Strait notes the change in a Christian palem thus:

> In this Christian *palem* (colony) we can see the bright blue sky. Our eyes are fastened upon the clothing, their hair neat and smooth, with brightly coloured flowers entwined in the braids giving the women and girls a dainty Christian appearance. (W.F. Strait quoted in Truman 1984, 90)

Strait goes on to say that hitherto jobs that were closed to the untouchables were open to them, such as school teachers, village headman and labourers in "mission industries."

Because of the Gospel, the Dalit converts could refuse beating traditional *tappetalu* (percussion drums) and refrain from Dalit *chindu* (a ritual dance) at Hindu ceremonies. Their refusal to beat drums and dance resulted in persecution. But, in the course of time, high caste people showed signs of change in their attitude towards Christians. Truman records that high-caste people:

1. Petitioned for a Christian preacher to replace the deceased headman of the village (see Truman 1984, 94)

2. Even allowed Christian Dalits teachers to reside in the village instead of restricting them to Dalit *palems* (Truman 1984, 95)

3. Allowed Dalit children to sit and study in government schools along with high-caste children

4. On the other hand, Brahmans and Sudras sent their children to Christian schools

Let us return to Dhryam's minutes. They do not specify a specific year, but it gives us evidence that Christianity was established in Madiri Puram village when eight people believed in the gospel and were baptised. These eight pioneers were baptised by Vayilala Janayya, the third preacher and an unidentified American missionary. The eight first believers were:

> Pedda Sanjanna (Yosepu), Ganganna (Daveedu), Pedda Kondanna (Benjamenu), Bayappa (Daniyelu), Pani Lasumanna (Lajaru), Dannada Pakeeranna, Elkuri Buddanna, and Dannada Bajari (Andreyya) (Secretary, *SV* [*Minutes*] 1951-2005, 2).

The gospel emphasised that "all men have come short of the glory of the Lord and have become sinners and under the wrath of God and needed to believe in the Lord Jesus Christ for the forgiveness of their sins." Sins such as *beedi* (country cigarette) smoking, drinking *Kallu* (country arrack), telling lies, going to cinemas, stealing, deception and adultery were stated as wrong. In addition, the church has the Ten Commandments written on the wall behind the pulpit (Exod. 20:1-17).[8]

The first four commands relate to God and his holiness. The rest of them command humans to love their neighbours and not covet anything that does not belong to them. The Ten Commandments were written in the context of Yahweh redeeming

---

[8] The Ten Commandments (NIV, Exod. 20:1-17): (1) And God spoke all these words: (2) "I am the LORD your God, who brought you out of Egypt, out of the land of slavery. (3) "You shall have no other gods before me. (4) "You shall not make for yourself an idol in the form of anything in heaven above or on the earth beneath or in the waters below. (5) You shall not bow down to them or worship them; for I, the LORD your God, am a jealous God, punishing the children for the sin of the fathers to the third and fourth generation of those who hate me, (6) but showing love to a thousand [generations] of those who love me and keep my commandments. (7) "You shall not misuse the name of the LORD your God, for the LORD will not hold anyone guiltless who misuses his name. (8) "Remember the Sabbath day by keeping it holy. (9) Six days you shall labor and do all your work, (10) but the seventh day is a Sabbath to the LORD your God. On it you shall not do any work, neither you, nor your son or daughter, nor your manservant or maidservant, nor your animals, nor the alien within your gates. (11) For in six days the LORD made the heavens and the earth, the sea, and all that is in them, but he rested on the seventh day. Therefore, the LORD blessed the Sabbath day and made it holy. (12) "Honor your father and your mother, so that you may live long in the land the LORD your God is giving you. (13) "You shall not murder. (14) "You shall not commit adultery. (15) "You shall not steal. (16) "You shall not give false testimony against your neighbor. (17) "You shall not covet your neighbor's house. You shall not covet your neighbor's wife, or his manservant or maidservant, his ox or donkey, or anything that belongs to your neighbor."

his people from the bondage of Egypt. Thus, Exodus is the "event" in which the Ten Commandments were "instituted" for Israel to follow, and the same are adapted by New Israel, the church. The statutes of the law are good and work as referents to all human affairs in the world. The institution of the Decalogue is the model for morality and it is the dynamic aspect that keeps reminding Israel and other nations to follow. On the contrary, there are human institutions that hurt humanity. For example, King Ahab wished to establish the worship of Baal in Northern Israel. My analysis will depend on the renowned Old Testament scholar, Walter Brueggemann. Having laid down a standard, let us get back to the morality situation in Madiri Puram village.

Morality

Within six decades of its Christian light (c. 1915-1977), Madiri Puram Church experienced gross immorality on the part of some of the believers. One such problem is loss of the church's land, over a period of ten years (1977-1986). Three of its members coveted 15 feet of church land. One of the three encroachers even consulted *Panchaangam* or "horoscopes" (see Paras 2005, 1) in approval of his evil desire. It must be mentioned, however, that there are those who feared God and did not encroach on church acreage. Why claim sanctuary land during 1977-1986 and not before or after? More so how would the church deal with this negligence?

Church Land Encroachment

The trespass is possible for a couple of reasons, greed being one of them. The leadership crisis in the church conference began in the eighties. Madiri Puram church entertained taking sides with the contending conference leadership, which itself was in crisis.

For example, do people side with Governing Council "A" or "B"? The Governing Council headed by Mr. "B" belonged to the Gadwal region, while Mr. "A" hails from beyond the *Pedderu* ["river Krishna" north of Gadwal]. Mr. "A's leadership was later approved by the Foreign Mission Board in 1984 (see *SV [Minutes] 1951-2005,* 52-54). Madiri Puram church returned to Governing Council "A" as it was approved by the Mission Board. During this dispute period, the Secretary and an influential government teacher in Madiri Puram church advocated supporting Governing Council "B". Governing Council "B" floated the idea of forming Gadwal as a separate Mennonite Brethren Conference. Gadwal as a single mission field has to its credit half the churches of the 850 (today) in the Conference until 1981 when Yemmiganoor was separated by geographic distance and for administrative purposes.

Image of Madiri Puram Circuit

One of the ways to ensure such a separate Church Conference was to declare new circuit headquarters, Madiri Puram being one. Madiri Puram would have nine neighbouring village churches under its care.[9] It was natural that their pastor was appointed "circuit leader" on 3 July 1981 (see *SV [Minutes] 1951-2005*, 38). Status as a circuit has enforced the church's ability to secure a "marriage license" by their Pastor "L". The Governing Council "A" had declined to write a recommendation letter to the government as part of their pastor's credentials to secure "marriage license", because the church leadership at the time supported Governing Council "B." Under the influence of a prominent teacher—a member of their church, and the secretary at that time—records that "the church was unanimous to spend from its treasury, whatever it takes to secure marriage license to their pastor" (see *SV [Minutes] 1951-2005*, 45). This became a prestige issue for the church to fight it out in the Magistrate Court.

All this meant that there were two parties within the church accusing one another. The dissenting group went to the extent of alleging that supporters of "A" from their church filed an objection in the Alampur Magistrate Court to stall the issuance of a marriage license to their pastor. The church spent over "twenty thousand Rupees" (c. $527 US) from its treasury for legal and incidental expenses. To date the church is very unsettled over the thought of such a large misuse of funds.

As matters worsened, the church also experienced an unwelcome scene of the pastor at that time, a trained wrestler, physically challenging the lead opponent, accusing him of siding with Governing Council "A" and stalling his marriage license. This season of dispute probably was read by some as an opportune time to move their

---

[9] The entire circuit consisted of 2,060 Dalit Christians in 1981. Nine villages under the Madiri Puram circuit were (1) Mandoddi, (2) Pacharla, (3) Tanagala, (4) Venkatapuram, (5) Vepadinne, (6) Vayilala, (7) Konkala, (8) Satarla and (9) Mundladinne.

boundaries and intrude upon the church land.[10] This gross moral lapse on the part of a few Christian Dalit households invited the hottest *Panchayat* disputes, misunderstandings and bitter relationships.

However, unlike the much politicised marriage license issue, the land encroachment dispute was not taken to the court of justice but resolved in a Church *Panchayat* under the chairmanship of the rich Reddy. The church land encroachment issue was settled with a human face. There is no minute, whether or not it was required, of the encroachers to pay the price of the occupied land or if a disciplinary action was taken against them. The land was lost to save human relationships. Concern even for the wrongdoer is one of the chief characteristics in the *Panchayat* way of dealing with justice than the "winner and loser" system in a court of justice. In this case, the resolution instead was to build a compound wall to protect the church land from further encroachments.

A description of the encroachment in feet is here in order:

Table 16: Church land encroachment

(All measurements in feet)

Source: see *SV [Minutes] 1951-2005*, 22 and pages 63-67.

Description	Actual Measurementment on 8 June 1977	Modified Measure-As on 4 Nov 1986	Encroachment in 10 years time	Comments
Near Mr. "P's" house	41	38	3	(1) in 10 years time, i.e., between 1977 and 1986 some members of the church could encroach 15 feet of Church land in total radius
North side of Mr. "P's" house to the west side midst of Mr. "T's" house	56	50	6	

---

[10] The dispute between the local pastor and the said member supporting Governing Council "A" was amicably settled in a reconciliation meeting held on 15 November 1982, see *SV [Minutes] 1951-2005*, 47-48. The Field Chairman, the Secretary and other executives were present in the meeting.

Contd., **Table 16**: Church land encroachment

Description	Actual Measure-mentment on 8 June 1977	Modified Measure-As on 4 Nov 1986	Encroachment in 10 years time	Comments
Between south edge of Mr. "P's" and Mr."R's" houses	64	58	6	(2). It cost Rupees. 20,565.80 [c. 527 US $] to construct the compound wall to halt future encroachments.
Front side of the church from the centre of "I's" house to west side of Mr. "S's" house	65	65	–	3. In 1986 the modified boundaries were fixed under the chairmanship of and signature of "M" Reddy and other [Minutes] 1951-2005, 65).
Road near Mr. "R's" house to west	3 width	3	–	
South corner to west corner of the church	14	14	–	
East of the Church	12	12	–	4. Compound wall on the West side was built (see SV 1951-2005 [Minutes], 66).
Back of the church (Near Mr. leej "M's" House), with Room for Ox Cart Movement	15	15	–	
Total loss			15	5. – Indicates no loss off land.

Some elders who voiced against such covetousness included the family that donated their house plot for the sanctuary. Such protests were naturally interpreted as envy by the offenders. How should we understand this event?

Sacred Space: Justice Deconstructed

As noted earlier, I am indebted to Walter Brueggemann's *Theology of the Old Testament* (1997) in the fleshing out of the issues discussed in this chapter. Brueggemann is a renowned Old Testament authority. I have adopted two of his concepts in understanding morality and life guidance. The two concepts are "event" and "institution" (Brueggemann 1997, 736). Event and institution are grounded in human-divine relationships and their interpretations. For example, Exodus (Exod. 12) was an event in the life of Israel and the giving of the Ten Commandments at Sinai was a righteous institution (Exod. 20).

Three people encroaching on the Madiri Puram village church land is an event of disgrace to the church's image. None of the non-Christian holy places are encroached upon in this village. There are a couple of issues here to consider.

Firstly, church land encroachment was an act of profanity against God. In this connection, Brueggemann rightly understands "theodicy" to mean God's passion for justice. Brueggemann maintains, "... justice for Israel is rooted in the very character of Yahweh" (Brueggemann 1997, 739). Postmodern Jewish writers such as Jacques Derrida emphasise justice and even question God. There is nothing left out that is not questioned; therefore, all meaning is a deconstruction. Brueggemann is right that justice according to the Jubilee year will turn world governance [institution] upside down. Brueggemann worries that the "haves" have played with the Jubilee regulation to their advantage in Israel and, by implication, the present world systems do the same. He worries:

> In the Old Testament, not everyone everywhere is an enthusiast for distributive justice. Distributive justice,[11] if taken seriously (as in the practice of Jubilee), is inherently destabilizing of the status quo, for redistribution means to place established interests in jeopardy. (Brueggemann 1997, 738)

---

[11] For Brueggemann, distribution and retributive justice are two sides of justice. My reference here is: Should not the land encroachers relinquish their occupation? One of the three has extended his house. So, the trouble is more acute and sensitive than one would think.

While this being the reality, there is also the Israelite passion to push God's love for justice to a penultimate status and invert it with justice for humans as ultimate. Brueggemann protests:

> While we might expect that Yahweh is ultimate and justice penultimate, in some of Isreal's most desperate utterances, matters are inverted. Justice is held up as ultimate, and Yahweh as an agent of justice is critiqued for failure of justice. That is, Israel is aware that there is more to Yahweh than justice: there is holiness and downright capricious irascibility. Sometimes Israel is awed and deferential before this staggering ultimacy of Yahweh In its texts of protest, however,Israel would seem to value justice more than Yahweh. This is not because Israel is legalistic, or because Israel prefers a set of principles to a live agent. On the contrary, it is because Israel is irreducibly committed to material, concrete well-being, and not even Yahweh's own character will talk Israel out of its passion for well-being on the earth. Thus Yahweh in heaven must 'get with the program' of *shalom* on earth! (Brueggemann 1997, 740)

An example of a human quest for justice above, Yahweh's character is seen in Job's passion for justice over his innocent suffering. The point I am making here is that the Madiri Puram village church could have gone to the extent of socially excommunicating the three households, at least levied an appropriate fine. Such action would have been counted as precise justice. But the church panchayat thought the issue was much bigger than greed. "They did not want to invite a schism in the church because of their disciplinary action," says R. Dhyryam, the long time Secretary of the Church (Dhyryam 2007[12]). So the question for the church was: Do we lose 15 feet of land or invite a potential schism in the church? They chose the loss of the land to a schism. But the church wisely put a full stop to such occurrences in the future by erecting [instituting] a boundary wall. In this case, it was a better form of justice than to lose brotherhood. The question then is: How do we define a sacred space? Is not God zealous about church land? Would He not curse the guilty?

It appears that land is important, but its symbolic value as divine gifting and as a sign of God's reaching humans prevailed in this case. Then is it okay to lose land dedicated to God's purposes? This demands us ask the important question: Are there gradations within Jerusalem about *pavitra stalamu* (sacred space)? As there is the Jerusalem temple hierarchy, there is also variation in the holy

---

[12] Mr. Dhyryam view over a phone interview on 28 December 2007.

of holies and the camps outside the tabernacle area. In the wilderness, the tabernacle was surrounded by the priestly and Levite families followed by other clans.

In her excellent volume *Jesus and Land* (2007), Karen Wenell has thoughtful ideas on how land was treated both as sacred and social space during the second temple Judaism. She begins by saying that, sacred space meant different things to different religious and secular groups in New Testament times. For example, the study of the *Torah* was pivotal to understanding sacredness for the Pharisees, difference from the importance of the "physical temple" for the Sadducees or as the relevance of "community hermeneutic" is for the Qumran people (see Wenell 2007, 79-91, 142-146). For the Qumran the temple was defiled by Antiochus IV, since he ordered abominable swine to be offered at the altar.

From the perspective of the history of religions, Mercea Eliade views sacred space as "an irruption of the sacred into the world, breaking with the chaos of surrounding profane space" (Eliade quoted by Wenell 2007, 4). In critique of Eliade, Wenell also notes Jonathan Z. Smith, who differed with Eliade, and thrust the importance of the "human role in the creation of sacred places" (*ibid.*). Wenell banks on Bruce J. Malina, a noted New Testament scholar's evaluation of New Testament understanding on sacred space as social construction: A territory is always the outcome of the social interpretation of space. In this sense, it is a social construction. It exists essentially in the repertory of symbols that constitutes the collective mind of a given social group (B J. Malina quoted in Wenell 2007, 144).

If church land is both sacred and socially constructed, is there gradation in understanding the most holy areas differently from the least holy areas within the Jewish ethos? Wenell does an excellent job of speaking to this issue. She draws on the *Graded Holiness* diagram presented by Philip Jenson, to illustrate the connections between the ideology of holiness, sacred space, people and sacrifice.

Figure 13: *Graded Holiness* by Philip Jenson

					(Increasing Holiness) →
Holiness Gradient	Most Holy	Holy	Clean	Unclean	Especially Unclean
Spatial Realm	Holy of Holies	Holy Place	Court	Camp	Outside Camp
People	High Priest	Priest Israelites	Levites, Impurities	Minor Impurities	Major
Sacrifice	Sacrifice to God	Sacrifice (priests)	Sacrifice (non-priests)	Purification 1 Day	Purification 7 days

Source: Wenell 2007, 66

The diagram given above is read from the right to the left. Movement to the left increases from the most common to the most holy category of spaces and/or persons. In the case of Madiri Puram village people, the encroached space is located as "Court area," in my judgment. The church has put up a boundary to halt further encroachments, i.e., up until the camp area, the fringe spaces are outside camp, like the "bore well" on the north and "bullock cart passage" in the south.

It is my understanding that in the secular world, the judge charges the client. But the reverse ethic has happened in this case. The Madiri Puram church has acted as both the judge and a definite loser. It has lost something of the holy that belongs to the entire community as well as spent a large amount of money and incurred a loss to its testimony (self-identity). While non-Christian temples or mosques have not lost their land by encroachment, it might be said that the Gilgal Mennonite Brethren Church compound in this village remains a monument to pronounce the loss and how to resolve critical moral issues. It has shown something about their most holy God who lost His son to save the world. In this sense, physical space did not matter to them as compared to leaving room for the erred households to remain in fellowship. In a collective society such as in India, shame and honour means death or life. In such situation, excommunication would mean loss of human dignity to the three families. For sure, not requiring compensation from the families is not the best solution, even in the eyes of Hindu or Moslem *dharma* (jurisprudence). But it proves my thesis that Christian Dalits are torn between the values of their former culture and of the gospel. In this sense, I would consider the church panchayat to have acted very wisely.

However, in essence, the church did chastise the wrongdoers. It has taken them to task in the church panchayat and resolved the issue under the chairmanship of the local Reddy (patron, high-caste village head). Their immorality has been exposed in the church minutes. This is a concrete response to (and a blow to) unjust households for violating its sacred space. One of the beautiful things is that the church has not pulled these householders to the court of justice. In the end, the church has saved its testimony and unity and kept its doors open for the encroachers to mend their ways. This is deconstructing justice in a reverse order by invoking "curses and blessings" as found in Deut 27:17 (see C J H. Wright 1996, 224, 277-278; Elmer A. Martens 1998, 299-315).

Finally, how did Jesus understand the sanctity of the Jerusalem temple and the land of Israel? Wenell concludes her thesis by putting two biblical references in juxtaposition, one from Genesis and the other from Matthew. One represents a promise to Abram, and the other the final commandment of Lord Jesus Christ. I agree with her, because these two verses truly represent my thesis of change and continuity of the physical land and the boundary less kingdom of God values that Jesus personified and proclaimed:

> On that day, the Lord made a covenant with Abram saying, 'To your descendants I will give this land from the river of Egypt to the great river, the river Euphrates, the land of the Kenites, the Kenizzites, the Kadmonites, the Hittites, the Perizites, the Rephaim, the Amorites, the Canaanites, the Girgashites, and the Jebusites' (Gen 15: 18-21).

> Jesus came to them and said, 'All authority in heaven and on earth has been given to me. Go therefore and make disciples of all nations, baptizing them in the name of the Father, the Son and the Holy Spirit, and teaching them to obey everything that I have commanded you. And remember, I am with you always, to the end of the age' (Matt 28: 18-20, NIV quoted in Wenell 2007, 146).

Thus, Jesus reinterpreted the sacred space while the church partners with him extended the kingdom values in praxis. In the Madiri Puram village, the church-land-encroachment issue was settled without humiliation. The church wrestled with losing land but gaining humans. This is how both "event and institution," as advocated by Walter Brueggemann, makes sense to me. The event of encroachment is a reality and the church never wanted such immorality institutionalised. It put an end to greed by constructing a compound wall, which amounted to costly discipleship (see *SV [Minutes] 1951-2005*, 67).

Land grabbing reflects a passion for materialism, seeking benefit for oneself and one's progeny, but at the expense of stealing land devoted to the Sanctuary. That is not all; there are evidences of sexual immorality in Madiri Puram, as elsewhere. Sexual immorality is against individuals, families and the body of Christ, while land encroachment is against God and against the community. I will expand on the womaniser's story.

A Womaniser

In and around Madiri Puram, village promiscuity is a luxury.[13] This has provided a pattern to a few others to indulge in licentiousness. One way to interpret morality is to base it on righteous or unrighteous life models in and around. A prominent Reddy in the past was a well-known womaniser. He would not let a woman go free if it was his pleasure to gratify his sexual urge with her. I even note a telling story of a gifted Christian Dalit administrator who declined to assume church "Chairmanship" owing to his immoral life. He personally quoted 1 Tim 3: 2, "Now, the overseer must be above reproach, the husband of but one wife, temperate, self-controlled, respectable, hospitable, able to teach ..." (see *S V [Minutes] 1951-2005*, 43-45). The point is that immorality is prevalent. The leader who declined had social status, political acumen and the monetary resources to maintain women.

In addition to (1) bad social models, Dalit culture also has the practice of (2) *basvi* (temple prostitution). Temple prostitution is dedicating a young girl to appease the deity. When mature, she would meet the sexual desires of the most influential or rich high-caste men and others. In one sense, the bulk of Hindu tradition encourages (3) multiple consorts. For example, *Krisna* (one of the ten incarnations of Vishnu) had many *gopikas* (consorts). Kings had many wives and (4) concubines, which is another model. Womanising is one such tendency among villagers. Thus, it may be said that the popular religious and social atmosphere encouraged promiscuity.

---

[13] In a neighbouring village called "Teerapu", two men of a Hunter family (in-laws) butchered each other for two generations over a harlot. The trouble started when a man slept with another's concubine, thus debauchery resulted in murders for two generations over a woman.

Nirmala—A Modern Jael (cf. Judg 4: 17-22)

Given such social background, a married Christian Dalit womaniser attempted to rape another's wife at midnight in the later part of the 1990s. Shyam, infatuated for Nirmala for a long time, made intentional plans to rape her. At this incident, Nirmala's mason husband was away at a cosmopolitan city to earn Christmas expenses for his family. Lying on her bed, Nirmala was singing spiritual hymns. Her hut had only a bamboo sheet door with a hang-in bolt. The intruder opened it very skillfully. "Shyam slipped in ... put off the light ... approached the woman down ... male above position." In this position, Nirmala recalled the offender's opening words and how she handled the situation:

> I have not let a woman go free whom I targeted to have sex with (her throat went gasping with tears in her eyes). She says, 'I pushed him aside with my large hands, and as the house owner I knew where the electric switch board lay. I reached my hand and switched on the light instantly. There ... I recognized the man. (Nirmala 2005, 46).

He was younger in age to her and a brother by distant relation. In a flash of thought, Nirmala connected the reason for Shyam's nighttime teasing sometime ago, while she was returning home from her field.

Nirmala pleaded with Shyam not to commit such a crime against her and pointed him to Genesis 20. In this chapter, King Abimelech took beautiful Sarah into his harem. She was the wife of prophet Abraham. God warned Abimelech in a dream that Sarah was married and he returned her to her husband, if not "... you may be sure that you and yours will die" (Gen 20:7). God also told Abimelech, that he was innocent and that God had kept him from sinning against Him (Gen 20:6).

But Shyam took Nirmala's points very lightly and said. "Ah! Those were ancient days; the Old Testament has no relevance today." Then Nirmala read to him from Matthew 5:27-30 (NIV):

> You have heard that it was said, 'Do not commit adultery. But I tell you that anyone who looks at a woman lustfully has already committed adultery with her in his heart. If your right eye causes you to sin, gouge it out and throw it away. It is better for you to lose one part of your body than for your whole body to be thrown into hell. And if your right hand causes you to sin, cut it off and throw it away. It is better for you to lose one part of your body than for your whole body to go into hell.'

Shyam snapped, "Uhn... evén the New Testament is outdated!"

Just then Nirmala got an idea: "to boil oil and pour on him." But she was clever with him and said, "*Ore! na maata neevinra, nennee matinta . . . akaliga vundi, bajji chesukoni tinta ... apudu nee asa neraverchukovachu*" (Younger brother, listen to my request, I am hungry I will bake something to eat and then you may fulfill your need [Nirmala 2005, 47]). Then she started singing the Christian song *Yesuto teeviganu podama ... sainyamandu ....* (let us walk with Jesus in confidence) and then she said, I sang all the four verses in the hymn,[14] including the below main verse, as I boiled the oil in the pan to make *bajji* (a dish of vegetables) and as I kneaded some flour:

> *Sodanalu manala chutti vacchina*
> *Satanu ambulenno tagilina-2*
> *Bayamu ledu manakika prabuvu*
> *Chenta nundumu-2 " Yesuto.. (Nirmala 2005, 47)*

(Translation: Though temptations overwhelm us, although Satan's arrows hit us, we fear no evil because we are in the company of Jesus.)

Lying on the bed, the trespasser was gazing at her all the time. Nirmala thought, "If I poured the hot oil while he is staring at me ... he may spill it over me instead." She wanted to divert his attention from her to something else. She took firewood and started to remove cobwebs above her head but moved a little away from the hearth and said to him, "My house is a poor hut, but God has given you a good house,[15] this diverted his attention enough towards the roof. In a spur of a moment, I lifted the pan with boiling oil and poured over him; then I ran to the West, he to the East towards his house. Due to unbearable pain, he poured water over his burns, the skin peeled off from his hands. His face had some burns but eyes spared" (Nirmala 2005, 47).

She said that his family rushed him to the village doctor for treatment that midnight. The doctor inquired how it all had happened.

---

[14] See MB Board of Evangelism and Church Ministries. 2007. *Stuti Aradhana Suvartha Keertanalu*. [Telugu Hymnal of MB Churches-India]. Mahabubnager, Andhra Pradesh. pp.169-170 for full hymn No.214.

[15] The violator has a brick house.

> The family members recounted that Nirmala did it, because this man
> went to spoil her. The doctor said, 'There is no virtuous woman like her
> in the entire Harijan wada.[16] Why did he go there? I have no proper
> medicine; rush him to District Hospital.' They rushed him to District
> Civil Hospital by next morning. 'He was admitted, treated, and is alive
> and back to life. I do not understand why God let him live' (Nirmala
> 2005, 48).

The story given above demonstrates that a devout woman has "fear of God" as her influence, which included her knowledge of the Scriptures and the value of spiritual hymns. The story also reflects how her glorious faith could influence her resistance. The hymns that she learned from the community gave her courage in times of helplessness. She is a living heroine of faith, a model for others. Sometimes there is no other way than to frustrate the designs of an evil person with harsh treatment. Nirmala acted in some ways like Jael in the book of Judges (Judges 4:17-22; 5:24-27). On the other hand, the life of the adulterer is immoral. Immorality and tolerant society were his influence. He even knew Bible stories and could converse with Nirmala on them.

The incident was reported to the police and a couple of Telugu Daily newspapers covered Nirmala's valiant story, but without highlighting her "fear of the Lord", the counsel she had offered to the immoral person and her identity. In the end, her question was, "Why does God let the wicked survive? In other words, why do the righteous suffer and the wicked prosper?" Her cry is akin to the prophet Habakkuk (Hab 1:1- 4). Let us unravel her agony.

Christu Bhakta: Woman Is Not a Dalit of Dalits

The term *Christu bhakta* is rich in its meaning. It means a living devotee or witness to Christ's risen power. The Christian Dalit woman is not weak, but a powerful hope to the world. Nirmala has created an "event," a name and an identity for Christian women. And she refused to "institutionalise" immorality in the case of her offender (Brueggemann 1997, 735-736). She resisted Shyam, the intruder: "I pushed him aside with my large hands, and as the house owner, I knew where the electric switchboard lay. I reached

---

[16] Harijan [= children of god] a term M. K. Gandhi coined to show equal treatment to low-caste people. But low-caste people refused to be called children of a lower god, questioning: Are Hindus then the children of the devil? Instead, they adapted the term "Dalit" to mean a people oppressed for at least 3,500 years in India by the caste system. Wada" is a section of the village

my hand and switched on the light instantly. There ... I recognized the man" (Nirmala 2005, 46). She exposed his male chauvinism to the world. She questioned his comfort zones. How could she do so?

Firstly, she did it in contravention to patriarchy in Hindu, Islam and Christian Dalit cultures. For example, the Hindu culture upholds male domination and degrades woman's status in society. According to Manu, the Hindu lawgiver (500-300 B. C.), a woman should "in her childhood be under the control of her father, in her youth under the control of her husband, if her husband is dead, she should be under the control of her son" (Ilaiah 2003, 173; Melanchthon 2007, 51 footnote 18). She is not supposed to think independently. She is the property of a man. She has no ritual status. Aruna Gnanadason, a woman liberation thinker from India and an activist in the World Council of Churches, protests:

> Aryans brought with them the patriarchal joint family as effective means of controlling women. Women came to be viewed as property of males — just as his field or property that belonged to him. Only sons could inherit property therefore the birth of sons became crucial. Women could not perform certain rituals (due to the impurity associated with their menstruation) and therefore the birth of a son was essential to continue the family name and to perform certain rituals — particularly to light the funeral pyre of his father, so as to ensure him a better life after death. (Gnanadason 1990, 134)

Secondly, Nirmala acted on the contrary to her own Christian Dalit culture. Dalit culture in line with the Brahmanical tradition, accepts that "man is superior to woman" (see Rajshekar 2002). A Dalit woman is treated as "dust of dust" within her own society (Nirmal 1987, 6). Within Dalit families, she experiences "domestic violence" (Gnanadason 1990, 130).

Thirdly, Nirmala, for sure, was responding to evil in obedience to her biblical faith. While she is semi-literate, she is a student of the Bible and is closely following the teaching of the church. These include her devotional hymns like *Yesuto teeviganu podama* (let us walk in confidence with Jesus even though Satan's arrows hit us). Shyam is known to have raped several other young and married women in the village. Nirmala was aware of his immoral history. She reacted to such human patterns and acted on renewed mind (Rom 12:1- 3). She spoke the truth in love. She gave Shyam enough time to leave her territory. Only when he would not listen, did she think of teaching him a violent lesson — by pouring boiling oil on him.

Fourthly, despite all this, her "why" question is legitimate. Her agony is: "He was admitted, treated, and is alive and back to life. I do not understand why God let him live" (Nirmala 2005, 48). This is a cry for justice and vengeance. The thing is that of all the crimes committed against humanity, sexual humiliation for a woman is the worst haunting shadow. Two prominent Indian women, N. N. Sarkar and Rina Sarkar, unravel the agony a sexually assaulted woman goes through. N. N. Sarkar works for the Department of Reproductive Biology at the All India Institute for Medical Sciences, New Delhi, and Rina Sarkar is Advocate, Ladies' Bar Room, High Court of Delhi. These two women have done an excellent scientific study estimating the impact of rape. They note:

> Sexual assault on women, unlike any other offence, e.g., theft, robbery or murder, leaves a deep-rooted effect or stigma in the body and mind of a woman who has to live the rest of her life in society with the unpleasant shadow of this incident. (Sarkar and Sarkar 2005, 407)

For them the post-event trauma for a woman include:

> ... sleep disorders, nightmare, anxiety, depression, suicidal ideation, and diminishing of sexual urge and pleasure among other disorders following sexual assault or rape. Recovery is slower in sexual than in non-sexual assault victims (*ibid.*).

Laudably, these two scholars have also given thought to recovery measures. The measures include "emotional support from friends, relations, social and community supports" (Sarkar and Sarkar 2005, 416). They also find that religion has a positive impact on coping with stressful life events.

Why Is God Silent?

Questions for Nirmala still remain: Is God silent to her cry for justice? Why is her violator and the violator of several other women allowed to live? (Habk. 1:1-4) There are no easy answers. Nevertheless, I propose a three-fold response. Firstly, in my thinking, it was her faith in God that provided her strength to resist the evil man's intent. The hymn and scriptures, including the ideas to frustrate the adulterer, came from the grace of God. God has started to wipe her tears away. He will answer her question in heaven too. I think, Brueggemann is right in saying that we cannot reduce (deconstruct) God's person below our demand for justice (Derrida in view for Brueggemann 1997, 740). Moreover, Nirmala and the entire village are aware that an attempt of rape was made but the act did not take place, though shame is equally cruel even in this case. So there is reason to praise God. This is how Nirmala's action is comparable to that of Jael (see Judg 4:17-22). Nirmala never meant to invoke violence in handling the situation, but she had to resort to shocking the offender. She wanted to break the customary tolerance of loose character, or of an institution.

Secondly, I am of the firm opinion that her trauma could have been reduced if the church panchayat had dealt with this violation. As per the records, they did not, which raised the question: Is it party with the tolerant culture? Some members of her community have consoled Nirmala, but that is not enough to experience community support.

Thirdly, when the police and newspaper reporters came, the church could have used the situation to highlight how Nirmala glorified God, even when sin tried to trample over her. Thus, it could have been an event of Christian witness rather than replicating an institution of silence.

A Transit Comment

One can be sure that, either in the case of church land encroachment or in attempted rape, some people were not under Christian influence. They were keen on horoscopes or sexual gratification. The three encroachers were united and defended each other. In the end, what it meant was that in the case of men encroachers of the church land, the panchayat met and resolved the issue, but when it came to women and justice, it was left to cultural toleration. On the contrary, Nirmala was graciously enacting principles of her faith to frustrate the designs of the womaniser. Therefore, Christian Dalits have differing self-identities. Some glorify their God, while others gratify themselves. However, there is more to human life than wickedness and resisting evil. People seek guidance in life crises.

Life Guidance

Again, a story is used to bring home the point and major issues at stake. Most people run to God for guidance in trouble. How Madiri Puram people exercise guidance is very interesting to know.

Peasant Theology of Prayer

Peasants seek God's guidance when monsoon rains fail them. Monsoon rains are supposed to come in the months of June through September each year. Sowing seeds and filling of water reservoirs or ponds would happen at this season through monsoons. But if rains fail them, they are troubled at heart because rain is their life. Their prayers are on behalf of all peoples, irrespective of religion, caste, tribe or sex. It includes the welfare of the birds of the air and the animal world.

If the monsoons fail, the Madiri Puram church *panchayat* declares fasting prayers for at least three days. Prayer participants enlist themselves and then the Secretary of the church allocates a Rota of ten minutes of prayer for each participant. The fasting prayers are said in the upper room. The rest of the congregation is involved in devotions, hymns and praises at the basement. Prayer participants take wooden steps to reach the upper room to pray and climb down to join the larger assembly. God answers their repentant prayers and sends rain in abundance, so the non-Christian villagers testify, "*Mee devudu vaana gurupistadu*" ("Your God, orders rain.").

Nature of Peasant Prayer

Sadhu is a layman. This eighty-year-old saint inaugurated the season of prayer by "invoking God of the Universe." It happened during *pagati aaradhana*, "morning worship" on Sunday, July 3, 2005.[17] Sometimes Sadhu's prayer is a "complaint," at other points he "reminds" God of [His] suffering humanity. His prayer makes a "statement" to God on how the speechless birds of the air and domestic and wild animals wait for his provision. Sadhu repeats the same phrases four times each time intensifying his appeal. Repetition is the Orientals' way of pleading for mercy. It rekindles God's compassion, sovereignty and "incomparable" salvific powers. Sadhu's prayer takes the names of Hindu gods and implies "their powerlessness" in sending rain. Sadhu's prayer "demands" that God opened the gates of His heavenly reservoirs. He questioned if God desired peasants to "commit suicide" by swallowing pesticides, owing to the unbearable burden of agricultural loans. The aged layman saint constrains his God to "gaze" at him, his village and the drying soil, and the parching environment unsafe for birds and animals. Sadhu begins to "press" the indignant God from withholding rain for three years in a row:

---

[17] Peasant churches usually worship at night, 9-11 pm. During daytime, they work in their fields. But participation in daytime worship (10 am-12 noon) is considered a measurement for deeper level of faith, though just 20 per cent of 600 households attend.

> na deva ... na deva ... na deva ... na de ... va .... Lokamanta (repeat)
> ...annamu leka, neellu leka ... nayana, manavulu neekakkarleda, na deva
> neekakkarleda, swamee neekakkarleda, deva ... neekakkarleda? (a long
> cry) .... akasa paksulu, noruleni jantuvalu, myata leka, tagadaniki neellu
> leka alaterutundavi. (Sadhu 2005, 7)

(Translation: My God..., my God..., my... God... my Go...d (a crying drag of God's name).... All people [repeat] are suffering without food and drinking water... ...Father 'have you abandoned humans, my God are you not in need of them, master, do you not need them, God, do you not care for them? ... The birds of the air and the speechless animals are troubled for want of grass and water to quench their thirst).

Sadhu, believes that God holds the keys and "demands" that He opened the floodgates of heaven:

> Nayana, akasa tumulippumu, anta nee setulavundi deva, nee setulavundi
> deva, akasatumulippumu, akasatumulippi vaananu guripinchumani
> vedukuntunnanu tandri, vaananu guripinchumu, na deva vaananu
> guripinchumu, na deva vaananu guripinchumani vdedukuntundamu.
> (Sadhu 2005, 7)

(Translation: Father, open the watergates, God, everything is in your hands... it is in your power God, open the floodgates in the sky and pour out rain... I plead with you, Father, God, order rain...)

Sadhu, a lifetime farmer, goes on to describe peasant woes: "Many farmers have sown millions of seeds, but the seeds have not sprouted... (a deep agony)... followed by his appeal to God the Father, to gaze at him."

> Naayana entamando boomilo kotla yittanalu yesinaru deva, yittanalu
> pandakunda agipoyinai..., yittanalu agipoyinayi swame, na deva... na
> deva, na deva, na deva ani ninni vedukuntunnanu deva, "na dikku
> sudumu," tandri. (Sadhu 2005, 8)

At a couple junctures in his fervent prayer, Sadhu uses cultural terms like *vaana devuni* (rain God) but adds emphasis to mean just the rain. For him none has power but the God of the Bible: *anta nee setulavundi deva, nee setulavundi deva* (Sadhu 2005, 7).

But all the non-Christian villagers who are listening to church prayers over the public address system consider that there is a "god of rain" called *Varunudu*. Sadhu appeals with long cries and "demands" God to open the "floodgates" in heaven. So it would be safer to interpret *vaana devuni* to mean "blessings of rain." Let us consider his prayer in his native tongue:

> Aakasa tumulippi "vaana devuni" daya cheyumani vedukuntunnamu
> swamee, vaananu guripinchumani vedukuntunnamu deva, vaananu
> gurupinchumu, aakasa tumulippumu, deva aakasa tumu... lippumu
> (demanding voice), deva aakasa tumulippumu swamee (Sadhu 2005,
> 8).

Sadhu prays to God. He is also indignant at his fellow believers for not being watchful and prayerful. However, before finding fault with some of his co-believers, Sadhu identified himself with them by uttering, *maanavunni tandri* to mean "father, I am only (a *sarx*, a flesh) a human apart from you." Then "Prayer Sadhu", as he is known, complains to God against some of his easygoing fellow believers... *ninda tintaru p andukuntaru* ([they] eat to their fill and slumber). By implication, Sadhu worries that their slumber will cause famine. They had better watch and pray or face drought. That year only 18 out of 600 household heads [men] enrolled in fasting prayers. The low participation is part of Sadhu's taunt; thus his concern for the health of the church. In this sense, he sees lethargy in place of vision, as an influence on most Christian Dalits. They do not foresee the impending famine and are, therefore, uncompassionate.

Sadhu sees the ensuing trouble and predicts farmers' suicides[18] as a possibility if God were not to respond to his prayer. He

---

[18] Though not in Madiri Puram village, yet in theirs and other states thousands of farmers have committed suicide, namely the states of Andhra Pradesh, Maharastra, Karnataka and Punjab in the 1990s and the trend remained unabated through 2006-2007. The causes and remedies for suicides are presented here below as per Wikipedia.

Causes: Absence of adequate support infrastructure at the level of the village and district, uncertainty of agricultural enterprise in India, indebtedness of farmers, rising costs of cultivation, plummeting prices of farm commodities, lack of credit availability for small scale farmers, relative absence of irrigation facilities and repeated crop failures.

Remedies: Government to actually implement the various money-lending Acts that already exist to prevent the alienation of the farmers land –holding, to make the crop Insurance Scheme more farmer friendly, with lower premia and less red-tape, renewal of the land's biodiversity to ensure the health of land and enable the farmer to cope with market ups and downs, better health facilities in the locality since expenditure on health has been one of the most important financial drain in the village, better education facilities at the school level in the villages to enable better coping with a more technologically oriented agriculture, quality checks on agricultural inputs like seeds, fertilisers and pesticides to prevent cheating of the farmer by unscrupulous suppliers of industrial inputs for agriculture, reliable agricultural advisories for farmers on farm-related practices and better access to markets for agricultural produce to get higher rates for farm produce. See "Farmers" suicides in India—*Wikipedia*, the free encyclopedia: *http://en.wikipedia.org/wiki/Farmers'_suicides_in_India.*

wonders if God would assume responsibility in the event of such deaths: "It (suicide deaths) may be your will, master, (but) not ours." His peasant agony mounts on this matter as he travails in prayer:

> adi nee sittamu swamee, ma sittamu gadu," makanta neeve .... Ma devudu maki sayamistadani asa vundi..., tandri, yee lokanni raksinse devudavu neeve, batikinche devudavu nive, pantalu pandinche devudavu nive, nevu dappa vere devudu ledani, prardhana jesi vedukuntunnanu deva. (Sadhu, R. 2005, 9)

(Translation: "It [suicide deaths] may be your will master, [but] not ours'; you are everything to us. We have full trust... that you would answer our prayers [Father, you are the one who let us live or die by emphasis, a protest against God's silence, for three consecutive years now]. You are the one to bless our crops, and we restate, we know no other God, but you... I submit my supplication).

Sadhu did not even close his prayer customarily, that is, "in the name of Jesus we pray... Amen!", but his hearers in the church and his living God understood it. His Elijah-like prayer set the stage for a "week of prayer" festival.

The preacher (researcher) of that day stressed commitment to God. He preached from the book of Malachi. He exhorted people to be faithful to God and to their spouse (Mal 2: 14). He asked them to test God by offering tithes and special offerings, and their own lives (3: 8-10). He questioned some people's disbelief in God's power to punish the wicked (3: 13-18).

The above two events made church elders summon the church *panchayat*, i.e., the male heads of the households to consider a season of fasting prayers.

Instructions to Prayer Partners

The church *panchayat* met and resolved to hold a three-day session of fasting prayers, from July 8-11, 2005. People were exhorted to prepare and enroll their names for those special days. The participants were reminded of the regulations as follows:

- Take bath each morning.
- Wear clean clothing.
- Be in the sanctuary 24 hours.

- Abstain from conjugal relations[19]
- Pray on your knees.
- Pray just for 10 minutes in the upper room.
- Stop when the reliever begins his prayer.

As part of the preparations, the church elders washed the entire sanctuary with water on the previous afternoon. Prayers began as planned. But there were no signs of rain until the middle of the second day. Murthy, one of the church elders, climbed down from the upper-room wooden steps, with heavy heart and tears rolling down from his eyes. He felt zealous about his Almighty God. Murthy came to one of the ministers near the pulpit and said: What will we say of our living God, if it does not rain by tomorrow? How will we face the non-Christians in the village? (Murty 2005)

His question and attitude melted the worshiping community. The lead minister announced Murthy's zeal for the name of the Lord and led the gathered assembly to kneel down and unite in a cry unto God. We did. By the evening, clouds formed and heavy rain pour started thereafter for three days. It rained so much that some of the dry crops, like millet in black soil, began to pale away due to an excess of water, and we had to plead God to give a break from incessant rain.

Impending severe famine was the context for the Madiri Puram village area. Life direction meant to seek God's face and to be a witness to His mighty acts in the village. Life guidance is revealed only when the community captures the burning zeal for God's name and only when they are united in heart. The resulting experience of God's grace raises their honour too. Such revelations usually start with one person being prompted by God to stir the community. And it happens only when people pray on behalf of all humanity, the birds of the air, the animals and the whole creation.

This is Elijah-like prayer. How does seeking guidance enact change and continuity and present us with identity markers of Christian Dalits in the Madiri Puram village?

---

[19] Women are discouraged from participating in fasting prayers, for the church has experienced a woman breaking her vow in the middle when she remembered her boiling milk pot. Another difficulty in breaking the males-only custom is lack of reliever women in the upper room. Traditionally, the church does not like women saints relieved by men saints.

Prayer as an Identity Marker

In this case, prayer is to seek God's favour in an impending famine, but prayer is much more. Prayer is engaging God in world affairs. For example, for a peasant, "fertility and rhythm of seasons" is central to life (Hiebert 2006, 158). He seeks pragmatic solutions to his problems. He is distressed when nature around him does not have green, fragrant grass and fruitful crops. As the crop grows, his spirit raises to heights. Therefore, he cries to God for mercy. In analysing prayer as an identity marker, I will bring insights from Elijah's prayer in 1 Kings 18:16-46 and apply it to Madiri Puram Christian Dalit intercession.

Who Is the Troubler?

When vegetation and human lives are parching for three consecutive years, who is to be blamed? This was the question king Ahab asked of Elijah. In such situations, people of all faiths analyse the reasons and come up with differing answers and remedies. King Ahab alleged that Elijah was the "troubler" of Israel: "When he saw Elijah, he said to him, Is that you, you troubler of Israel?" (1 Kings 18:17). Note that Ahab did not give reasons for his argument, but accused Elijah for the trouble. Elijah's response to Ahab, instead, presents a history of reasons, "But you and your father's family have. You have abandoned the LORD's commands and have followed the Baals (1 Kings 18:18). Yahweh's honour was attributed to "worthless idols" (1 Kings 16:26), Baal and Asherah. The troubling situation had to be dealt with. The warning of drought was given through Elijah in 1 Kings 17:1 "As the Lord, the God of Israel, lives, whom I serve, there will be neither dew nor rain in the next few years except at my word." It culminates in three years with the event on Mount Carmel. What can be read is that Ahab under the influence of Jezebel, his wife, was instituting Baal worship in Israel. Jezebel ensured her religious establishment by killing many prophets (1 Kings 18:4).

On the contrary, for Elijah, his God was zealous for events of faith every time Israel approached Him. In the end, it meant the contest and Elijah killing 450 of Baal's priests fed by Jezebel, in retribution (1 Kings 18:4). True prophets were often known as troublemakers. In this case, Ahab was to be blamed for the severe drought. Brueggemann's definition of "troubler" is as follows:

> The troubler is one who disturbs the well-being of the community by acting for self against healthy social relationships. The prophets were often perceived as troublers because they dissented from conventional reality and raised awkward questions. Thus Hosea is dismissed as a "fool" who is "mad" (Hos 9:7); Jeremiah is reckoned to be a traitor for undermining the war effort (Jer 38:4). And surely Elijah is a profound social disturbance. The work of prophets is to raise questions and expose what is taken for granted when it is in fact destructive (Brueggemann 2000, 222).

A drought is a "curse" and a definite sign of a "discredited king" (Ahab) as opinioned by Brueggemann (2000, 219). A king's righteous rule was to ensure rain (Ps 72:6). For Brueggemann, the episode of Elijah killing 450 Baal priests underscores the severity of the issue and the lack of any sense of compassion. However, Brueggemann notes that:

> The narrative is about the radical transformation of the realm of Israel from drought to rain, from curse to blessing, from death to life. In an arid climate, where all vegetation is vulnerable because of water shortage, this transformation is nothing short of a resurrection. The deep turn to life is evoked by Elijah, but it is enacted solely by Yahweh, so that the narrative as a whole, in its dramatic force, is a doxology to Yahweh newly acknowledged, acknowledged through the process of the drama. In the end, the entire narrative moves toward the acclamation of the people:
>
> Yahweh, it is he who is God;
> Yahweh, it is he who is God (18:39) (Brueggemann 2000, 227-228).

In this case, some of the non-praying Christian Dalits were the troublers. How would the Dalits dishonour God? There are two backgrounds to Christian Dalit beliefs. In a Dalit humanist understanding, Dalits are "godless" people. Their gods are ancestor heroes who died while defending their people. In his misjudgment, Kancha Ilaiah, a political science professor and a renowned Dalit liberation activist, "reduced" even Christ to one such martyr who died for his people.

> Though Sammakaka and Sarakka[20] emerged as Goddesses from the battlefield, unlike the Hindu Gods, they are martyrs not victors and subduers. It is common for martyrs to be transformed into divine spirits. They story of Christ himself is one example. . . (Isaiah 2007, 97)

The implication here is that non-Christian Dalits dishonour Christ as one among their ancestors, in proof of their humanism. True,

---

[20] Sammakka and Sarakka were tribal mother and daughter goddesses. They lost their lives in defending their people against unjust laws of Kakatiya [Hindu] invaders in Warangal District of Andhra Pradesh, c. 998 AD. In memory of these there is a biannual jatara.

Christian Dalits of Madiri Puram were in the past, "godless people",[21] but now they are a people of living God and they declare the praises of Him through prayers: *"But you are a chosen people, a royal priesthood, a holy nation, a people belonging to God, that you may declare the praises of him who called you out of darkness into his wonderful light. (1 Pet. 2: 9)*

A second way to dishonour God is with non-Christian "pride." Dhyryam, well- versed in social issues in my research village, says, "It did not rain in 2004 even though we fasted and prayed," and because God needed to break somebody's boasting:

> In 2004 as we started to pray for monsoon rains in the church, the non-Christian friends also started to pray in their temple [with Public address systems going louder and competing oneanother's prayers]. We sent a word, 'since we have started first let us finish and then you may start your season of prayers. They refused to oblige, we and they continued prayers simultaneously. So to teach them a lesson, God did not send rain that year. The real intention of non-Christians was to steal the glory of God by boasting "Look! It rained since we prayed, it is not your God but ours too sends rain". ...Rest of the years whenever we prayed it rained. All this happens to show to the nations that Jesus is the only God (Dhyryam 2005, 43).

Dhyryam says that today these people may not admit this truth that "our God rains," but some of them encourage us to pray for rains. Some even send their first fruits to the church. Dhyryam adds, "All this is said to testify that we have developed since we accepted Christ as our Savior. There is no doubt about this fact" (*ibid.*).

Thirdly, the Christian Dalits were also at fault by not being concerned for the suffering humanity. Sadhu, the praying saint of the village, was upset about such persons in his own community: *"ninda tintaru pandu kuntaru"* (they eat to their fill and sleep). In addition, we need to question who the troubler is since no rains fell in the first of the three consecutive years. It must be the Christian Dalits. God's power or grace cannot be institutionalised. Faith in Him needed to be dynamic always. This was also confirmed to us when Mr. Murthy moved our hearts with his zeal to honour God: "What will we say of our living God, if it does not rain by tomorrow? How will we face the non-Christians in the village?"

---

[21] In the introduction to this chapter, I have expanded the godlessness of the Dalits. This included Dalit beliefs in spirits, like Narsappa and their respects to "mother" as life-giver.

This was the provocation in the good sense of the term for the church to unite their hearts as part of their identity. Unity in prayer and heart is necessary to a witness for God. The result was that God's name was glorified and the rain came in abundance.

Summary

This chapter has attempted to answer the question: "In what ways do Christian Dalits of Madiri Puram Village enact change and continuity in morality and life guidance?" Firstly, we have considered that three households put together encroached 15 feet of sanctuary land, over a period of ten years (1977-1986). Encroachment of land, for me, is an "event" in the words of Brueggemann (1997.736). The church panchayat had put an end to such gross negligence by erecting compound wall, which cost them dearly (c.527 US $).

This, to me, means a righteous step, an "institution" blotting out encroachment in the future. In this case, the church did not require of the intruders to pay compensation for the land. Perhaps they should have. Moreover, they let the doors of fellowship open to the wrongdoers. This they did in order to avoid a potential schism in the church. They valued loss of land is better than loss of brotherhood.

In understanding "sacred space", I have brought in lessons from Karen Wenell's (2007) book, *Jesus and Land*. She understands sacred space as holy, as well as socially, construed. She concludes her argument by putting the tension between the promise made to Abraham and the last commandment of Lord Jesus Christ, i.e., Gen. 15:18-21 with Matt. 28:18-20. I agree with her that sacred space for the Kingdom is boundary-less, while it must be tangible as well. There is a tension. So, while the Madiri Puram church shut out the encroachers' greed by erecting a compound wall, the very wall continues to witness to an identity crisis in a village where there is no loss of land among the non-Christian temples or mosques.

Secondly, Nirmala's story projects how she enacted her Christian morality in response to a sexual assault on her. Her biblical faith, spiritual hymns and God's grace have helped her to treat the intruder with harsh treatment, but to the glory of God. The intruder showed his nominal Christianity.

Thirdly, we have seen how peasant Christians seek God's mercy for monsoon rains. Within the story, we see signs of lethargy and watchful saints praying to God. In the end, even people of other faiths admit that the Christian Dalit God is the One who orders rain, saying, *mee devudu vaana guripistadu*. Again, Walter Brueggemann has helped me bring insights from the prayer of Prophet Elijah in 1 Kings 18:16-46. The God of Israel desires "events" of faith at each juncture in life, but king Ahab, under the evil influence of Jezebel, his wife, wanted to establish Baal worship.

The result was that the king and his family were the "troubler" of Israel and not Elijah. The story is clear that Ahab had provoked God's anger and He answered it with heavy rain within three years, but this meant destroying Baal worship and its 450 priests. The next question we face is: How do the Christians of Madiri Puram village reach consensus in their church *Panchayat* (legal assembly)?

Chapter 7

CONSENSUS AND CHURCH PANCHAYATS

Introduction

Merriam-Webster's Online Dictionary (1843) defines, "consensus" as "group solidarity in sentiment and belief." Previously, I focused on how the Madiri Puram village church reached consensus in settling the church land encroachment dispute. The church has suffered loss of a part of its land, but was intentional about retaining the integrity of the church. This chapter will further expand on "how Christians of Madiri Puram village reach consensus in their church *Panchayats*" (legal assemblies, RQ 4). I will use a few events in the life of the church as evidence for different types of consensus. The events will cover issues of divorce, church discipline and political consensus.

"Panchayat" means a traditional village council consisting of five elders. A Panchayat is usually headed by a charismatic leader called a *sarpanch*. Traditionally, this headman of the village is an aged person, a high-caste individual and has earned his respect through his impartial judgments over the years (see Hiebert 1974, 103).

The traditional Panchayat runs on consensus, while a court of justice is based on discerning truthfulness from falsehood. In a court of justice, "winner-loser" is the main factor, while in traditional panchayat, the focus is on justice and life together in a village. Traditional panchayat has been functional for thousands of years in village India. Noted missiologist, Paul G. Hiebert, has done an excellent study on the *Konduru* village in South India and has an excellent chapter on panchayat. The chapter has rich stories about how consensus is derived (Hiebert 1974, 101-130). Hiebert notes, for village India, kings and kingdoms rise and fall but the panchayat way of leadership is what keeps the village going. Hiebert has a fine grasp of what ancient wisdom in panchayat means. Panchayat leadership functions on the basis of "consensus" reached between major factions:

> Their leadership is a function of their ability to bring the assembled
> elders to some common consensus, which will have the support of all
> or most of the major factions involved. If they fail to do this, their
> decisions are ineffectual, for their power lies ultimately in effective social
> ostracism, and not in the fines levied and the punishments decreed
> (Hiebert 1974, 103).

When the dispute is amicably settled, elders of the panchayat as well the disputants celebrate with a traditional wine called *kallu* (sap of a palm tree). This drink is usually purchased with part of the monies levied as fine on the guilty person or party. With the drink celebration, harmony is restored between disputants and the village Panchayat elders (Hiebert 1974, 107-111).

Types of Legal Systems in Madiri Puram Village

There are five kinds of legal systems that exist in Madiri Puram village: First, the "*kula* or caste or clan panchayat." Clan panchayat deals with extramarital relations in the life of Prakash and Pentamma couple. Second, there is the "Christian Dalit panchayat." Christian Dalit Panchayats will deal with church discipline in correcting some of the misbehavior of its members. But it will show that their panchayat is most human in the final analysis. Third, I will explore "village panchayat" dominated by Reddy and Christian Dalits. In relationship to this, I will talk about how the "Court of Justice" (for example the Supreme Court of India) has declared a land case in favour of Pakanati Adi Sheshi Reddy in his efforts to secure 205 acres of government land for Christian Dalits. British colonisation, education, press and transportation have impressed India with their jurisprudence through courts of law (Dey 1992, 63). Fourth, in this chapter, court of justice and the Reddy and Christian Dalit "political consensus" intersect.

I elaborated on the church trying the Court of Justice to secure marriage license for their pastor. I indicated that the church had spent Rs 20,000 (c.USD 527) and, to this day, the church is uncomfortable about this huge expenditure. In the end, the marriage license issue was settled outside the court, within the church, with the help of the regional head of the church, in a panchayat way. In this chapter, I will describe how Pakanati Adi Sheshi Reddy has moved from the lower to the Apex Court in securing 205 acres of government land for Dalit Christians.

Fifth, I find justice administered by the *rytu sangham* (farmers' guild). I will not be able to deal with *rytu sangham* legal disputes. However, a brief note of explanation is needed. Since 1958, most of the land in Madiri Puram village has come to benefit the Rajolibanda Diversion Scheme canal water. *Rytu Sangham* looks into litigations such as someone grazing someone else's crop, or disputes regarding sharing of canal water, or changing borders or the welfare issues of the farmers in this guild.

The post-independent (1947) India village has come to experience a second type of Panchayat called, *naya* (modern) panchayat. Traditional panchayat is the most effective system in my research village even today, while modern Panchayat is present in a big way in electing their *Sarpanch* and ward members. A major difference between traditional and modern Panchayat is the years of service of a Panchayat. In traditional panchayat, the choosing of elders is for a year. Naya Panchayats elect their leaders for a period of five years. *Naya Panchayat* is based on democratic principles and a majority vote system. Majority vote can be manipulated by the rich and the influential as in this village. For example, a Dalit can also become a Sarpanch either by election or, on rare occasions, by consensus.

This chapter will emphasise three types of "consensus" and how they are reached at Christian Dalit Panchayats:

1. Kula Panchayat
2. Christian Dalit Panchayat
3. Reddy-Christian Dalits Panchayat

Every caste or clan has its own legal system, called *kula panchayat* (caste council). Dalit caste panchayat still functions outside the parameters of the church. But its *myatarlu* (caste council elders) are Christian Dalits. For instance, traditionally, the church did not deal with issues such as *vidakulu* (divorce). Divorce issues are settled in their caste panchayat on consensus. Should divorce not be a concern of the church is a different question altogether, but in this village, Christian divorce is an anathema.

Kula Panchayat

Let us talk about *kula panchayat* (caste council). In Madiri Puram, there are three clans: Tekuri meti (clan), Ganganna meti and Ashanna meti. Personal jealousies, land litigations and political rivalries do take place between clans. Disputes and imbalances can sometimes get out of hand leading to violence. This is where the *kula myatarlu* (clan heads) resolve the disputes. For example, clan heads discuss and resolve issues of extra marital relations on consensus.

In a neighbouring village, there was a critical and sensitive litigation. R. Danam, one of the experienced *kula myatarlu* (clan head), told me the following story. Prakash and Pentamma were married for five years. They had no children. Prakash, the husband, was affected by polio in his childhood. From his waist down, he was crooked and so unable to have sex. But, being the only son, his parents got his cross-cousin to marry him. The passion for progeny made his parents find a woman. There were rumours that Pentamma, Prakash's wife, had extra-marital relations. The adulterer's family was slandered and his parents sought the decision of the *kula* panchayat (caste council). The woman and the adulterer's families were summoned.

The clan council elders sought an explanation from Pentamma. She replied, "I have my husband's permission to commit this act in an effort to continue his lineage." How do we resolve this crisis? Danam, a Christian Dalit and a caste council elder, went on to say that in this case, the caste council had consensus on a three-point approach:

1. We should help the Prakash couple live together, even if we need to tell thousand lies.

2. Adultery is sin, but divorce is also not healthy for the woman's family. They need a progeny.

3. When disturbed, a stone (spouse) meant for a platform should be re-adjusted back to the same platform and not dislocated to any other platform. (Danam 2005, 26).

The adulterer then was charged with a fine so that everyone understood that this matter was brought up to the caste court, the entire situation was heard and a ruling was given. This meant that the *Kula* (clan) panchayat provided a way out for the woman to bear a child that legally belonged to Prakash, her husband.

Then the question for Danam was: On what grounds do you sanction *vidakulu* (divorce) and order a remarriage? As a clan judge, his answer was typical:

- In the event of a proven impotence of a husband,
- Or if a spouse falls chronically ill, or
- In the event of adultery (Danam 2005, 26).

When reminded of the case of the woman with a disabled husband who had extra-marital relations (Prakash couple), he said, "We pray as Christian Dalit caste elders before we start to hear a case, but we resolve according to the need and the caste values" (Danam 2005, 25). In this sense, a clan Panchayat is mostly humanistic in its decisions. It punishes, but most of the time retains the integrity of the family. However, the basic factor here is that the Panchayat's decision presents us with split-level Christianity.

Thus, Hiebert is in concurrence with the noted social anthropologist M. N. Srinivas, who opinioned, "that it is not that justice administered by the elders is "always or even usually more just than the justice administered by the judges in urban law courts, but only that it is better understood by the litigants" (Srinivas quoted in Hiebert 1974, 130). Thus, *Kula panchayat* in this village points to the existence of Dalit as well as Christian jurisprudence in creative tension. From a clan panchayat, let us move to the Christian Dalit way of discerning justice. Has it changed in any way because of biblical influences?

Christian Dalit Panchayat

In Madiri Puram village, Mennonite Brethren Church, "consensus" is a recurring theme. Consensus is most pronounced in electing its leadership annually. Consensus is also applied to put social pressure on a wayward householder in fulfilling his responsibility to the peasant church. For instance, it will apply pressure if a household is due its share towards the support of their pastor and has not fellowshipped with the church for long.

Consensus is required when confusion has occurred. Chaos is intense when their pastor leaves for his higher seminary training without making appropriate arrangements for the smooth functioning of the church. This has compelled the church to choose panchayat leadership in a formal way. The long time Secretary of Madiri Puram church notes:

> ...Pastor left the church for Devarakonda [town] for further seminary training without making proper arrangements. This has left the church suffer for leadership care, as well left it guessing how much is in the treasury. Thus as the church was experiencing lukewarm situation, the youth of the church at the time assembled the entire church and chose its five leaders, *'ekagreevamuga'* (on consensus).... (Secretary, *SV [Minutes] 1951-2005*, 7).

This does not mean that their pastor did not have informal elders to work with him before he left for Seminary education; it means he did not provide leadership for the life of the church in his absence. But that gave the church an opportunity to break new grounds.

The above depiction of a "directionless" situation makes them take initiative. It is noteworthy that the church assembly focused on two basic needs (1) church leadership and (2) economic stability [treasury]. Moreover, we should note that it was (3) the lukewarm situation of the church that concerned the youth. It is the (4) youth who took initiative for the welfare of the church. All this means, it is the *laos*, the people of God, who felt the need for direction to the church over and above the clergy in this instance. As a truly indigenous church, it has come out of its shackles of dependence to govern itself and take responsibility for self-support in the words of Henry Venn and Rufus Anderson. The big factor I note is that the church chose its leadership (5) *ekagreevamuga* (on consensus[1]). They chose *five* leaders in the pattern of a panchayat. Typically, a pastor is not one among the elders' council, though he may be invited to sit in the council. The five first leaders chosen by consensus in the pattern of panchayat were:

- Treasurer, R. Thamasu
- Secretary, R. Jakarayya
- Elders, R. Davidu, R. Eliya and R. Rubenu (Secretary, *SV [Minutes] 1951-2005*, 7)

These five elders served the church for 12 years (1951-1962). However, there were no elections held for the years 1955-1962 and 1964-65, which meant the same leaders were leading the church or the elders malfunctioned. But with the resignation of the Treasurer in 1965, the treasurer had to be replaced.

Why would a pastor leave his church without making proper arrangements? A few reasons may be advanced. In village India, in the early 1950s, a *pantulu* (pastor) was the best-educated person. Village Christians were students of a pastor to learn how to read

---

[1] *"ekagreevamuga"* can mean "unanimously," if literally taken into English. But it suffers the real sense of the term. In the case of Madiri Puram church councils it means *"consensus,"* as it will be clear from the rest of this chapter. Consensus means differences subsumed ·in unity.

and write. In Indian culture, students dared not, at the time, question their guru (teacher). Moreover, the pastor may have been an important leader, like a white missionary holding sole authority in his hands, or thought it below his dignity to talk to the church elders about alternative arrangements. But the youth taking up the matter in consensus speaks of their determination to serve their Lord and direct the church.

In the Gadwal area, a village church panchayat would provide leadership, governance and economic stability, take disciplinary actions and provide social protection with the help of the local Reddy. The church does even hire or fire pastors. Church panchayat in Madiri Puram village has taken a couple of fronts for its function, such as self-support and governance.

Self-reliance and Naagu

The long-time Secretary to the Church records how eight of its pioneer believers consented to tenant farm a land in the years 1951-1954. God blessed their effort and gave a great yield. In gratitude, these god-fearing elders brought some of the produce to the Church as a free-will offering.

> The eight pioneer elders were: (1) Chinna Kondanna, (2) Bayappa, (3) Chinna Sanjanna, (4) Ganganna, (5) Chinna Jammanna, (6) Dannada Ashanna, (7) Pedda Sanjanna, (8) and Chinna Alisab. The source from free will offering was lent to Chinna Kondanna for four consecutive years and thus the grain, in other words the Church treasury increased. (Secretary, *SV [Minutes] 1951-2005*, 3)

This grain was lent on interest. Thus began the history and practice of *Naagu* [lending grain on interest]. Thus, "to record these barrowings and repayments, a treasurer and elders were elected" (R. Zachariah, *SV 1951-2005[Minutes]*, 3-4)." Up until then, the "pastor-teacher" of the church was the sole recorder. That is why the peasant church was unaware of the treasury. It appears that under pastors the church grew in spirit and education but not in leadership and self-support. Thus, beginning in the 1950s, the church was intentionally run by elders. It is governed by a Panchayat (Elders Council).

To ensure economic independence, the church introduced lending grain. Culturally, lending "seed–grain" is called *Naagu*. Lending is on half interest. Grains like paddy and millet are lent to a borrower at the time of sowing. The borrower repays at the time of harvest (four months duration) adding half to the measure taken. For instance, if a borrower takes 100 kilograms of paddy, he repays 150 kilograms at the time of harvest. The half measure interest becomes income to the church. This income, in kind, is redistributed as the *Naagu* next year. When the *Naagu* accumulated reached more than what the community needed, the church "hoarded" (stored) the grain and sold it for profit when market prices shot up. To facilitate this social system, a portion of the parsonage serves as *gummi* or "storage space" to the church, even today. *Gummi* is a large, round bamboo basket, six feet in radius and about twelve feet in height. Traditionally, villagers store grain in these containers for long periods.

The other forms of support to the church include *panduga patti* (membership fee), first fruits and *mokkubadi sanda* (free-will offering).

Table 17: Sources and Types of Income and Expenditure for 1999-2005

S. No.	Sources of Income	Types of Expenditure
01	Festival offerings– Christmas and free will; Good Friday and free will; New Year and free will; Harvest festival and free will	Petromax lamps – Kerosene – gas cylinder refilling
02	Donations– to honour the Reddy family and to pay the sweeper of the church by Christians and people of other faiths.	Electrical equipment– – repairs or replacement
03	Marriage-related contributions/fee– - engagement fee - bride or groom fixing contribution - wedding fee	Support to Pastor– Full salary, official travel, - firewood, house repairs/additions– - Christmas gift for clothes– - Christmas groceries– - incidental expenses (spouse funeral) Partial: -medical help, children, marriage help
04	Paddy sale proceeds– paddy interest proceeds	Donation to other churches

Contd., **Table 17**: Sources and Types of Income and Expenditure for 1999-2005

S. No.	Sources of Income	Types of Expenditure
05	Millet/jawar sale proceeds — Empty jute/plastic bag sale proceeds	Church building and premises upkeep: • Wall clocks repair · • Wall text writing • White wash • Festival decoration • Bore well repairs • Gates, doors and locks
06	Rent proceeds of caste vocation land (Mudda Manyam)	To MB Conference Ministries • Bible Schools • Bible Colleges
07	Sunday Offerings— Worship and Free Will	Communion expenses

08	Support to Pastor
	   (3 times in a year)
	   (1) 32 measures of paddy
	   (2) Good Friday contribution
	   (3) Christmas contribution
	Occasional expected:
	• Christmas Carol Contributions,
	• house warming, hair cutting, or muhurtam of cotton crop
		Festivals—expenses
		Decorations PA system rentals
		• Christmas
		• Good Friday
		• New Year
		• Harvest
		• Refreshments

09	Women Fellowship offerings	Chain Prayer —Refreshments
10	Youth fellowship offerings	Stationary
11		PA System —Purchase and Repairs
12		Musical instruments — Purchase and Repairs
13		Honorariums —To P.M. Reddy— To daughter of P. M. A. Reddy
14		Church Sweeper

Source: Treasurer; 1999-2005 Income and Expenditure Registers

But if the crops fail, the borrower shall pay double the measure taken on the next year. Violators of such a covenant are socially boycotted. For example, the church panchayat ruled in consensus that "if a family fails to contribute, for two years in succession toward the support of their pastor–the church and church council shall not participate in any function of the said family" (Secretary, *SV [Minutes] 1951-2005*, 85). But after repeated warnings, such a household is restored to fellowship upon full payment of the dues. As per reports, in October of 2006, the Church stopped lending grain because people troubled the elders with all kinds of lame excuses. One borrower blamed the other saying, "If such and such one repaid, I will."

Another factor that stopped the practice of *Naagu* (lending grain on interest) was in famine years; the poor peasants felt it was taxing. Instead, the church started buying grain during harvest on fair prices, hoarding it and selling it when market prices were profitable. In this sense, the peasant Church serves as a farmers' society. It teaches self-help and self-support systems to the congregation. This is a reason why most of the Gadwal field churches live in two spheres — self-support and self-governing, but in general lack training and guidance (as elsewhere) in self-propagation. However, churches are active in self-theologising, the fourth sphere, as evidenced in the land-grabbing dispute.

The above paragraphs show that churches grow out of hard-earned money and free-will offerings. Its financial stability depends on innovative methods, but is based on available resources. Youth take initiative in the welfare of the church. The church seeks innovative ideas, such as auctioning free-will offerings, such as eggs, animals and fowls (like hens), or renting out paddy *Kolakadava* (measuring iron pot). It is recorded that R. Danam "auction-rented" the *Kolakadava* for 155 seirs (a seir is 1.4 kilograms of grain) during 1973-1974 (see *SV [Minutes] 1951-2005*, 14). The church's pioneer elders take risks. They are "models" to emulate. Such leaders form part of the church's ancestors of faith in addition to the white missionaries and the national pastor-teachers. Further, leadership is necessitated to record the contributions of God's people. The church Panchayat is accountable to the annual General Body held either in December or January each year.

In this procedure, the church as a society does face incidences of discipline. How would it practice its social discipline? The church is united against a head of the household in transgression. It resolves in consensus to issue such a member a notice of social ostracism until he rectified the matter.

Panchayat and Church Discipline

There are a few incidences of mismanagement of the church treasury. A treasurer in 1972 was "taken to task" by the special general body (see *SV Minutes 1951- 2005*, 13). By 1974, the system of a *Standing Committee* was constituted in addition to panchayat leadership to process and implement disciplinary action against violators, but the Standing Committee works under the church elders; violations such as abusing elders and evading contributions towards the support of the pastor cause disciplinary actions.

A member of the church did not care to fellowship with the church and did not bother to pay his yearly contributions. In 1975, his daughter was to be married. So the family head had to send word to the church elders. In return, the church elders required of him to consent to pay his dues and yearly contributions:

> That Mr. 'S' consent to pay his dues; rupees hundred, and pay his yearly contribution in kind to the support of pastor and renew his fellowship with the church panchayat (Secretary, *SV [Minutes] 1951-2005*, 17).

Only upon the assent of this member did the church panchayat see his daughter's marriage solemnised by their pastor under the auspices of the church. It is quite a social pressure and a question of identity and influence for individual families.

Twelve years have passed peacefully since Mr. "S" was disciplined. In early 1987, after the above event, an influential and wealthy member of the church went too far and hurt the image of the church panchayat and its pastor. Mr. "P" conducted the marriage of one of his son's and solemnised it by hiring a town pastor, at his residence. The church panchayat took it to heart, interpreted it as sowing seeds of schism and a trespass of the peasant church ethos. Moreover, on the day of the wedding, the chairman of the Gadwal Field Association visited the village church. Thus, the trespass was also against the regional Church Head. The Madiri Puram church would not let it go until the member in question asked for forgiveness in public in the presence of two local Reddys and the regional Church Head at a later date. The church Panchayat issued a social ostracism warning to Mr. "P", saying:

> You have violated the church's social harmony by conducting your son's marriage at your residence, that too by hiring a pastor from outside

> without the permission of the church. Hence, you are advised to rectify
> the matter in the presence of the Gadwal Field Association leadership
> and the local village patron P. M. Reddy and R. Reddy of Konkal village,
> until such time the church cannot fellowship with you (Secretary, *SV*
> *[Minutes] 1951-2005*, 61).

The influential member understood the seriousness of the issue and image loss for his household and asked for forgiveness of the regional church Head in the presence of local and neighbouring village Reddys on 26 June 1987, "What I have done is in violation of the church principles, forgive me." (Secretary, *SV Minutes 1951-2005*, 61)

Some members deliberately go against social integrity either as simple disobedience as in the case of Mr. "S," or due to planned spiritual and economic superiority complexes like in the case of Mr. "P." Unlike societies where individualism is exercised, in both the above-mentioned cases, the community would not tolerate it and the members in question could not stand the threat of social isolation for long. But there is a way to regain honour, if one repents. In this sense, the peasant panchayat way of disciplinary action is restorative, in contrast to the punitive justice exercised in industrial societies. The next model is the "Reddy-Christian Dalit Panchayat" in Madiri Puram village.

Reddy-Christian Dalit Political Consensus

Christian Dalits in the Gadwal region are known as "Reddy-Christians," more so in the Madiri Puram village. Reddys, as landlords, oppressed Dalits for centuries in Andhra Pradesh. The Reddy's are the *kshatriya* (ruler caste) in Madiri Puram village. Kshatriyas are second in the caste hierarchy. Mr. R. Danam claims that Pakanati Adi Sheshi Reddy was of "royal blood" from the Pakanati Somanadri family. Late prince Pakanati Somanadri was renowned as a mighty warrior at Gadwal Fort (Danam 2005, 20).

The late Pakanati Adi Sheshi Reddy (1904-1970) was one such bond labourer of the Dalits. A a *zamindar* (landed man), he treated Christian Dalits as untouchables. He hired forty Christian Dalit bond labourers all through his life. Yet, he was exceptionally benevolent to poor Dalits. He fought to secure 205 acres of *gairani bhoomi* (government land) for Christian Dalits. He fought it against the rest of his high-caste contestants for the same land led by *Akula Linganna* of the Nayak family. Influential regional high-caste people, including the wealthy Reddys, joined muscle and might with the

Akula Linganna family. Pentanna, Tolla, an intelligent Christian Dalit priest at Maremma temple, says:

> Adi Sheshi Reddy rivals included, Tanagala Yama Reddy, Alampur Chandra Shekar Reddy, and Rajoli Ramadas (maternal uncle of Mr. M.S. Damodara Rao of Madiri Puram) and Sunkesula Ananta Reddy. But Adi Sheshi Reddy never left the fight in between (Pentanna, Tolla, 2006, 14; cf. Damodara Rao 2006, 3).

Tanagala village Reddys are known for their wealth. Alampur and Rajoli were erstwhile princely states. Sunkeshula village has rich landlords. Venkat Rao, the Brahmin and the grandfather of Damodara Rao, was the revenue collector over seven villages.[2] The Damodara Rao had served Madiri Puram village as *karnam* (revenue collector) for 29 years. The Damodara Rao family owned 1,000 acres of land in Madiri Puram, while Adi Sheshi Reddy had just over 220 acres (besides, of course, many acres in Rangapuram and Paipadu villages).

But all the above-mentioned mighty landlords and their political influences were no match to Pakanati Adi Sheshi Reddy's determination and *laulikamu* (political acumen).[3]

It took Pakanati Adi Sheshi Reddy 12 long years (1949-1961) to win the case to secure 205 acres of government land. He spent about Rs 70,000 (c.1795 US dollars) to pursue the case, moving from the lower to the Apex Court in the country. He charged nothing in return from Christian Dalits, except that they stand united with him in consensus all along and that they bear individual travel expenses whenever the court summoned them. The Christian Dalit elders at that time never abandoned their Reddy. In fact, about 40 Dalit youth provided their Reddy with personal security round the clock. Moreover, the elders of the church at that time met and prayed everyday for 12 years in their hut church[4] for the success of the Reddy cause. Their consistent prayers were evidence of consensus.

---

[2] Venkatrao was "*karnam*" [revenue collector] for the following seven villages: 1). Rajoli 2). T. Garlapadu 3). Tummilla, 4). P. Garlapadu, 5). Madiri Puram, 6). Mundladinne, and 7). Tummalapalle.

[3] *Laulikamu* has three shades of meaning: social and legal diplomacy or acumen, winsome nature, and proactive leadership. Laulikamu is a colloquial Telugu term for "laukikamu" which means secular shrewdness. It represents one's ability to navigate through rough political weathers.

[4] The present sanctuary was built in 1973.

During these years, when his opponent Reddy captured some of his Christian Dalits at Alampur, their magistrate town, and forced them to deny allegiance to their benefactor [Sheshi] Reddy, they would not give in. In such situations, Pakanati Adi Sheshi Reddy made it plain to his opponents: "If you can make one Dalit of my village turn against me, I will wear bangles and will go by female form of my name, "Sheshamma" (Danam 2005, 4).

The case was declared in favour of Pakanati Adi Sheshi Reddy in 1961 by the Apex Court in Delhi, the capital of India. In light of the Supreme Court judgment, the Mahabubnager District Collector ordered the Revenue Department to "distribute 205 acres of *gairani bhoomi* (government land) as per the discretion of Pakanati Adi Sheshi Reddy" (Rao, 2005, 3-4). Damodara Rao, who served the village as *karnam* (revenue collector) for 29 years (1962-1983, 1999-2002), alleges that Pakanati Adi Sheshi Reddy forcibly "grabbed" the land for Dalits. However, Rao recalled the progression in the case from his revenue records that Pakanati Adi Sheshi Reddy registered the land to six Christian Dalit family heads:

(1) Pani Lasumanna S/OAshappa

(2) Ganganna S/O Buddanna

(3) Samelu S/O Sanjanna

(4) Dannada Ashanna S/O Pakiranna

(5) Kondanna S/O Dollappa and

(6) Tekuru Timmanna S/O Naganna. (Rao 2005, 4)

Thus, each of the above-mentioned households received about 33 or 34 acres of land for free. Landless Dalits became landed people. Hailing the good side of Pakanati Adi Sheshi Reddy, Rao continues to note, Adi Sheshi Reddy,

- Was a man of determination (see also *Akula* Linganna 2006)[5]

- Had forgiving spirit if his opponent humbled himself

- Harassed but never ordered elimination of his opponent and never encouraged theft (Rao 2005, *ibid.*)

---

[5] Akula Sheshanna, the younger brother of Akula Linganna [the staunch opponent of Adi Sheshi Reddy] compared the character of Adi Sheshi Reddy to that of *Bhismachari*, the warrior guru to both Kauravas and Pandavas in Epic *Mahabharata*. Sheshanna goes on to say that there was none who will be born with the determination like that of Adi Sheshi Reddy.

The description given above indicates that Pakanati Adi Sheshi Reddy is a benevolent Sarpanch to the Christian Dalits because he secured 205 acres of land for them for free. Thus, Christian Dalits in the village coined a proverb to describe their bonds with the Reddy, *puliki malavasaramu, malaku pulavasaramu*; it means "tiger and thicket are inseparable" (Danam 2005, 1). Thicket provides the tiger with a place to hide and hunt game. The presence of a tiger (Adi Sheshi Reddy) makes the de-foresters to be cautious about indiscriminately felling the trees or bushes (Christian Dalits). The key here is Christian Dalit identity with the Reddy in political consensus. It can also mean that the church was in agreement with the Reddy in pursuing the case in a law court. This shows that Christian Dalits are in agreement with the patron Reddy, seeking justice in national courts apart from village panchayat.

The social-political consensus between Christian Dalits and Pakanati Adi Sheshi Reddy also meant that they play down their Christmas celebration. During the entire period of his fight for the government land, Pakanati Adi Sheshi Reddy had a vow that if he succeeded, he would offer his hair to his lord Sri Venkateswara at the Tirupati pilgrimage centre. The Apex Court judgment came in favour of him around Christmas in 1961. Christian Dalits very much desired his presence in the Church on Christmas Day. The Reddy instructed them to play down the Christmas festival, but said, "We will celebrate the New Year's Day in a big way" (Dhyryam 2005, 5). Then he left for Tirupati, the most famous Hindu pilgrim centre in South India. He had his long hair offered to his god. When he returned from fulfilling his vows, Christian Dalits received him with *tappetlu* (percussion drums),

> Interestingly, the Reddy upon his return from Tirupati, went straight to visit the church and sought the prayers of Rev. N. R. Samuel, the pastor of that time. He should usually go visit and break coconut at every major Hindu temple in the village but to our knowledge, he did not do so. From the church, he went to his home (Dhyryam 2005, 5).

This suggests that he had some respect for the God of the Christian Dalits and, for some reason, dropped the idea of visiting his Hindu temples. Pakanati Adi Sheshi Reddy and Christians had a huge New Year celebration that year. This shows the bonds between the Reddy and the Christians. When I raised the issue with Dhyryam, the most resourceful key informant, of the propriety of playing down the birth of Jesus Christ [Christmas] for the sake of a Reddy, his reply was significant: "Well that was only for that year [1961], not a tradition, and there is nothing wrong with celebrating New Year with a person who fought for us and our upliftment" (Dhyryam 2005, 5).

Madiri Puram Christian Dalits go by the word of Pakanati Adi Sheshi Reddy for a second reason; Reddy had compassion for the poor. His household gifted (1) a *Mangala Sutra* (marriage ring) to every couple that got married (Isaac 2005, 8). Even if there were ten marriages a day, the Reddy would gift ten *Mangala Sutras*. *Mangala Sutra* is prepared by the groom's family. It is the "sign" that a woman is married. Traditionally, a groom ties a cotton thread soaked in turmeric paste around the neck of his bride. *Mangala Sutra* is a gold piece (cup shape) in a thread hanging on the chest of the bride. This is a symbol; it declares that her man is alive. It is meant also to set boundaries for men besides her husband. It is a mark of chastity. Absence of it is caused either by the death of her husband or upon breaking her marital vows with him. Disregard for *Mangala Sutra* by a woman is unwelcome by society. Disrespect to *Mangala Sutra* brings dishonour to the lady and her family. Losing it is a serious matter. (2) The Reddy family was also charitable in another way. When a Dalit woman gave birth to a child, *Reddamma* (the wife of the Reddy) used to send "a blouse piece, about three kilograms of rice and some peanut oil" (Isaac 2005, 8). This is a sign of care and appreciation as mothers in society.

Reddy-Christian Dominant Class

There is a third angle for Reddy-Christian Dalit political consensus. Late Pakanati Adi Sheshi Reddy provided Christian Dalits with social and physical protection. Pakanati Adi Sheshi Reddy and Christian Dalits formed the "dominant class" unlike in any other village. He stood for their cause.

Figure 14:
P. Adi Sheshi Reddy
(1904-1970)

In one of the following years after, the 205 acres of land dispute was settled in favour of the Reddy, a Christian Dalit *Pelli uureginpu* (marriage procession) was to reach the Reddy house to pay their respects to him. The newlywed couple bows down in respect to the Reddy and his patron help (like marriage loan). The procession is usually taken during the cool of the day, on bullock carts. The bullock carts are well decorated and people are in their best dress and in jovial mood. The marriage procession is a great celebration. The procession needs to pass through the *Boya* (hunter) caste section of the village to reach the Reddy mansion. But the bullock carts were forcably blocked by the *Boya*s (hunter/sudra caste) near their section of the village. During the heated exchange, Sudras even broke the yoke of the ox carts. The *Boyas* were among the ones who lost the court case.

The violence was reported to their Reddy. He encouraged the Christian Dalit leadership: "Show your manliness or wear bangles"[6] (Danam 2005, 6) and asked them to teach the Sudras a lesson. That night he supplied money to the Dalits to buy *lathis* (clubs) and *vankayalu* (crude bombs). Additionally, some Christian Dalit leaders are skilled cobblers, so they produced enough leather slings over night. Christian Dalit women gathered stones and spread them along the road as small mounds, in the disguise of developing the main road. No Sudra doubted their intention.

Every day, most of the *Boya* farmers pass through the Dalit section of the village to reach their farmlands. At the dawn the next day, while the *Boyas* (hunter caste) were driving their oxen with farming goods to their farmlands, Christian Dalits attacked the *Boyas* with their slings and gravel stones chasing them back to their section of the village and pursued them until they drove them out

---

[6] *Magatanamu choopandi leda gajulesukondira* in Telugu

of the village. From then on, Sudras do not touch the Christian Dalit community. This is how the proverb, *puliki malavasaramu-malaku pulavasaramu*, i.e., "tiger and thicket need each other" is reinforced.

During my interview, recollecting village events, a former pastor raised his right hand to enact how people would commit their allegiance to the Reddy in the affairs of the church and the village, "*Ha! Reddy etla jeppite atla jestamu* ["Alas! As the Reddy says, so we will act."] (See Isaac 2005, 8) To this date, it is an unwritten law.

Emergence of a New Hierarchy in Church Panchayat

It may be mentioned that due to their social bonds with the Dalits, the Reddys of Madiri Puram village have some regard for the Christian God. This entire story shows the emergence of a hierarchy of a different nature in matters of church polity. The Reddy sits in major decision-making assemblies of the church. In one sense, it is an opportunity to proclaim the gospel. But it is also an occasion for stifling its witness[7] since the pastor of the church receives minimal respect as compared to what exists between the Reddy and his Christian Dalit supporters. As a result, a hierarchy is created representing a pyramid as follows:

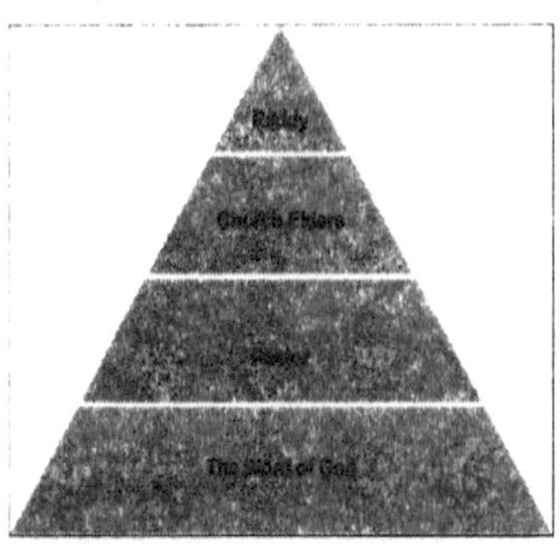

Figure 15: Reddy-Christian Dalit Panchayat Hierarchy

This brings me to consider the following realities in Church Panchayat. In a way, the church cannot be separated from the power

---

[7] No Reddy has worshiped the God of the Bible, so far. However, rumor has it that Manikya Reddy was affected with leprosy because he denied his vow to Jesus Christ. This Reddy received the "*deevena*" of Sadhu Yosepu to beget children. When children were born he promised to donate a Jeep to the service of the Christian healer. But he never fulfilled it. And it is said that as a result he was struck with leprosy, from which the Sadhu was healed before he became a servant of Jesus Christ.

blocks in the village. It must work with them and point to their Creator and Lord of Lords.

It may be concluded that:

- Due to their social bonds with the Dalits, the Reddys of Madiri Puram village have some regard for Christian God.

- The role of Reddy creates a clear hierarchy of a different nature in matters of church governance. But it does present the church with unique opportunities to witness.

- Close relations with the Reddy have resulted in apprehensions of Shudras and Brahmans on Christian Dalits. This also includes limitations in relation to Christian witness to high-caste people.

- The pastor's word is marginal in decision making in general throughout Gadwal and Alampur provinces. He is treated as "an employee of the church" and has "limits in nurturing the congregation" (Pradeshi 2005, 21). This is one of the negative impacts of the panchayat way of church governance.

- When the Reddy and Elders of the church are "superior" to the pastor, insights from the Scriptures are down played.

However, there is welcome news of the "Reddy-Christian Dalit" combination of polity. That is, they are Christian in faith as well as "Reddy-Christian" in the polity of the church. Their combination forms the "dominant class" in the village. Why would they align with the Reddy for justice? In his dissertation, Krishna M. Ajjarapu deals with the reasons for this association. Ajjarapu states three reasons why Dalits remain as subordinates:

- Their continuous economic dependence on the landlords.

- The system of tenure maintained by the landlord and the eviction enacted in the event of trespassers have kept the lower castes immobilised.

- The tendency to refer their disputes to the high castes kept them inferior (Ajjarapu 2001, 190).

Nevertheless, a dominant class category is not as strong as ethnic or caste councils, but since 1949, the Reddy-Christian Dalit dominance is an unwritten norm in Madiri Puram village. See Figure 16 below.

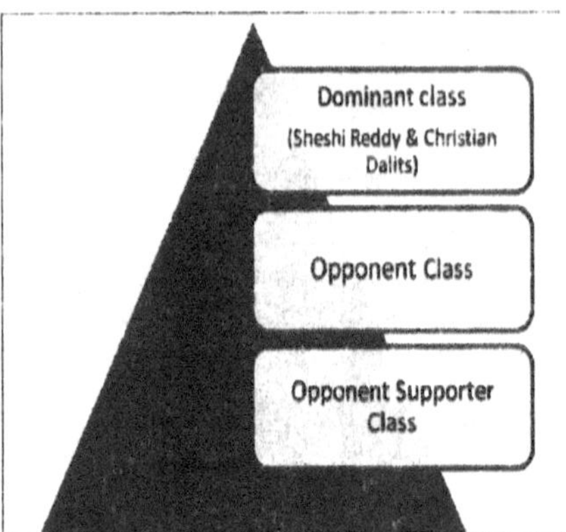

Figure 16: Reddy-Christian Dalit Dominant Class

Figure 16 depicts that the dominant class has opponent classes.

The dominant class consists of Reddy and Christian Dalits from the low caste. Their local opponent class consists of priest, trades, hunter and Sudra castes. We also have the supporting non-local opponent supporter class, which is mostly Reddy and Brahmins from the neighbouring region and villages. Dominant class creates and maintains status-quo. The distinction that we need to keep in mind is that Christian Dalits needed to keep their colony together for the cause of acquiring the 205 acres of ceiling land. They needed to maintain consensus within their section of the village. Consensus does not mean that every household among Christian Dalits agrees with the decision of the Reddy-Christian "dominant class" panchayat.

An example of this difference is shared by two households. Mr. Paras recalled that his father *vadlapani* (carpenter) Chinna Sanjanna was supposed to get a share of 205 acres of land, but he was denied it by the benevolent Reddy because his father refused to swear falsely against the land ownership of a Nayak family in the village. Nayak families opposed tooth and nail the Adi Sheshi Reddy's fight for 205 acres of land for the sake of Christian Dalits. Mr. Paras said,

> Chinna Sanjanna, my father, refused to swear falsely against a Nayak, the legal owner of a certain piece of land in the village. He did this in order to keep his Christian conscience clear. At this, Adi Sheshi Reddy got furious and was waiting for an opportune time. The Reddy then reminded my father's Christian commitment to deny him a portion of 205 acres of *gairani bhoomi* (government land, Paras 2005, 3).

In another case, Adi Sheshi Reddy harassed R. Sadhu, a Christian Dalit. R. Sadhu was head servant of the wealthy Brahman family in the village. This Brahman family was party to opponents of Adi Sheshi Reddy. At that time, R. Sadhu only had a couple of his 25 years of bond service left. The Reddy summoned R. Sadhu to break his service during a sowing season. R. Sadhu pleaded:

> I am sorry patron Reddy, this is a sowing season and it will be too hard for the Brahman farmer to run the affairs without my head servantship. Moreover, I am at the close of my service years, let me finish my commitment years and then I will stop serving the *Karnam* family. Adi Sheshi Reddy got angry with me and he ordered the plunder of my ripe peanut crop that year (R. Sadhu 2006, 3).

In the above two cases, neither R. Sadhu, nor carpenter Sanjanna (both Christian Dalits) could stop Adi Sheshi Reddy from his hurtful resolves. Nor could they join his opponent party or resist the broad consensus of support among Christian Dalits for the Reddy. They could only experience hurt, but not resist the "Reddy-Christian Dalit hegemony."

Analysis: Consensus and Hierarchy Replicated

My interest in this chapter is to demonstrate consensus in the Christian Dalit panchayat in Madiri Puram village. Three categories have emerged from my foregoing data. Firstly, Christian Dalits still maintain *kula* (caste) panchayat along with the church panchayat in that they pray to God but decide on the basis of Dalit customs. R. Danam has said, "We pray as Christian Dalit caste elders before we start to hear a case, but we resolve according to the need and the caste values" (Danam 2005, 25).

Secondly, they have church panchayat; and thirdly, there is also the village Panchayat. Church Panchayats have mostly been in regard to self-support, self-governance and disciplinary actions with human face.

In a village in South India, everyone knows everybody else. There is seldom anything hidden. A family's history, its economic status and health conditions are known to the village council. Unless a household rebels, panchayat judgments are pro-life in a village. In extreme cases, a renegade household is socially ostracised, but when they repent, fellowship is restored to the wronged person. Panchayat is a human way of settling issues. It is different from the tribal councils where there is the likelihood that just one or two tribes are in dispute. In a South India village, there are a number of ethnic communities and each caste has its own Panchayat.

Thirdly, we have seen how the Reddy-Christian Dalit "political consensus" functions in the village. All this raises important missiological questions.

Replication and Consensus in Church Panchayat?

Theoretically, replication of consensus in the pattern of the Hindu Panchayat is contested in my research village. Their social order can neither be put into nor understood apart from Hindu *dharma* (rules) structures. Hierarchy, as a social system, aims at bringing social harmony as well as social disturbance. For example, Dalits in India regard caste hierarchy as subjugating their human dignity. I have cited examples to that effect (see Chapter 5; "two names to one").

Michael Moffat has written an influential work titled, *An Untouchable Community of South India (1979)*. The chief argument of Moffat is that Dalits (*harijans*[8]) live in consensus with the wider Indian culture by replicating virtually every relation and institution from which they have been excluded by the higher castes. Moffat says that untouchables are also included in the Hindu social system by accepting their low social roles as *complementary*. Moffat's thesis is substantiated by his ethnographic study among the untouchables of Endavur village in Tamil Nadu, South India. Moffat was inspired by Louis Dumont (*Homohierarchicus* 1966), an authority on Hindu social order.

Robert Deliege, Professor, has convincingly critiqued Moffat's conclusions. I agree with Deliege, for his reasoning agrees with my research findings at Madiri Puram village.

For my purposes, I am testing whether consensus in the Christian Dalit panchayat at Madiri Puram is also a replication of caste hierarchy and whether it follows Hindu cultural values. In order to do this, I need to look briefly at Deliege's critique of Moffat. Firstly, Moffat's finding is that Dalits *replicate* Hindu social structures. In matters of Dalit peoples, one way to understand Hindu caste categories is to look at it as a system of "inclusion" and "exclusion." Dalits are part of the system when they are taken as structurally subservient and excluded from ritual purity-impurity functions. Dalits are impure because they touch (clear) the ground as agriculture

---

[8] "Children of God" as called by Mahatma Gandhi.

labourers and remove carcasses. On the contrary, they complement in purifying the village from impurities. However, unfortunately for Moffat, Dalits do not have a separate "subculture" from the majority Hindu culture. Thus, they are in *consensus* with the Hindu system:

> They do not possess a separate subculture. They are not detached or alienated from the 'rationalizations' of the system. Untouchables possess and act upon a thickly textured culture whose fundamental definitions and values are identical to those of more global Indian village culture. The 'view from the bottom' is based on the same, principles and evaluations as 'the view from the middle' or 'the view from the top.' The cultural system of Indian Untouchables does not distinctively question or revalue the dominant social order. Rather, it continuously recreates among Untouchables a microcosm of the larger system (Moffat quoted in Deliege 1992, 156).

Secondly, Moffat finds that Dalits *replicate* purity and impurity practices when they are in their own caste section of Endavur, Moffat's research village. That is, when separate from the high-caste section of the village, Dalits are in "consensus" with the majority culture. The emphasis here is that when excluded, Dalits are more conscious about caste distinctions within themselves. Moffat wrote:

> The Untouchables of Endavur replicate among themselves, to the best of their materially limited abilities, almost every relationship from which they have been excluded by the *uur* (village high[9]) Castes. And this replicatory order is constructed in the same cultural code that marks highness and lowness, purity and impurity, superodination and subordination, among the higher Castes. It thus implies among the lower Castes of Endavur a deep cultural consensus on the cognitive and evaluative assumptions of the system as a whole (Moffat in Deliege 1992, 156).

What all this means is that replication of popular "power grids" is the stronger indicator for "consensus" that Dalits are Hindu (Indian culture).

Deliege summarised three arguments of Moffat over his "replicatory" principle among Dalits ("Harijans" Deliege term) as follows:

> First, the untouchables are divided into different castes, which replicate the main caste order; secondly, the Paraiyars, the main Harijan caste within Endavur, are themselves divided into hierarchized grades; finally, Harijan religion, to a large extent, replicates the cult of Hindu deities found among higher Castes (Deliege 1992, 157).

---

[9] My addition to explain the term *uur* and the author's sense here.

Then Deliege precisely differs with Moffat by saying that the untouchables are different people-exteriors. Deliege writes,

> One should notice that the very idea of replication implies some exteriority. To replicate is to reproduce someone else's institutions or to move some practices from one context to another…The very concept of replication thus implies that there is something different about untouchables. If it were not so, this concept would be quite meaningless. I find it useful precisely because it translates the ambiguity of the untouchable's position, at the same time similar and different, inside and outside society (Deliege 1992, 160).

Dalits have different power models or customs to judge. But why do they replicate the popular social structure (replication) and culture (consensus) as proposed by Moffat? Deliege offers three reasons why Moffat's concept of replication and consensus should be rejected. Firstly, Dalits did not create the caste system or Hindu religion.

> Furthermore, replication, even when it clearly occurs, cannot be taken as the sole and ultimate evidence for consensus. It is true that untouchables are both Indian and Hindu: they speak the language of the majority, eat the same food when they can afford it, follow the same customs when they are allowed to; they are divided into Castes, and worship village deities. Yet Harijans did not create the caste system or Hindu religion (Deliege 1992, 166).

The question in my mind is how we can then reckon with the Reddy-Christian hierarchy in Madiri Puram. The answer Deliege provides me is:

- Dalits did not create the Hindu caste hierarchy; therefore, the Reddy-Christian hierarchy is not a "replication" of the Hindu structure in Madiri Puram.

- The Reddy-Christian dominant class in Madiri Puram is unique. There are no such models as far as this research goes or in my experience in the village of my birth or the village of my growth.

- Deliege is right in saying that even if Dalits replicate caste structures, they do it not as part of their belief system, but because they are forced to. (Deliege 1992, 166)

It may be mentioned that the caste hierarchy is a Hindu category employed to contextualise the Reddy-Christian Dalit consensus. I am using it to explain how Adi Sheshi Reddy and Christian Dalits function differently in Madiri Puram village.

It is also true that Adi Sheshi Reddy always felt that he was superior in caste to the Dalits for whom he risked his time and money (c. US$ 1750) for 12 long years. Why did he fight for 205 acres of government land for so many years while he knew he was (1) working against his own caste structure (hierarchy) sanctioned by his religion (*Rgveda* 10.90 and *Manu dharma Sastra* I.91 (Manu's Law Code) and that (2) the entire village and the regional high-caste people opposed him tooth and nail? (3) That Adi Sheshi Reddy, all through his life, trusted the Christian Dalit consensus to support his cause. They even prayed every day for 12 years for the success of the case in law courts.

In all probability, in some ways, it seems that Adi Sheshi Reddy was used as an instrument of God as Cyrus the Emperor was in the Old Testament.

> Yahweh said, of Cyrus, He is my shepherd and will accomplish all that
> I please; he will say of Jerusalem, 'Let it be rebuilt,' and of the temple,
> 'Let its foundations be laid' (Isa 44:28).

Likewise, Pakanati Adi Sheshi Reddy did not believe in Jesus Christ, the Lord of the Christians in Madiri Puram. The prophet Isaiah clarified the matter further for us:

> I am the Lord, and there is no other; apart from me there is no God.
> I will strengthen you 'though you have not acknowledged me' (Isa 45:5).

I judge that this is what the Christian Dalits of Madiri Puram feel when they say, *Puliki malavasaramu-malaku Pulavsaramu* (tiger and thicket are inseparable). When he won the c ase, Adi Sheshi Reddy had instructed them to play down the Christmas festival and that "we will celebrate the New Year's Day in a big way" (Dhyryam 2005, 5). As noted earlier, he then went to fulfill his vows to his god Sri Venakateswara at Tirupati.

When he returned, it was a big celebration of God's grace, the joy of owning land, as well as a celebration of their consensus for 12 years. A point that should be clear here is that Adi Sheshi Reddy did not believe in Jesus Christ as his Saviour as per my respondents. God is not concerned about our shallow concerns for conversions. Yahweh does not compel anybody, but does expect us to recognise his sovereignty as there is "no other God besides Him" (Isa 45: 5). In this sense, the meaning of *every knee shall bow, every tongue shall confess* (Phil 2: 20-11) could mean that even those who did not trust Jesus as their Lord while on earth, will also acknowledge Jesus as sovereign on the day of judgment. God uses some, even though they have not "acknowledged him" (Isa 45: 5), as His way of opening up Himself to them.

The two other ways that we can understand Adi Sheshi Reddy's benevolence is to say that he wanted to prove himself a big man, since he was a migrant to the village from Ranga Puram (Rayalaseema, a different geographic region). As an alien, he sought the protection of Christian Dalits, his obedient bond labourers and not his high-caste compatriots who could question him. Yet, another way to interpret his character is to say that since he had blood, he proved to be one of those benevolent persons. It must have become an issue of image for him to stand with the Christian Dalits, while others opposed him. In any case, I trust that all regents must come under the rule of Yahweh. This was highlighted when Chinna Sanjanna refused to swear falsely against Adi Sheshi Reddy when summoned:

> Chinna Sanjanna, my father, refused to swear falsely against a Nayak, the legal owner of a certain piece of land in the village. He did this in order to keep his Christian conscience clear. At this, Adi Sheshi Reddy got furious and was waiting for an opportune time. The Reddy then reminded my father's Christian commitment to deny him a portion of 205 acres of *gairani bhoomi* (Government land, Paras 2005, 3).

So, the Christian character (not to swear falsely) was superior to the Reddy standards. However, a majority of Christian Dalits were in consensus with the harassment of the Reddy against innocents like Sanjanna. Dhyryam again helps us go a little deeper in our insights into Adi Sheshi Reddy's disposition. Dhyryam says:

> I personally know that as a rich landlord, Adi Sheshi Reddy misused his power by grabbing lands of some of his non-Dalit (high caste) clients by multiplying interests to the money he lent to them. He created documents to that effect. These people were robbed of their land to the tune of 50 acres of land. Adi Sheshi Reddy was good to Christian Dalits but not to the rest of the village (Dhyryam 2005, 6).

The truth, then, is that Christian self-identity is split between the powerful Reddy majority consensus and the minority Christian ethics such as the conscience—the issue raised by carpenter Sanjanna. Consensus in the world is against God at times. In order to be a big man, one creates opponents to the extent that he becomes blind to their needs. However, Adi Sheshi Reddy has shown a big heart, he sent a word to Sudrulu upon winning the case in the Supreme Court:

> I am willing to share the 205 acres of government land with you opponents also, provided you come and partake in the *uura bhojanam* (meal fellowship for the entire village). But the high Castes did not show up owing to hurt feelings (Danam 2005, 5).

Uncritical Contextualisation in Kula Panchayat

The other thing we noted in the field data is about the *kula* (caste/ clan) panchayat resolution. With regard to the Prakash-Pentamma couple, the *kula* panchayat was most human in understanding their need for progeny. They charged a fine to the adulterer, but condoned her (husband included) adultery in the end. They judged in accordance with Dalit jurisprudence. The answer could be that Christian Dalit judges have a greater responsibility for teaching and leading people to understand that "adoption" is a better way than committing adultery for procreation, though Prakash was disabled by polio.

Perhaps Prakash's parents could have been counseled in the first place to think about the issue of marriage for Prakash and may be adoption of a child, in addition to their disabled son, could have modified the situation. However, in this case, the most difficult question is addressing the sexual needs of Pentamma, since progeny is not the only issue at stake here.

I wish the Kula panchayat had merged into the church panchayat to think through the Prakash-Pentamma crisis. This may have meant that the church panchayat had consensus to pardon the sin of the woman, her adulterer, and her disabled husband, but advised all parties to "sin no more" (Jn 8: 11). The church panchayat has a place in the mission of God.

Principles of Critical Contextualisation: Hiebert

In the words of veteran missiologist Paul G. Hiebert, the *Kula* (clan) Panchayat headed by Christian Dalit judges has opted for uncritical contextualisation in condoning "adultery" (the old customs). Hiebert wrote that uncritical contextualisation has two weaknesses:

> First, it overlooks the fact that there are corporate and cultural sins as well as personal transgressions. Sin can be found in the institutions and practices of a society in the form of slavery, oppressive structures, and secularism. It is found in the cultural beliefs of people and exhibited as group pride, segregation against others, and idolatry. The gospel calls not only individuals but societies and cultures to change. Contextualization must mean the communication of the gospel in ways the people understand, but that also challenge them individually and corporately to turn from their evil ways (Hiebert 2000, 185; cf. 1995, 168).

The second weakness that alarms Hiebert about uncritical contextualisation (e.g the kula panchayat judgment) is that it opens the door to syncretism of all kinds (Hiebert 2000, 185). Instead, Hiebert has four very practical principles in doing critical contextualisation. A summary of those are hereunder. His basic concern for critical contextualisation comes from Christendom's neglecting to study people in difference to studying the scriptures and theology (see Hiebert 1999, 369-370). I will quote only the main concepts from his *Anthropological Insights for Missionaries* (2000):

> First, an individual or church must recognize the need to deal biblically with all areas of life. This awareness may arise when a new church is faced with births, marriages, or deaths and must decide what Christian rites, weddings, or funerals should be like . ... (2000, 186).

> Second, local church leaders and the missionary must lead the congregation in *uncritically* gathering and analyzing the traditional customs associated with the question on hand.... The purpose here is to understand the old ways, not to evaluate them. If we show any criticism of the customary beliefs and practices at this point, the people will not openly talk about them for fear of being condemned. We will only drive the old ways underground (*ibid.*).

> In the third step, the pastor or missionary should lead the church in a Bible study related to the question under consideration.... It is important, however, that the congregation be actively involved in the study and interpretation of Scripture so that they will grow in their own abilities to discern truth (*ibid.*).

> The fourth step is for the congregation to evaluate critically their own past customs in the light of their new biblical understandings and to make a decision regarding their use. . . Leaders may share their personal convictions and point out the consequences of various decisions, but they must allow the people to make the final decision if they wish to avoid becoming policemen. . . (*ibid.*, 187; 1995, 171; 1994, 64, 75-92, 88-91).

A final word of caution that Hiebert suggests is well taken:

> The missionary may not always agree with the choices the people make, but it is important as far as conscience allows, to accept the decisions of the local Christians and to recognize that they, too, are led by the Spirit of God. Leaders must grant others the greatest right they reserve for themselves, the right to make mistakes. The church grows stronger by consciously making decisions in the light of Scriptures, even when the decisions may not always be the wisest, than when it simply obeys orders given by others (*ibid.*, 190).

With regard to church leadership or panchayat, it finally boils down not just to ask who the in-charge is, but who the Lord of the church is. And I agree with Lesslie Newbigin that it is not even truth, justice or the worldviews that change people, but the truth of the person of Jesus Christ that will transform church governance, the world and its affairs:

> That truth is not a doctrine or a worldview or even a religious experience; it is certainly not to be found by repeating abstract nouns like justice and love; it is the man Jesus Christ in whom God was reconciling the world. The truth is personal, concrete, historical (Newbigin 1989, 170).

This person of Jesus has begun to change the Christian Dalits of Madiri Puram from their old traditions. He will mature not only them, but also the whole world in recognising that Jesus is Christ.

Summary

The aim of this chapter has been to show how the Madiri Puram Mennonite Brethren church does its panchayat/administration. We have considered three examples of how it practices its justice. Firstly, we found that this peasant church still continues to hold on to clan (*kula*) panchayat on consensus. We considered the case of the Prakash and Pentamma couple. Pentamma was condoned of her extra-marital relations since the *kula* panchayat decided from the human perspective that Mr. Prakash should have a progeny through her. The joy of progeny through one of the spouses opens the door for adultery. This is a continuing non-Christian Dalit practice. Instead, we suggest that the clan court merge with the church Panchayat and discuss the situation in detail and solve the issue based on biblical principles. The best way to continue the progeny is through adoption, which was an ancient and biblical way of continuing a family name (e.g., Abram was willing to consider Eliezer as his heir, Gen 15:3).

Secondly, the church Panchayat has rightly assumed its responsibility to find creative ways to choose its leadership of self-governance. And the elders of that time found the ways and means for self-support. Thus, the Gadwal area churches are mostly self-supported. They have very minimal ecclesial politics and influences. It was also pointed out that in this case, the pastor of that time had left for his seminary training to Devarakonda town without making proper arrangements for the running of the church. This is considered as an old way of shepherding churches as an important man. The youth of that time took initiative in choosing their leadership on consensus. *Naagu* (lending grain on ½ interest per crop) is one way they increased in giving. Free-will offerings, special offerings, annual contributions to the support of their pastor are other ways that they make their church self-supporting.

Church panchayat has also threatened its wayward members when they tried to evade church discipline and its social integrity. For instance, Mr. Paras was chastised for solemnising his son's marriage in front of his house by hiring pastor from a nearby town. The issue was so serious that he had to ask for forgiveness in the presence of the local Reddys and the regional church head. These issues are recorded in their minutes.

Thirdly, it was pointed out that the major disputes of the Madiri Puram village church are still settled under the chairmanship of the local Reddy. The thing is that Pakanati Adi Sheshi Reddy has shown them exceptional favours. He fought for 205 acres of government land and distributed it among them for free. This is where church governance needs to grow. The Adi Sheshi Reddy who graced them with land is no longer alive. Moreover, some people in the village say that due to his unjust activities (land grabbing and womanising), there is no progeny left to him. His cousin's children are the ones who rule the village. The pointer is that Adi Sheshi Reddy was unjust when compared to the biblical heroes. For example, St. Paul has exhorted his Corinthian congregation that in church disputes, it is God who should be our judge and not any human. Paul went to the extent of saying that the church even judges the fallen angels (1 Cor 6:1-11).

Paul wrote:

> Do you not know that the saints will judge the world? And if you are to judge the world, are you not competent to judge trivial cases. Do you not know that we will judge angels? How much more the things of this life! (v.2-3)

All this leads me to make some recommendations in my next chapter.

CONCLUSION

This part of the book will make some concluding remarks and offer a few areas for further research on the Indian village. Based on my ethnographic data and the foregoing research, I conclude that "change and continuity" are complementary yet conflicting worldviews intersecting in Madiri Puram, my research village. Madiri Puram is a pseudonym for a Mennonite Brethren Christian Dalit community in South India. Change or continuity is enforced by certain factors, the Good News of Jesus Christ being the primary influence since the 1920s in the village. Thus, their faith and practice forms are identity markers, while they continue some of their old beliefs and practices as well.

The late M. N. Srinivas (1967), a noted social anthropologist, has rightly identified two prominent "agents" of social change and continuity, namely "Sanskritisation" and "Westernisation." Sanskritisation is an aspiration to ritually upgrade one's caste status from a lower to a higher category. Such aspirations make some positional changes in a particular locality. But universally speaking, Srinivas, himself a Brahman, asserts that Brahman supremacy is unchallengeable. Thus, the caste system retains structural continuity (Srinivas 1967, 3).

Westernisation (modernisation) for Srinivas meant the changes ushered in by British Rule in India (1750-1947). The British have introduced their technology, jurisprudence, transportation and education, and they were made available to all sections and sexes of society, including the Dalits. One of the results of such efforts was the birth of the "new elite" like Raja Rammohan Roy, Mahatma Gandhi, the Tagores and the Vivekanandas. The new elite are open to "new ideas" thus affecting change in political and cultural spheres.

---

[1] Williams D. Premkumar looks at Evangelical Theology in Church architecture. He feels "The Church in the Spirit is God s presence in the world and its attention to architecture is a new creation product, a spiritual sacrifice." See Premkumar 2005, v. However, my view is that apart from viewing church architecture from a poetic point of view, we need researches on how Christian Dalit art forms enhance national integrity.

These new elite were open to new political and cultural ideas and were seminal in ushering new India:

> In the political and cultural front, westernization has given birth not only to nationalism but also to revivalism, communalism, "casteism," heightened linguistic consciousness and regionalism. To make matters more bewildering, revivalist movements have used western-type schools and colleges, and books, pamphlets and journals to propagate their ideas (Srinivas 1967, 55 -56; Bose 1994, 394).

Secondly, Westernisation paved ways to Dalit conversions to Christianity. Srinivas observes that converts to Christianity did not influence Indian society for three reasons:

1. They generally hailed from lower castes.
2. Conversion alienated them from majority society.
3. Conversion did not change their customs but just their faith (Srinivas 1967, 60).

The third impact of Westernisation is abolition of a few of the traditional practices, such as *suttee* (widow burning) in 1829, "female infanticide," "human sacrifice" and "slavery" in 1833 (Srinivas 1967, 47; Agnihotry 1987, 15; Srinivasan & Gary R. Lee 2004, 1115). Thus, the stage was set for my study.

Research Questions

In the light of the above claims and conflicting ideas, I have focused to study the Gilgal India Mennonite Brethren Church in Madiri Puram village from four perspectives. These perspectives serve as identity markers, namely:

1. How is change and continuity exhibited in the religious symbols of Madiri Puram village and how does this define their Christian identity?

2. How do Christians of Madiri Puram village resolve conflicts created by socio-economic status?

3. In what ways do Christians of Madiri Puram village enact change and continuity in morality and life guidance?

4. How do Christians of Madiri Puram village reach consensus in their church Panchayat (legal assembly)?

The core chapters of this book are developed to address the above four questions. In chapter 4, I have exhibited that the church has adapted "Norman architecture" from the local Reddy cattle shed and his residence for its porches. These porches are silent but a powerful symbol of their indigenous theology and identity. The elders of the construction of the sanctuary at the time (1973) have toured two districts (Kurnool and Mahabubnager) to consider Baptist and Mennonite Brethren church architectures but finally chose to adopt the local form. Norman architecture, plus synagogic replicas with wall text writing like the Ten Commandments and the photo icon of living healer-saint Sadhu Yosepu, (1962) adorn the church with beauty. Two specific identity markers are earmarked in their art and architecture.

Firstly, in difference to Srinivas' observations ("Western influences", Srinivas 1967, 60), the church porches are intentional about national or social integrity. It also proves that conversion to Christianity did not alienate Dalits from their "majority society" (contra Srinivas 1967, 60). Their association with the majority culture in the village is reinforced by their political alignment with the prominent Adi Sheshi Reddy. Thus, theirs is what I call "Reddy-Christian Dalit Panchayat" or governance. Further, the church porches also indicate that Christian Dalit customs are "modified" (refer to Srinivas 1967, 60) as evidence of change in their core faith and practices. For example, their exclusive faith in Jesus and the scriptures.

Secondly, the community is doing its critical contextualisation by adapting just three porches to represent the Christian trinity. Thirdly, on the contrary, I have also pointed out that when Maremma, the ferocious chief deity of the Dalits, is adapted and Sanskritised by the high castes in the village, her ritual status has been raised (Sanskritised), but her people and her Christian Dalit priest are degraded or de-Sanskritized (Srinivas 1967; Colpe 1987, 511). This is how the Christian Dalit ceremonial status is in tension between change and continuity.

In the chapter entitled, "Two Names to one Child: Socio-Economic Status in Creative Tension," I have addressed my second research question: "How do Christians of Madiri Puram village resolve conflicts created by socio-economic status?" A Christian Dalit child begins to live with two names: Viswas and Vikas, the former for the church circles and the latter for the purposes of the school. These two names mean two different worldviews as the child grows. "Viswas" refers to his Christian identity while "Vikas" satisfies his Scheduled Caste economic, educational and political necessities. In India, a Christian Dalit, most of the times is compelled to live in tension because of official and caste hegemonies. All this boils down for a Christian Dalit to say, "We are Christian by faith, but Hindu by religion" (*Vaarta*—a Telugu newspaper, Thursday, 7 November 1996, 10). I have identified these as existential compulsions. I have then reflected on this theme and said that these existential compulsions should not bind the Christian Dalit from seeing a higher obligation to His sovereign Lord and acknowledge His upliftment.

This would include efforts to secure reservation benefits to the Christian Dalits on par with Dalit converts to Buddhism or Sikhism, as well as losing economic benefits if it means to stand with Christ. For me the tension lies in between the two. It is not an easy task. It is a matter of judgment call when it matters Christian discipleship, which equally calls the nation to do justice to Christian Dalits.

In the chapter entitled, "Morality and Life Guidance", I have unpacked three events in the life of peasant Christian Dalit church of Madiri Puram. Morality has two sides: land grabbing and how a woman believer courageously faced a sexual assault on her life. The first event focused on how three households encroached 15 feet of sanctuary land. This is discontinuous with their Christian conscience. One of the three even consulted horoscopes to proceed with his evil design. Such an act is disgraceful, not even Hindu or Muslim sanctuaries are subject to such encroachments.

Interestingly, the church has not initiated disciplinary action against the land grabbers but arrested institutionalisation of such immorality by erecting a compound wall that cost the church c. 527 US dollars. The church's action has saved itself from a probable disintegration of the church. However, the church has recorded this immorality in its *Minutes* book. The church has settled this dispute under the chairmanship of the Reddy.

Secondly, on the reverse, I have highlighted Nirmala's Christian character. She has resisted a sexual assault on her person by a wayward Christian Dalit womaniser. This is a laudable Christian identity marker. Theoretically, Walter Brueggemann (*Theology of the Old Testament* 1997) has helped me analyse the concepts in this chapter. For him Exodus is an event in the life of Israel and the Ten Commandments at Sinai instituted their covenant with the Lord. Nirmala's story unravels how she teaches a harsh lesson to the womaniser. Her brave act is a telling story to the world that sin cannot be "institutionalised" (Brueggemann1997). It must be resisted (Heb 4:7).

Thirdly, in the matter of life guidance, I have discussed the peasant theology of prayer for monsoon rains. The church has the reputation, from non-Christian friends, that the Christian Dalit God is the one who orders rain, "*Mee devudu vana guripistadu.*"

The chapter entitled "Consensus and Church Panchayats" focused on three main types of administering justice among others. Firstly, I have documented that Christian Dalits in Madiri Puram still practice *Kula* Panchayat (clan justice system). I have examined how "Prakash and Pentamma" couple raises human concern for progeny after five years of married life. Prakash was terribly affected by polio in his childhood and was not able to have sex with his wife. Then Pentamma commits extra-marital relations, with the consent of her husband. In this case, the caste council had consensus on a three-point approach:

(1) We should help the Prakash couple live together even if we need to tell many lies.

(2) Adultery is sin, but divorce is also not healthy for the woman's family. They need progeny.

(3) When disturbed, a stone (spouse) meant for a platform should be re-adjusted back to the same platform and not dislocated to any other platform (Danam 2005, 26).

Secondly, I have depicted that, based on consensus, the church Panchayat has dealt with issues of self-governance, and self-support. The youth of that time (1951-1954) took the responsibility of choosing the Panchayat way of church leadership when their pastor left them directionless to further his seminary training. Church panchayat implements *Naagu* (lending grain on half interest per crop) as a way to strengthen the church's economic stability.

Further, unlike the five-year term in *Naya* (modern) panchayat, the peasant church chooses its elders each year on the pattern of a traditional Panchayat. It practices social ostracism as a way to punish wayward members. For example, someone who arranged his son's marriage ignoring the collective society and its elders' council was chastised. Mr. Paras, the trespasser, repented, "What I have done is in violation of the church principles, forgive me," (Secretary, *SV Minutes 1951-2005*, 61), then the fellowship was restored to Paras' household.

Thirdly, I have described how "Reddy-Christian" political consensus prevails even today. Adi Sheshi Reddy had fought for 205 acres of government land for 12 long years (1949-1961). Adi

Sheshi Reddy had moved the case from a lower to the Apex Court in the country. He fought it against his high caste contestants for the same land. The Reddy-Christian Dalit political consensus has led to "Reddy-Christian Dalit dominant class" unlike in any other village, as I know it. What this means is that all the major disputes of the church are settled under the headship of the local Reddy. Theoretically speaking, based on Robert Deliege, I have said that this is a unique combination and not a "replication" of the Hindu dominant caste hierarchy in India (Deliege 1992, 166). However, I sincerely feel, whether *kula* or church or dominant class, or any kind of consensus must come under the leadership of Christ

Further Research

My study is limited to just four areas of Christian Dalit life in Madiri Puram, a South Indian village. The dissertation has offered some insights into the areas of architecture, socio-economic struggles, morality and life guidance and the Panchayat way of administration. But there are a number of other areas that need further research.

According to the chapter on "art and architecture", the Madiri Puram village church was intentional about enhancing social bonds with the majority society. But this is just one limited piece that I could write about. There is more to explore on how Christian Dalits are contributing to the integrity of the nation. Such research will reduce the criticism of Indian Christianity for its alleged western thought forms, worship patterns and so on.

For example, noted social anthropologist M. N. Srinivas had defined Christian influence as part of Westernisation. We need critical responses to such broad statements. Srinivas, in fact, chooses the term "Westernisation" to "modernisation" and thus supplying the Hindu fanatics with ideas to hate Christianity as foreign in faith and practice. So, my suggestion is that several scholars should explore how Indian Christians are passionate about building social harmony through their art and other forms of worship in churches (See Williams D. Premkumar 2005[1] and cf. Wenell 2007).

The second theme that emerged from this chapter is "Sanskritisation" of Maremma to Kattameedi-Maremma but de-Sanskritization of Christian Dalit priest and her people. Sanskritisation is a ritual procedure for moving up the ladder within the caste hierarchy; it is also a ritual procedure for regulating the Untouchables where they belong.

This has meant that the Hindu majority in the village do fear Maremma, the chief deity of the Dalits. But such fear of the ferocious Maremma has not altered their view of the Dalit priest and her people. The Dalit priest can officiate at Kattameedi Maremma, but can only be seated below the platform, distanced from the deity. This would mean the priest is not really allowed to officiate at the altar.

As evidenced in my dissertation, the Christian Dalits are further de- Sanskritised with the high castes' ceremonial attitudes towards the low-caste converts. Thus, the system keeps the sacred and profane boundaries intact. Therefore, further research should be done on the religious status of the Dalits and conscientising the larger Indian masses for true freedom and change. Such research may be geared to finding how to articulate social protest and how to empower the Dalits to gain human dignity. I personally would like to pursue responding to M. N. Srinivas' undue categorisation of Christianity as part of "Westernisation."

Chapter 5 deals with, how Christian Dalits suffer from social and economic discriminations within a caste-ridden bureaucracy and society. Such inhuman treatment has compelled the Christian Dalits to find ways and means to justify their actions, such as seeking Scheduled Caste certificates. Unfortunately, as a result, these life struggles have made the dalits to state, "we are Christian by faith but Hindu by religion" (*Vaarta*—a Telugu Daily News Paper, Thursday, 7 November 1996, 10).

Anyone who knows the Christian Dalit struggles in India is constrained to work for their upliftment and empowerment. The situation calls for a Moses-like participation in redeeming the Dalits from Hindu cultural hegemonies. For me, it means incarnational involvement to identify with and enlarge the Christian Dalit vision and network, including projects for their economic upliftment (e.g. providing farming loans on a low interest rate).

A concern here is that Christian discipleship is not simple; it demands maturing believers by participating in their struggles and motivating the church at large to support the economic and human dignity struggles of poor peoples. Such concern for me should include working for all sections of society, Dalit and non-Dalit alike. Further research in this regard shall include not being judgmental about this telling weakness within Christian Dalit communities, but finding non-violent methods to protest, engage, empower and influence the majority society. It would include making sacrifices to finding constitutional rights to extend reservation benefits to Christian Dalits, because they are part of the sons and daughters of the nation.

In chapter 6, I have discussed issues related to peasant Christian "morality and life guidance." I have analysed three issues. First, three Christian Dalit households have occupied 15 feet of sanctuary land in total. This I have considered to be against their Christian conscience. Second, contrary to the land grabbers, Nirmala has lived out her fear of God in resisting the Christian Dalit womaniser. Third, I have examined Sadhu's prayer for monsoon rains and his worry over non-praying fellow believers.

As a second-generation Christian Dalit missiologist, I see the dire need to write scientific missiologies based on real-life stories. India longs to see Christ-like lives of Christians more than hermeneutically correct preaching. Mahatma Gandhi, the father of our nation, held to such views on Christianity (Ellsberg, Robert. ed. 1991. *Gandhi on Christianity*, xv).

The land-grabbing event was not a good model, but it represents how rural Christians resolve critical issues. They upheld human relationships over and above punitive justice. I suggest such models be further examined by theologians, national jurisprudence and national security departments such as the army and the police.

The chapter on "Consensus and Panchayat" projected the five legal systems of Madiri Puram village, namely (1) *Kula* or caste panchayat, (2) Christian Dalit panchayat, (3) Reddy-Christian Dalit panchayat, (4) Court of justice (5) and *Rytu Sangham* (farmers' guild).

I have discussed in detail just three of the above five legal systems, which involve Christian Dalits-kula, Christian Dalit and Reddy-Christian Dalit Panchayats. The court of justice has intersected in the case of Pakanati Adi Sheshi Reddy fighting for 205 acres of government land, which was distributed free of cost among the Christian Dalits. The church had also approached the court of justice to secure marriage license to their pastor. But the church withdrew from such efforts, because the matter was finally settled in a consensus way.

With regard to *Rytu Sangham* (farmers' guild), I have clarified the issue, but there is a need for researching further on the nature, function and impact of farmers' guild on the dynamics of village life.

In chapter 7, I have suggested that the Kula and Church Panchayats merge and together do critical contextualisation. In this context, I have said Madiri Puram could have condoned the adulterous life of the Prakash-Pentamma couple (per Kula panchayat), but laid down the "sin no more" biblical principle (Jn 8:11) on all the parties. The merging of Dalit and Christian Dalit Panchayat needs further research.

This book demonstrates evidences of continuity and change in the lives of Madiri Puram village Christian Dalits. Many of their actions and adaptations utilise local customs and practices. Some of their core beliefs and practices uphold their ownership of church architecture, of issues of self-support and self-governance. These Christians adapt some changes out of existential compulsions, such as seeking Scheduled Caste certificates for reservation benefits. However, such practices induce internal tensions. A lot depends on further research and how seriously we take the task of disciplining rural congregations, which comprise the majority church in India.

Appendix I

Interview Questionnaire

Research Question 1

How do religious symbols exhibit change and continuity of Madiri Puram village Christian identity?

1. List three important holy places in your village and why are they holy to you?
2. Did forefathers go to receive *"prasadam"* from the village Hindu priest?
3. Name your family gods and goddesses. What do you like in their image?
4. How do religious symbols exhibit your community identity or discontinuity?
5. What made change or not change your house gods (conversion)?
6. When you are sick who do you visit apart from a medical doctor?
7. Say in a few words what makes your life meaningful.
8. In what ways does your Church encourage training younger generations for leadership?
9. Does your Church reach out to neighboring villages with the gospel?

Research Question 2

In what ways do Christians of Madiri Puram village enact change and continuity in morality and life guidance?

1. How often does your pastor visit you and talk over your family problems?
2. When your crop fails and you land in debt where do you go for advice?

3. Please describe how you express your religious devotion to God?

4. In what ways do members contribute to the support of the church?

5. When people commit adultery how does the church handle it?

6. How does the church deal with spirits and black magic?

Research Question 3

How do Christians of Madiri Puram village resolve socio-economic status conflict?

1. How many acres of land do you own?

2. What did your parents own: a bullock cart, oxen, a mud house or thatched roof house? What do you own: a brick house, a wrist watch, a bicycle, a scooter?

3. Did your parents know how to read and write or were they orally literate (e.g a dramatist, poet etc) ?

4. What work do you do to earn your living?

5. Does Christian integrity and clean environments help raise your seating in a village council?

6. Where do you sit while paying your land revenue to the village *karnam*?

7. In what ways, did or did not your conversion to Christianity raise your social status? Do the low Castes and high Castes share the same cups in hotels? Do students from all caste backgrounds eat midday meals together at school?

8. In Kabaddi or Volley Ball game do low caste boys play with the high caste boys? In a marriage dinner, does a Reddy and Christian teacher eat at the same table?

Gender Issues

9. Who is the most educated woman in your village?

10. Is your wife or husband a partner in marriage negotiations for your son or daughter?

11. According to your tradition list some religious activities that a woman believer can do?

12. Describe some things that women are not supposed to do in a Church or temple or dargah worship?

13. If a husband beats his wife repeatedly where does she go for advice or settlement? In the event of a spouse committing adultery how does your community resolve the issue?

Research Question 4

How do Christian Dalits of Madiri Puram village reach consensus in their church *Panchayat* (legal assembly)?

1. How do you choose your Christian pastor?

2. Do you choose your *Sarpanch* under *Naya Panchayat* system or old Panchayat system?

3. When there is a land dispute who do you appeal Caste council, or *Panchayat* or church council?

4. Under what circumstances do you refuse to use the services of a pastor or religious leader or a Sarpanch?

5. During assembly elections which political party or who do you vote and why? In what ways do political parties influence Church affair?

Appendix II

Informed Consent Letter

CHANGE AND CONTINUITY: Influences on self-identity of Madiri Puram village Christian Dalits in South India (1915-2005)

Dear friend,

I am researching Influences of change and continuity on Christian and non-Christian Dalits of Madiri Puram village. Persons like you in Mundladinne, Shantinagar, Julekal and Waddepally villages are also interviewed for a comparative study with that of Madiri Puram village. I believe understanding India from the perspective of ordinary people is one best way to learn about India. Therefore better understand the village church in India. I am also doing this research for my doctoral dissertation. I consider your worldviews and reflections and experiences valuable in this effort.

I am asking you to give your consent to be interviewed about your background and views as you see them. The interview will last between 1 and 2 hours. You will be contacted at a later date for follow-up or clarifications.

This research will be used to write papers for journals, graduate courses, a dissertation and possibly a book. Any profits made from the publication of this research will be shared in the development village church in Mahabubnagar district.

The information you provide will be held in strict confidence. Your name will not appear in any published documents, nor will the village in which you live be mentioned (pseudonym will be used). Your involvement is completely voluntary and you are free to withdraw at anytime during this study.

Thanking you for your consideration, (Etala D avid Solomon)

I have read and understand the nature and purpose of this study, and I freely consent to participate.

Name (print) ____

Signature ____________________________ Date ________________

REFERENCES CITED

Agnihotry, S. A. 1987. Education for social change among Indian women. *Scientific World* 31, no. 1: 13-16.

Ajjarapu, Krishna M. 2001. Perspectives of pure-impure opposition among Brahmin, Shudra, and Harijan Christians in the city of Hyderabad. Ph.D. diss., Trinity International University.

Akula, Linganna. 2006. Opinion on Pakanati Sheshi Reddy. Interviewed on 31 October.

Alasuutari, Pertti. 1995. *Researching culture: Qualitative method and cultural studies.* New Delhi: Sage Publications.

Ambedkar, B. R. 1948. *The untouchables-who are they? And why they became Untouchables?* New Delhi: Amrit Book Co.

Arunodaya, M. I. 2005.Christian as well Hindu Festivals in Madiri Puram Church. Interviewed on 5 September.

Assistant Statistics Officer.2005. 2001 census report of Waddepally Mandal. *Mandal Revenue Office.* 13 September.

__________. 2005. Rain fall in Waddepally Mandal 2000-2005. *Mandal Revenue Office.* 13 September.

Azariah, Masilamani. 2000. *A pastor's search for Dalit theology.* Delhi: DLET/ ISPCK.

Bailey. Carol A. 1996. *A guide to field research.* New Delhi: Pine Forge Press.

Bernard, Russell H. 1995. *Research methods in anthropology. Qualitative and quantitative approaches.* 2d ed. New Delhi: Altamira Press.

Bhatti, S. S. 2005. State, Market and Society: Issues and Interface in Rural and Urban India. In *State, Market and Civil Society: Issues and Interface.* ed. Rajesh Gil. 75-96., New Delhi: Rawat Publications.

Booth, Wayne C, Gregory G. Colomb, and Joseph M Williams. 2003. *The craft of research.* 2d ed. Chicago: The University of Chicago Press.

Bose, Ashish. 1994. Gender issues and population change: Tradition, technology and social turbulence. *International Social Science Journal* 141: 304-5, 387-95.

Bowker, John, ed. 1997. Urs. *The Oxford dictionary of world religions.* Oxford, New York: Oxford University Press, 1009.

Brueggemann, Walter. 1997. *Theology of the Old Testament: Testimony, dispute, advocacy*. Minneapolis: Fortress Press.

__________. 2000. *1 & 2 Kings*. Smyth & Helwys Bible Commentary. Macon, Ga.: Smyth & Helwys.

Colpe, Carsten. Sacred and the profane, the". In *The Encyclopedia of Religion*,Vol.12, ed. Mircea Eliade, 511-526. London: MacMillan Publishing Company. 1987.

Covell, Ralph R., with contributions from Jean–Paul Wiest and the China group. 2001. Ricci, Matteo", In *A dictionary of Asian Christianity*, ed. Scott W. Sunquist.703-705. Cambridge: UK. William B. Eerdmans Publishing Company.

Damodara Rao, M. S. 2005. My family and village history and culture. Interviewed on 27 December.

Danam, R. 2005. Pakanati Sheshi Reddy. Interview, 16 October.

__________. 2005. Family Origin of P. Sheshi Reddy. Interview 16 October.

__________. "Sheshi Reddy is from a royal family". Interview on 16 October.

Definition of "Continuity". Accessed 12 November 2007. Available from wordnet.princeton.edu/perl/webwn; Internet. "History of slums in Bombay", http://theory.tifr.res.in/bombay/history/slums.html. Accessed on 20 December 2007. Internet.

Definition of "Life" on the Web: (en.wikipedia.org/wiki/Morality, cited in wordnet.princeton.edu/perl/webwn). Accessed on 4 January 2008. Internet.

Definition of "Life".2008. Accessed. Available from (en.wikipedia.org/wiki/Morality, cited in wordnet.princeton.edu/perl/webwn). Accessed on 4 January. Internet.

Definition of "Morality" .2008. Accessed. Available from en.wikipedia.org/wiki/Morality. cited in wordnet.princeton.edu/perl/webwn). Accessed on 5. Internet.

Definition of "Social Change" Accessed 12 November 2007. Available from: en.wikipedia.org/wiki/Social change; Internet.

Deliege, Robert. 1992. Replication and consensus: Untouchability, caste and ideology in India. *Man*, n.s., 27, no.1: 155-173.

Devadanam, G. 2005. Correspondence with government officials at Alampur (1996-1998).

Devanandan, P. D., and M. M. Thomas, eds. 1960. *The changing pattern of family in India*. Bangalore: CISRS,

Dey, S. K. 1962. *Panchayati Raj: A synthesis*. Bombay: Asia Publishing House.

Dhyryam and R. Philip. 2005. "Intercession to frog goddess for rain". Interview with R. Dhyryam and R. Philip. August 16. Tape Recorded.

Dhyryam, R. 2005. History of Rajolibanda diversion scheme. Interview with R. Zachariah. Interviewed on 26 December.

__________. 2005. Dire poverty in Madiri Puram 70 years ago (1940s). Interview on 13 August.

__________. 2005. Reddy Christians. Interview with R. Dhyryam. 26 December.

__________. 2005. Why it did not rain in 2004. Interview with R. Dhyryam. 16 August. Tape recorded.

Directorate of Economics and Statistics. 2006. Rain fall in Waddepally Mandalam 2000-2005. Hyderabad: AP.

Dumont, Louis.1998. *Homo Hierarchicus: The caste system and its implications.* Complete Revised English Edition. Delhi: Oxford University Press.

Editor, 2007. Lower Castes genetically closer to Tribals. *Deccan Chronicle* (The largest circulated English daily published in Andhra Pradesh). Monday 15 January: 1-2.

Editor. 1996. Adugaduguna daga padutunna dalitulu [Trans. Dalits exploited at every step of life]. *Vaarta-* A Telugu Daily News Paper, Thursday, 7 November: 10).

Editorial. 2006. Just what is the Gospel? *International Bulletin of Missionary Research.* 30, no.1 (January): 1-2.

Elders, MB Church- Paipadu Village.1996. Transfer Pastor R. Yesiah. A Letter to the Chairman and Secretary of Gadwal MB Field Association. Dated 23 October.

Ellsberg, Robert. ed. 1991. *Gandhi on Christianity.* Maryknoll, New York: Orbis.

Elmore, W. T. 1984. *Dravidian gods in modern Hinduism.* New Delhi: Asian Educational Services.

Erickson, Millard J. 2001. *The concise dictionary of Christian theology.* Wheaton, Ill.: Crossway Books.

Executive Engineer of RDS Division at Uppal and the Project Administrator & Superintending Engineer at Rajolibanda Diversion Scheme Joint Declaration. 2005. *Priyadarshini Jurala Project Circle*, Gadwal. Pp.1-3.

Executive Engineer. Rajulabanda Diversion Scheme. 2005. *Uppal Camp-RDS Division*, Ieej Mandal. AP.

Farmer, H. 2005. Honor to Christian and Hindu rites and practices Interviewed on 31 March.

__________. 2006. Belief in heaven and hell- reaping good now and after life. Interview with Farmer. 10 October.

Farmers suicides in India- Wikipedia, the free encyclopedia. 2008. http://en.wikipedia.org/wiki/Farmers _suicides_in_India. Accessed on 26 December. Internet.

Freed, Stanley A., and Ruth S Freed. 2002. *Green revolution: Agriculture and social change in a North India village*. New York: Anthropological Papers of the American Museum of Natural History, no. 11.

Frykenberg, Robert Eric, ed., 2003. *Christians and missionaries: Cross-cultural* communication since 1500, with special reference to caste, conversion, and *colonialism*. Grand Rapids, Mich.: William B. Eerdmans Publishing Company.

Gattanna, S. 2005. S. Timmayya in my experience. Interview, Boyyala Guddam village. 24 September. Tape recorded.

Geertz, Clifford.1973. *The interpretation of cultures: Selected essays*. New York: Basic Books.

Ghurye, G.S. 1952. *Caste and class in India*. New York: Philosophical Library.

Gnanadasan, Aruna. 1990. Dalit women-The Dalit of the Dalit. in *A reader in Dalit theology*. Ed. Arvind P. Nirmal and V. Devasahayam, 129-138. Madras : Gurukul Lutheran Theological College & Research Institute for the Dept. of Dalit Theology.

Google search, Definition of morality on the Web: en.wikipedia.org/wiki/Morality. Cited in wordnet.princeton.edu/perl/webwn). Accessed on 5 January 2008. Internet.

Govindu, Akula (S% Akula Linganna). 2006. The fight for 205 acres of government land. Interview 31 October.

__________. 2006. The opponents to Sheshi Reddy on 205 acres of government land. Interview 31 October.

Hassan, J. 2006. Belief in mother as devata (divinity). Interviewed on 27 October.

Hastings, James,ed. 1915. *Encyclopedia of religions and ethics*. Vol. VIII (Life-Mulla).Edinburgh: T & T Clark: 325-327.

Hiebert, Paul G. 2006. Transforming Worldviews. Deerfield, IL: Trinity Evangelical Divinity School. Unpublished File in ICS Room.

__________. 2000. *Anthropological insights for missionaries*. Grand Rapids, Michigan: Baker Book House. Fifteenth Printing.

__________. 1994. *Anthropological reflections on missiological issues*. Grand Rapids, Michigan: Baker Book House.

__________. 1974. *Konduru: Structure and integration in a South Indian village*. Minneapolis: University of Minnesota Press. Second Printing.

Hiebert, Paul G, R. Daniel Shaw and Tite Tienou.1999. *Understanding folk religion. A Christian response to popular beliefs and practices.* Michigan: Baker Books.

Hiebert, Paul G, and Eloise Hiebert Meneses. 1995. *Incarnational ministry: Planting churches in band, tribal, peasant, and urban societies.* Michigan: Baker Books.

Hiltebeitel, Alf. 1987. Mahabharata. In *The Encyclopedia of religion*, M.E., 9:118-119. London: Macmillan Publishing Company.

Hopkins, Washburn E. 1915. Mahabharata. In *Encyclopedia of religion and ethics,ed. J. H.*, 8: 325-327. Edinburgh: T & T Clark.

Ilaiah, Kancha, 2007. *Why I am not a Hindu: A Sudra critique of Hindutva philosophy, culture and political economy.* Second Edition. Calcutta: Samya.

__________. 2003. *Devudi Raajakeeyatatvam: Brahmnatvampai Buddhuni Tirugubaatu* (God as political philosopher: Buddha s challenge to Brahmanism). Telugu Translation by Prabhakar Mandara. Hyderabad Book Trust. [English original, 2000 by Samya, Calcutta].

__________.1989. *The state and repressive culture – The Andhra experience.* Hyderabad: Swecha Prachuranalu.

Isaac, M. A. 2005. Pastors should live by proclaiming the Lord and not by writing Scheduled Caste Certificates to Christians. Interview 5 September.

Jones, C. R. 1981. Art and Architecture, Hindu. In *Abingdon dictionary of religions*, ed. Keith Crim., 55-57. Abingdon: Nashville.

Kraft, Charles H.1996. *Anthropology for Christian witness.* New York: Orbis Books.

Krishnaiah, P. Collector and Magistrate-Mahabubnagar.1990. *Mahabubnagar District Gazette. Extraordinary Publication by Authority.* Mahabubnagar: Monday, April 23.

Kumar, Girish. 2006. *Local democracy in India: Interpreting decentralization.* Thousand Oaks: Sage Publications.

Lemuel R.S. 1988. *Mennonite Brethren Local Church and Field Association Statutes- GC.* Mahabubnager. Section VI. 10, Page 7.

Macquarrie, John. 1987. Existentialism. In *The encyclopedia of religion.* Ed. M.E., 5: 222-225. New York: Macmillan Publishing Company.

__________. 1971. *20th century religious thought: The frontiers of philosophy and theology, 1990-1970.* Bloomsbury Street, London: Scheduled Caste Press Ltd.

Mahabharata date. Accessed 12 November 2007. Available from www.ece.Isu.edu/kak/Mahabharatall.pdf_; Internet.

Mahabubnager District Teachers Federation (DTF). 2005. Map of the Mandal with schools, distance from head quarters and vacant posts. Status in November.

Martens, Elmer A. 1998. *God's design: A focus on Old Testament theology.* Third Edition. N. Richland Hills, Texas: Bibal Press.

Massey, James. 1994. *Roots: A concise history of Dalits.* Revised Edition. Bangalore: ISPCK.

__________. 1996. *Roots of Dalit history, Christianity, theology and spirituality.* 3d enl. ed. Delhi: ISPCK

__________. 1997. *Down trodden: The struggles of India's Dalits for identity, solidarity and liberation.* Geneva: Risk Book Series, WCC Publications.

Mazumdar, A. K. 1993. Society, social change and Vivekananda. *Journal of the Asiatic Society* 35, no. 4: 14-22.

MB Board of Evangelism and Church Ministries. 2007. *Stuti Aradhana Suvartha Keertanalu.* Mahabubnager, Andhra Pradesh. Telugu Text.

Mekanan, Dan. 2007. *Touching the world: Christian communities transforming the society.* College Ville, Minn.: Liturgical Press.

Melanchthon, Monica Jyotsna. 2007. Akkamahadevi and the Samaritan Woman. In *Border crossings: Cross-cultural hermeneutics.* Ed. D. N. Premnath, 35-54. Maryknoll, N.Y.: Orbis Books.

Menacheri, George, ed. 1982. *The St. Thomas Christian encyclopedia of India.* Vol.1. Trichur.

Meneses, Eloise Hiebert. 2007. *Love and revolutions: Market women and social cange in India.* Lanham, Md.: University Press of America.

Mookherji, Debnath. 1982. A Profile of slums in Third World city: Calcutta. *Ekistics* 297 (Nov/Dec): 476-479.

Nagaraju, B. 2005. „Sangati Timmayya , a written document by Nagaraju. Nanadavaram village. 26 September.

Nageswarrao, Marishetti, and Marishetti Rambabu.2002. *PeddaBaala Shikhsa.* Rajahmundry: Gollapudi Veraswami Sons. Telugu Text.

Newbigin, Lesslie. 1989. *The Gospel in a pluralist society.* Grand Rapids, Mich.: Wm. B. Eerdmans Publishing Co.

Nirmala, G. 2005. Victory over attempted rape- a modern Jael (Judg 4:17-2; 5:24- 27). Interview on 18 August.

Oxford English reference dictionary. 1996. New York: Oxford University Press.P.1514.

Pajares, F. Available from "Elements of a proposal". http://www.des.emory.edu/mfp/proposal.html. Accessed 12 November 2007. Internet.

Paras, R. 2005. Boyyala Guddam Timmayya, the first evangelist to Madiri Puram Village. 17 July.

__________. 2005. Reddy denied government land to my father. Interview 29 December.

__________. 2005. Survey on models for Church Architecture. Interview on September 16.

Patel, Tulsi. 2005. *The family in India: Structure and practice*. Thousand Oaks, Calif.: Sage Publications.

Paulayya S. 2005. Sarpanch of Tummilla Village. Interview 27 September. Tape Recorded.

Pentanna, Tolla R. 2006. Pakanati Kings migration to Madiri Puram. Interview 17 October.

__________. 2006. Greatness of Maremma. Interviewed on 17 October.

Pradeshi, L. S. 2005. On Scheduled Caste certificates and other issues. Interview 24 July 2005. Tape Recorded.

Prabhakar, Vani. 2004. *Women in India*. New Delhi: Dominant Publishers and Distributors.

Pradeshi. L. J. 2005. Elders rule over the Church. Interview 24 July.

Prasad, Ravi D. M. 1997. *Dalit youth: A sociologist study*. New Delhi: APH Publishing Corporation.

Priest, Robert J. 2006. Experience-near Theologizing in Diverse Human Contexts. *Globalizing theology-belief and practice, era of world Christianity*. ed. Craig, Ott. And Herald Netland., 180-195. Grand Rapids, Michigan: Baker Academic.

Qaisar, Jan. 1993. The profane and the Sacred: "Judgment of Paris" and "God the Father" in the Mughal School of Art. In *Art and architecture: Felicitation volume in honor of Professor S. Nurul Hasan*, ed. Ahsan Jan Qaisar and Som Prakash Verma., 81-89. Centre for Advanced Study, Department of History, Aligarh Muslim University. Jaipur: Publication Scheme.

R. Sadhu M. 2005. Reddy harassment. Interview 27 December.

Rajshekar, V. T. 2002. *Brahminism: Fascism, racism, Nazism, Zionism* Bangalore, India: Dalit Sahitya Akademy.

Rayan, Samuel. 1996. Inspired Images. In *Culture, religion and society: Essays in honor of Richard W. Taylor*. Ed. S. K. Chatterji and Hunter P. Mabry. 2-40. Delhi: ISPCK.

Research Problem. Accessed 12 November 2007. Available from http://www.petech.ac.za/robert/respropl.htm; Internet; Internet.

Richard, H. L. 2001. De Nobili, Roberto. (ed.) In *A Dictionary of Asian Christianity, ed.* Scott W. Sunquist., 233-234. Cambridge, UK: William B. Eerdmans Publishing Company.

Ruud, Arild Engelsen. 2003. *Poetics of village politics: The making of West Bengal's rural communism*. New York: Oxford University Press.

Sabharwal, Deshraj. 2001. New agro-technology and change. *Man in India* 81, nos.1/2: 179-95.

Sadhu. R. 2005. Elijah like Prayer. Interview on 3 July. Tape Recorded.

Samuel, Edith. 2002. Dowry and dowry harassment in India: An assessment based on modified capitalist patriarchy. *African and Asian Studies* 1, no. 3: 187-229.

Sarkar, N. N and Rina Sarkar. 2005. Sexual assault on woman: its impact on her life and living in society. *Sexual and Relationship Therapy*. 20, no. 4 (November): 407-419.

Schull, Randy. Accessed 12 November 2007. Available from. http://www.vernalproject.org; Internet.

Secretary. 2005. *Samaavesha Vivaramulu, (Minutes) of Gilgal India Mennonite Brethren Church -Madiri Puram Village (1951-2005)*. Mahabubnagar District, Andhra Pradesh. South India.

Sen, Amartya K., and Jean Dreze. 1999. *Poverty and famines, hunger and public action, India: Economic development and social opportunity-omnibus*. New Delhi: Oxford University Press

Spradley, James P. 1979. *The ethnographic interview*. New York: Harcourt Brace Jovanovich College Publishers

__________. 1980. *Participant observation*. New York: Holt, Rinehart and Winston. Srinivas, M. N. 1967. *Social change in modern India*. Berkeley and Los Angeles: University of California.

__________. 1998. *Village, caste, gender and method-essays in Indian social anthropology*. Oxford: Oxford University Press.

Srinivasan, Padma, and Gary R. Lee. 2004. The dowry system in Northern India: Women's attitudes and social change. *Journal of Marriage & Family* 66, no. 5: 1108-17.

Subbamma, D.2006. Caste Vocation of Dakkalis. Interview over phone, 23 December.

Sudarshan, Ramaswamy. 1997. Law and democracy in India. *International Social Science Journal*. 49, no. 2: 271-278.

Suenobu, Keiko. 2008. Definitions of Life. Available from en.wikipedia.org/wiki/Life (manga). cited in wordnet.princeton.edu/perl/webwn). Accessed on 5 January. Internet.

Sundar Rao, PSS. Dr. 2005, 2006. Medical Missionary Association: A firm foundation. *Christian Medical Journal of India – A Quarterly Journal of*

Christian Medical Association of India 20 & 21, no. 4 (Oct – Dec 2005) and no. 1 (Jan – Mar 2006): 18-25.

Suraj, V. A. 2006. Belief in heaven and hell- unsure. Interview with A. Vijaya Bhaser. 10 October.

Talwar, Prem P. Urbanization in India: Facts, issues and recommendations. Available from http://www.auick.org/database/apc/apc02701.html. Accessed 20 December 2007. Internet.

The academic proposal. Accessed 12 November 2007. Available from http://www.utoronot.ca/writing/ proposal.html; Internet.

The Governing Council of the Mennonite Brethren Church of India. 1972. *India Mennonite Brethren Church at cross roads.* Mahabubnagar: Mennonite Brethren Press, AP. India.

Treasurer. 2005. 1999-2005 Income and Expenditure Register. Gilgal IMB Church: Madiri Puram Village.

Truman, Suez B. H. 1984. *A study of the Ongole mass movement of 1878 and its impact on the converts-Madigas.* Th.M. thesis, Bangalore: United Theological College.

Vahanam, V. A. 2005. Tormenting Narsappa and other gods. Interview on 10 October.

Vedulla, K. Rufus. 1992. *Strangers in Maharastra: Mennonite Brethren historical foundations.* Th.M. thesis, Trinity Evangelical Divinity School.

Vice-President, Alampur-ABDR.1997. Letter to Pastor G. Devadanam. Madiri Puram Village. Dated 13 September.

Victoria, M. 2006. Belief in heaven and hell: Action reaction nature. Interview on 19 October.

Waddepally Mandal Revenue Office.2005. Waddepally Mandal general information. A Display on Office Wall. 23 September.

Wadley, Susan S. 2002. One Straw from a broom cannot sweep: The ideology and practice of the joint family in rural North India. In *Everyday Life in South Asia,* ed. Sarah Lamb and Diane Mines, 11-12. Indiana University Press.

Waligo, John.1991. Inculturation. In *Dictionary of ecumenical movement,* ed. Nichol Lossky., 506-507, Geneva: WCC Publication.

Walls, Andrew F. 2004. *The mssionary movement in Christian history: studies in the transmission of faith.* Maryknoll: Orbis Books.

Webster, John C. 1999. *Religion and Dalit liberation: An examination of perspectives.* Delhi: Manohar.

Williams, Premkumar D. 2005. *Shaping Sacred Space: Toward an Evangelical Theology of Church Architecture.* Ph.D, diss, Trinity International University.

Wright, Christopher J. H. 1996. *Deuteronomy*. New International Biblical
    Commentary. Based on the NIV. Peabody, Mass.: Paternoster Press.

SCRIPTURE INDEX

SUBJECT INDEX